Quick Knits
Cool Projects™

HOUSE of
WHITE
BIRCHES

PUBLISHERS
SINCE 1947

QUICK KNITS: COOL PROJECTS

Copyright © 2006 House of White Birches, Berne, Indiana 46711

EDITOR	Jeanne Stauffer
ART DIRECTOR	Brad Snow
PRODUCTION MANAGER	Brenda Gallmeyer
ASSOCIATE EDITOR	Dianne Schmidt
ASSISTANT ART DIRECTOR	Nick Pierce
COPY SUPERVISOR	Michelle Beck
COPY EDITORS	Nicki Lehman, Mary Martin, Judy Weatherford
GRAPHIC ARTS SUPERVISOR	Ronda Bechinski
GRAPHIC ARTISTS	Erin Augsburger, Joanne Gonzalez
PRODUCTION ASSISTANT	Marj Morgan
PHOTOGRAPHY	Tammy Christian, Don Clark, Matthew Owen, Jackie Schaffel
PHOTO STYLISTS	Tammy Nussbaum, Tammy M. Smith
PUBLISHING DIRECTOR	David J. McKee
EDITORIAL DIRECTOR	Gary Richardson
BOOK MARKETING DIRECTOR	Dan Fink

Printed in China
First Printing: 2006
Library of Congress Control Number: 2006924143

Hard cover:
ISBN-10: 1-59217-136-2
ISBN-13: 978-1-59217-136-1

Soft Cover:
ISBN-10: 1-59217-158-3
ISBN-13: 978-1-59217-158-3

1 2 3 4 5 6 7 8 9

Knitting today is big, beautiful and bursting with fun and style!

Girls and guys are knitting throws on big needles in the dorm lounge, and at slumber parties 3rd graders are knitting scarves out of novelty yarns. Yarn companies have gone wild with colors and kinds of yarn with more new yarns and trendsetting colors available every season.

In these pages you'll find flirty fashion accents, trendy summer knits, sweaters rich with style and afghans sleek and cozy. Knitting has never been more fun! Whether you are new to knitting or you've been knitting a long time, these quick knitting designs will provide you with cool projects that will double your pleasure. You'll enjoy knitting them, and you'll enjoy wearing them. Let's get rolling on knitting!

CONTENTS

FLIRTY FASHION ACCENTS

TRENDY SUMMER KNITS

CONTENTS

AFGHANS SLEEK & COZY

FLIRTY FASHION ACCENTS

From simple to sensational, these trendy
scarves, hot-looking hats and fabulous
bags are ready for you to knit!

TERRIFIC TEXTURE SCARF

A soft yarn and big needles will zip this chic and sassy scarf off your needles.

DESIGN FROM PATONS DESIGN STUDIO

Finished Size
Approx 6 x 65 inches

Materials
- Patons Pooch 63 percent acrylic/27 percent wool/10 percent nylon super bulky yarn (36 yds/70g per ball): 3 balls auburn #65530
- Size 15 (10mm) needles or size needed to obtain gauge

Gauge
8 sts and 12 rows = 4 inches/10cm in St st
Exact gauge is not critical to this project.

Scarf
Cast on 12 sts.
Knit 3 rows, marking first row as WS.
Row 1 (RS): Knit.
Row 2: K2, purl to last 2 sts, k2.
Rep Rows 1 and 2 until scarf measures approx 64 inches from beg, ending with a RS row.
Knit 2 rows.
Bind off knitwise on WS. ◆

DASHING SCARF

Fringe is added along the entire length of this easy garter stitch scarf.

DESIGN FROM PATONS

Finished Size
Approx 6 x 50 inches
(excluding fringe)

Materials
- Patons Bohemian 81 percent polyester/19 percent acrylic super bulky yarn (68 yds/80g per ball): 2 balls wandering wines #11430
- Size 13 (9mm) needles or size needed to obtain gauge

Gauge
8 sts and 20 rows = 4 inches/10cm in garter st
Exact gauge is not critical to this project.

Scarf
Cast on 16 sts.
   Work in garter st until work measures 50 inches from beg.
Next row: K2, bind off next 12 sts. Fasten off securely, leaving last 2 sts unworked.

Fringe
Drop first and last 2 sts; unravel these sts for fringe along sides of scarf. ◆

CLEVER COLLAR SCARF

It won't take long to make this perfect wardrobe enhancer to brighten up any outfit!

DESIGN FROM CARON INTERNATIONAL

Finished Size

Width (at back of neck):
7 inches
Length: approx 43 inches

Materials

- Caron International Feathers 65 percent acrylic/35 percent nylon bulky weight yarn (70 yds/50g per ball): 3 balls macaw #0012
- Size 8 (5mm) needles or size needed to obtain gauge
- Size I/9 (5.5mm) crochet hook
- Row counter (optional)

Gauge

14 sts and 21 rows = 4 inches/10cm in St st with larger needles
To save time, take time to check gauge.

Special Techniques

Wrap and Turn (wrp-t): Beg on RS, bring yarn forward to the purl position, sl next st to RH needle, take yarn back to the knit position, return sl st (which is now wrapped) to LH needle; turn, leaving rem sts unworked.

Short Row Shaping: Each short row = 2 rows, a RS row and a WS row. For this scarf, all short rows beg on a RS row, where the st is wrapped, and end with a WS row which returns to the starting point.

Work the number of sts indicated in the instructions, wrp-t, return to starting point. On the next RS row, work wrap tog with wrapped st, as follows: Insert the RH needle into wrap at base of wrapped st from below, bring RH needle up and into st on LH needle knitwise; k2tog (the wrap and wrapped st)—this prevents a hole from forming where short row ended.

Pattern Note

All shaping takes place along the same edge, at the beg of RS rows.

Scarf

Cast on 2 sts.
Beg and end with a WS row, work even in St st for 3 rows.

Shape scarf

Beg on this row, inc 1 st at beg of row [every 4th row] 6 times. (8 sts)
Inc 1 st at beg of row [every RS row] 14 times, ending with a WS row. (22 sts)
Work even for 34 rows. Scarf should measure approx 17 inches, ending with a WS row.
*Short row: K11, wrp-t; purl to end.
Work 14 rows even, knitting wrap tog with wrapped st on first row.
Rep from * twice, then work short row once more (4 sets of short rows).
Work even for 34 rows. Scarf should measure approx 33 inches, ending with a WS row.

Reverse shaping

Beg with a RS row, dec 1 st at beg of row [every RS row] 14 times, ending with a WS row. (8 sts rem)
Dec 1 st [every 4th row] 6 times. (2 sts rem)
Work 4 rows even. Bind off rem sts.

Finishing

Using crochet hook, work 1 row single crochet around all edges. ◆

BIG NEEDLE SCARF SET

A self-fringing scarf and a matching hat are ideal projects for the novice knitter.

DESIGNS BY LAURA ANDERSSON

Size

Hat: Adult small (medium, large) Instructions are given for smallest size, with larger sizes in parentheses. When only 1 number is given, it applies to all sizes.
Scarf: One size fits most

Finished Measurements
Hat circumference: 28 (20, 22) inches
Scarf: Approx 4 x 51 inches without fringe

Materials
- Brown Sheep Handpaint Originals 70 percent mohair/30 percent wool worsted weight yarn (88 yds/50g per hank): 4 hanks mountain majesty #HP100 (A)
- Brown Sheep Nature Spun Worsted 100 percent wool worsted weight yarn (245 yds/ 100g per skein): 3 skeins butterfly blue #N59 (B)
- Size 11 (8mm) 16- and 24-inch circular needles or size needed to obtain gauge

Gauge
11 sts and 16 rows = 4 inches/10cm in St st
To save time, take time to check gauge.

Pattern Stitch
Texture Time (multiple of 5 sts)
Rnd 1: *K1, p4; rep from * around.
Rnd 2: *K2, p3; rep from * around.
Rnd 3: *K3, p2; rep from * around.
Rnd 4: *K4, p1; rep from * around.
Rnd 5: Knit.
Rnd 6: Purl.
   Rep Rnds 1–6 for pat.

Pattern Notes

One strand of A and 2 of B are held tog for entire hat and scarf.

Scarf is worked across the width; long strands are left at either end to form the fringe.

HAT

With 3 strands of yarn held tog, cast on 50 (55, 60) sts.

Join without twisting, place marker between between first and last st.

Knit 10 rnds.

Work 12 rnds of Texture Time pat.

Work even in St st until hat measures 5½ (6, 6½) inches.

Shape top

Rnd 1: *K3, k2tog; rep from * around. (40, 44, 48 sts)

Knit 1 rnd.

Rnd 3: *K2, k2tog; rep from * around. (30, 33, 36 sts)

Knit 1 rnd.

Rnd 5: *K1, k2tog; rep from * around. (20, 22, 24 sts)

Rnd 6: Rep Rnd 5, ending with k2 on small size, (k1 on medium size, k2tog on large size). (14, 15, 16 sts)

Rnd 7: K2tog around. (7, 8, 8 sts)

Cut yarn leaving a 12-inch end. Draw yarn through rem sts twice and pull tightly.

SCARF

With 3 strands of yarn held tog, cast on 175 sts, leaving a 10-inch tail at beg of row for fringe.

Work Rnd 1 of Texture Time pat. Cut yarn leaving a 10-inch tail at end of row. Slide sts to opposite end of needle.

Leaving a 10-inch tail at beg and end of each row, and sliding sts to opposite end of needle before beg each new row, continue in pat for 17 more rows (3 reps of pat).

Bind off loosely.

Finishing

Make an overhand knot with tails, using 6 strands of yarn for each knot.

Trim fringe evenly. ◆

REVERSIBLE WINTER WARMERS

Stay warm this winter and learn basic knitting skills while working on a toasty three-piece set.

DESIGN BY LOIS S. YOUNG

Size

Scarf: 7 x 64 inches, excluding tassels

Hat: Woman's, one size fits most

Mittens: Woman's, one size fits most

Materials

- Berroco X-press 60 percent wool/40 percent acrylic bulky weight yarn (42 yds/50g per skein): 10 skeins moss green #3614
- Size 11 (8mm) 16-inch circular and double-pointed needles or size needed to obtain gauge for hat and mittens
- Size 13 (9mm) needles or size needed to obtain gauge for scarf
- Stitch marker
- Stitch holder
- Tapestry needle

Gauge

10 sts and 16 rows = 4 inches/10cm in Double Moss st with larger needles for scarf
11 sts and 19 rows = 4 inches/10cm in Double Moss st with smaller needles hat and mittens
To save time, take time to check gauge.

Pattern Stitches

A. Garter Stitch (worked in rows)
All rows: Sl 1, k19.

B. Garter Stitch (worked in rnds)
Rnd 1: Purl.
Rnd 2: Knit.
Rep Rnds 1–2 for pat.

C. Double Moss Stitch (worked in rows)
Row 1 (RS): Sl 1, *k2, p2, rep from * across, end last rep k2, p1.
Row 2: Sl 1, *p2, k2, rep from * across, end last rep p2, k1.
Row 3: Sl 1, *p2, k2, rep from * across, end last rep p2, k1.
Row 4: Sl 1, *k2, p2, rep from * across, end last rep k2, p1.
Rep Rows 1–4 for pat.

D. Double Moss Stitch (worked in rnds)
Rnds 1 and 2: *K2, p2, rep from * across.
Rnds 3 and 4: *P2, k2, rep from * across.
Rep Rnds 1–4 for pat.

Pattern Note

For scarf, sl first st of each row purlwise to produce chained edge.

SCARF

Cast on 20 sts. Work 8 rows garter st.
   [Work 18 rows Double Moss st. Work 8 rows garter st] 9 times.
   Bind off in knit.

Tassels

Make 6

Cut 3 pieces of yarn, each 7 inches long. Holding pieces tog, fold in half.
   Cut an 8-inch piece. Starting at the center of this piece
of yarn, wrap both ends around tassel several times, ¼ inch from fold. Knot this yarn tightly in a square knot. Pull ends to inside to blend with tassel. Trim ends evenly. Attach one tassel to each corner and center of scarf ends.

MITTENS

Cuff

With dpn, cast on 20 sts, divided on 3 needles. Pm and join, being careful not to twist.
   Work 8 rnds in garter st. Purl 1 rnd.

Hand

Work 11 rnds in Double Moss st.

Beg thumb opening

Work 3 sts in established pat, k3, sl next 3 sts to holder, cast on 3 sts, work to end of rnd.
   Purl 1 rnd.
   Work 4 rnds garter st. Work 18 rnds Double Moss st.

Shape top

Rnd 1: *P2, k2tog, rep from * around. (15 sts)
Rnd 2: *P2, k1, rep from * around.
Rnd 3: *K2tog, p1, rep from * around. (10 sts)
Rnd 4: *K1, p1, rep from * around.
Rnd 5: *K2tog, rep from * around. (5 sts)
   Cut yarn, leaving a 6-inch end.
   With tapestry needle, draw yarn through all remaining sts twice. Pull tightly and darn in end.

Thumb

Sl 3 sts from holder to dpn. Working on these 3 sts, p1, k2, pick up and knit 1 st along side of thumb opening, 3 sts from cast-on edge, 1 st from 2nd side of opening. (8 sts)
   Place marker, work 8 rnds Double Moss st, continuing pat as established on first 3 sts of rnd.
Dec rnd: [K2tog] around. (4 sts)
   Cut yarn, and draw through remaining sts twice. Pull tightly and darn in end.

HAT

With 16-inch cn, loosely cast on 52 sts.
   Work in garter st for 30 rnds. Work in Double Moss st for 22 rnds.

Shape top

Rnd 1: *P2, k2tog, rep from * around. (39 sts)
Rnd 2: *P2, k1, rep from * around.
Rnd 3: *K2tog, p1, rep from * around. (26 sts)
Rnd 4: *K1, p1, rep from * around.
Rnd 5: * K2tog, rep from * around. (13 sts)
   Cut yarn, leaving a 6-inch end. Draw through remaining sts twice.
   Pull tightly and darn in end.
   Make tassel to match scarf and attach to top of hat. ◆

WINTER WALKS

Pooches and the people they take on their walks will look fashionable while keeping warm in these quick knits.

DESIGN BY BONNIE FRANZ

Dog Sweater Size

Fits small/medium dog

Finished Measurements

Neck to tail: 13½ inches
Chest/belly: 18½ inches unstretched (ribbing will stretch quite a bit if necessary)

Materials

- Lion Brand Jiffy Thick & Quick 100 percent acrylic super bulky weight yarn (84 yds/140g per skein): 6 skeins Cascade Mountains #211
- Size 17 (12mm) straight and 16-inch circular needles or double-pointed needles or size needed to obtain gauge
- Stitch marker
- 2 large buttons, 1 large toggle for sweater
- Sewing needle and thread

Gauge

9 sts and 10 rows = 4 inches/10cm in pat
To save time take time to check gauge.

Pattern Stitch

Ribbing (multiple of 3 sts + 1)
Row 1 (RS): K1, *p1, k2; rep from * across.
Row 2: *P2, k1; rep from * to last st, p1.
Rep Rows 1 and 2 for pat.

DOG SWEATER

Beg at back, cast on 31 sts. Work Rib in rows for 4½ inches, ending with a WS row.

At beg of next RS row, cast on 16 sts. (47 sts)

Beg with k2, work these sts in established Rib, maintaining Ribbing of body.

Next row (buttonhole row): Work in pat to last 3 sts, k2tog, yo, p1.

Maintaining established Rib, work 8 rows, then rep buttonhole row. Work 1 more row in Rib. On next RS row, bind off 16 sts of underbody band in Ribbing. (31 sts)

Work 4½ inches in Rib on rem sts.

Neck strap

On next WS row, bind off first 27 sts in Rib. Work on rem 4 sts in established Rib for 4 inches.
Buttonhole: On next WS row, k1, k2tog, yo, k1.

Resume Rib for 2 rows, bind off in Rib.

Finishing

Sew buttons to underbody opposite buttonholes, sew toggle to body opposite buttonhole on strap. For best fit, if possible, try sweater on dog before sewing on buttons and place buttons accordingly.

SCARF

Cast on 18 sts, beg Rib pat, ending k1. Continue in established pat until scarf measures approx 60 inches, bind off all sts loosely in Rib.

HAT

Pattern Stitch

Ribbing (multiple of 3 sts)
Rnd 1: K1, *p1, k2; rep from * to last 2 sts, p1, k1.
Rep Rnd 1 for pat.

Hat

Using circular needles or dpns, cast on 39 sts. Join without twisting, place marker to indicate beg of rnd.

Work Rib pat in rnds until hat measures approx 8 inches from beg.

Shape top

Rnd 1: K1, *p1, k2tog; rep from * to last 2 sts, p1, knit last st of rnd tog with first st of next rnd.
Rnd 2: *P1, k1; rep from * around.
Rnd 3: Knit.
Rnd 4: [K2tog] around.
Rnd 5: Knit.
Rnd 6: [K2tog] around.

Cut yarn, leaving a 10-inch end. Thread through rem sts and pull tight, fasten off. ◆

TWO-COLOR SCARF & HAT

Fluffy pompoms adorn the ends of a scarf; the matching hat boasts a quirky topknot.

DESIGNS BY UYVONNE BIGHAM

Size
One size fits most teens and adults

Finished Measurements
Scarf: 6½ x 60 inches
Hat Circumference: 19 inches

Materials
- Plymouth Encore 75 percent acrylic/25 percent wool worsted weight yarn (200 yds/100g per skein): 3 skeins hot pink #1385 (MC) and 1 skein off white #146 (CC)
- Size 8 (5mm) double-pointed and 16-inch circular needles or size needed to obtain gauge
- Stitch marker
- 4-inch piece of cardboard

Gauge
17 sts and 24 rnds = 4 inches/10cm in St st
To save time, take time to check gauge.

HAT
With MC and circular needle, cast on 80 sts. Join without twisting, place marker between first and last st.

Work even in St st until hat measures 26 inches.

Bind off.

Tie overhand knot in top of hat.

Roll up cast-on edge.

SCARF
With MC and dpn, cast on 80 sts, leaving a 12-inch end for later sewing. Join without twisting, place marker between first and last st.

Work even in St st until scarf measures 3 inches.

Beg stripe pat
Work in stripe pat of 4 rnds CC, 5 rnds MC, 5 rnds CC.

Work even with MC only until scarf measures 55 inches.

Beg stripe pat
Work in stripe pat of 5 rnds CC, 5 rnds MC, 4 rnds CC.

Work even with MC only for 3

inches more.

Cut yarn, leaving a 12-inch end.

Finishing
Draw end through all sts twice and draw up tightly. Pull end to inside.

Rep along cast-on edge, running reserved end through all sts.

Pompoms
Make 2
Wind CC around cardboard approx 75 times. Tie 1 end, cut other end. Shake pompom to fluff up.

Attach 1 pompom to each end of scarf. ◆

ROLLED BRIM HAT & MITTS

The use of Stockinette stitch throughout this pair causes the edges to roll naturally.

DESIGN BY UYVONNE BIGHAM

EASY

4

MEDIUM

Size
Adult

Finished Measurements
Hat Circumference: 17 inches
Mitten Length: 9½ inches, with cuff unrolled

Materials
- Plymouth Encore Worsted Colorspun 75 percent acrylic/25 percent wool worsted weight yarn (200 yds/100g per skein): 2 skeins blue/purple #7304
- Size 8 (5mm) double-pointed and 16-inch circular needles or size needed to obtain gauge
- Stitch markers
- Stitch holders

Gauge
19 sts and 26 rnds = 4 inches/10cm in St st
To save time, take time to check gauge.

HAT
With circular needle, cast on 80 sts. Join without twisting, pm between first and last st.
Work even in St st until hat measures 6 inches.

Shape top
Rnd 1: *K8, k2tog; rep from * around. (72 sts)
Rnd 2: Knit.
Rnd 3: *K7, k2tog; rep from * around. (64 sts)
Rnd 4: Knit.
Continue to dec every other rnd as established, having 1 st less between decs until 14 sts rem.
Knit 1 rnd.
Cut yarn leaving a 12-inch end. Draw yarn through rem sts twice. Pull tightly and secure.

MITTENS
Make both alike
With dpn, cast on 32 sts. Join without twisting, pm between first and last st.
Knit 40 rnds.

Thumb opening
Next Rnd: K1, sl next 4 sts to holder, cast on 4 sts, k to end of rnd.
Knit 38 rnds.

Shape mitten top
Rnd 1: [Ssk, k12, k2tog] twice. (28 sts)
Rnd 2 and all even-numbered rnds: Knit.
Rnd 3: [Ssk, k10, k2tog] twice. (24 sts)
Rnd 5: [Ssk, k8, k2tog] twice. (20 sts)
Rnd 7: [Ssk, k6, k2tog] twice. (16 sts)
Rnd 9: [Ssk, k4, k2tog] twice. (12 sts)
Knit 1 rnd.
Rearrange sts so there are 6 sts on each of 2 needles, having a dec st at each end of needle.
Sew sts tog, using Kitchener method.

Thumb
Pick up and k10 sts around thumb opening. Divide onto 3 needles.
Work even in St st for 1½ inches.
Next rnd: *K2tog around.
Cut yarn leaving a 6-inch end.
Draw yarn through rem sts twice. Pull tightly and secure.
Press thumbs to right or left for appropriate mitten. ◆

UNISEX SCARF

This scarf would be right at home in a man's overcoat or any lady's wrap—unobtrusive without being mundane.

DESIGN BY JULIE GADDY

Finished Size
Approx 8 x 68 inches

Materials
- Plymouth Indiecita Baby Alpaca D.K. 100 percent baby alpaca light weight yarn (125 yds/50g per skein): 5 skeins tan #208
- Size 6 (4mm) knitting or size needed to obtain gauge
- Stitch markers

Gauge
28 sts = 4 inches/10cm in pat (blocked)
Exact gauge is not critical to this project.

Pattern Notes
Scarf is reversible.
  Slip first st of every row purlwise.

Pattern Stitch
Diagonal Rib (multiple of 4 sts)
Row 1 (RS): *K2, p2; rep from * across.
Row 2: Rep Row 1.
Row 3: K1, *p2, k2; rep from * to last 3 sts, p2, k1.
Row 4: P1, *k2, p2; rep from * to last 3 sts, k2, p1.
Row 5: *P2, k2; rep from * across.
Row 6: Rep Row 5.
Row 7: Rep Row 4.
Row 8: Rep Row 3.
  Rep Rows 1–8 rows for pat.

Scarf
Cast on 54 sts.
Rows 1–4: Sl 1p, knit across. (3 garter ridges on each side of work)
Beg pat: Sl 1p, k2, place marker, work Row 1 of pat over 48 sts, place marker, k3.
  Continue in this manner, working 3-st garter st border at each side and center 48 sts in pat until scarf measures approx 67½ inches or ½ inch less than desired length, ending with Row 8.
  Knit 5 rows (garter st), continuing to sl first st of every row.
  Bind off all sts knitwise.
  Block scarf to finished measurements. ◆

RAINBOW EYEGLASS CASE

You'll never lose your glasses in this colorful buttoned case. Single crochet adds the finishing touch to this beginner-level project.

DESIGN BY EDIE ECKMAN

Finished Size
4 x 7 inches

Materials
- Lorna's Laces Bullfrogs & Butterflies 85 percent wool/15 percent mohair worsted weight yarn (219 yds/100g per skein): partial skein child's play #62
- Size 9 (5.5mm) needles
- Size I/9 (5.5mm) crochet hook
- Novelty button or bead

Gauge
20 sts = 4 inches/10cm in pat
To save time, take time to check gauge.

Pattern Stitch
Granite St (multiple of 2 sts)
Row 1 (RS): Knit.
Row 2: *K2tog, rep from * across.
Row 3: [K1, p1] into same st, rep from * across.
Row 4: Purl.
   Rep Rows 1–4 for pat.

Case
Cast on 20 sts. Work even in pat until piece measures approximately 15½ inches from beg, ending with Row 2. Bind off loosely. Cut yarn.

Finishing
Referring to Fig.1, fold case along A–B and pin. Starting at B, single crochet through both layers to C, then around flap only to D. Single crochet 3 in corner st at D, single crochet to E. Ch 8, or number needed to go around button, single crochet in same st, single crochet to F, 3 single crochet in corner st at F, single crochet to G, then through both layers to A. Fasten off. ◆

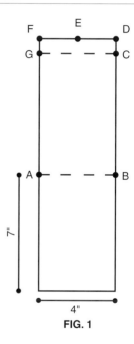

FIG. 1

WOOL FELTED PURSE

Produce a lightweight and very durable purse by machine—washing machine!

DESIGN BY SHARI HAUX

Finished Size

Approximately 27-inch circumference after felting

Materials

- Reynolds Lite-Lopi 100 percent wool worsted weight yarn (109 yds/50g per skein): 9 skeins #430
- Size 13 (9mm) 29-inch circular needle or size needed to obtain gauge
- Size K/10½ (6.5mm) crochet hook
- Stitch holders
- Stitch markers
- Safety pin
- 1 large shank button
- Laundry detergent
- Small mesh laundry bag
- 3-gallon pail for shaping

Gauge

10 sts and 14 rows = 4 inches/10cm in St st when using two strands of yarn held together. Gauge can be approximate. It is not critical in this project.

Special Abbreviation

Make 1 (M1): Inc by making a backward loop on right ndl.

Pattern Notes

Use 2 strands of yarn held tog throughout.

Use 100 percent, non-superwash wool only. Only animal fibers will felt.

Bag

Leaving a 15-inch tail for sewing later, Cast on 54 sts. Join without twisting, pm bet first and last sts and bet 27th and 28th sts.

Rnd 1: Knit.

Rnd 2: *K9, M1, rep from * around. (60 sts)

Rnds 3–7: Knit.

Rnd 8: *K10, M1, rep from * around. (66 sts)

Rnds 9–13: Knit.

Rnd 14: K2, *k4, M1, rep from * to end of rnd. (82 sts)

Insert safety pin in next st to mark beg of bag body. Knit every rnd until 12 inches from pin.

Divide for strap

Row 1: K41, turn. Place rem 41 sts on holder.

Row 2: Purl.

Rows 3 and 4: Rep Rows 1 and 2.

Row 5: K2tog, k to last 2 sts, k2tog.

Row 6: Purl.

Rep Rows 3–6 until 11 sts rem, ending with a WS row. Work 10 rows St st. Bind off loosely, leaving a tail for sewing.

Place sts from holder back on needle. With RS facing, rejoin yarn and work 2nd strap to match.

Finishing

Sew bound off edges of straps tog. Using same yarn and size K hook, single crochet in every other st of strap down to space where straps join. Single crochet tog last st of one strap and first st of other strap to stabilize. Ch 10, sl st in same st to make button loop, continue to single crochet around to start. With hook, sl st across wrong side of strap top, single crochet around strap as for other side, omitting button loop.

Sew bottom of bag and weave in ends.

Felting

Place purse in mesh bag. Set washer to *hot wash, cold rinse, lowest water level, long cycle.* Wash, using a small amount of detergent. Check frequently. When bag has felted to desired size, remove from washer and stretch over 3-gallon pail. Let air dry. Sew button opposite loop. ◆

CHIC LITTLE TOTE

This one-piece bag is so much fun you'll want one in each of your favorite colors!

DESIGN BY SCARLET TAYLOR

Finished Size
Approx 9½ x 5½ inches (Size will vary depending on yarn used and amount of felting.)

Materials
- Brown Sheep Nature Spun 100 percent wool worsted weight yarn (245 yds/3.5 oz per skein): 2 skeins butterfly blue #N59 (A)
- Lion Brand Fancy Fur 55 percent polyamide/45 percent polyester bulky (chunky) weight eyelash yarn (39 yds/1¾ oz per skein): 1 skein brilliant blue #209 (B)
- Size 9 (5.5mm) needles
- Size 11 (8mm) straight and double-pointed needles or sizes needed to obtain gauge
- Stitch holders
- Snap fastener

Gauge
Unfelted: (Knitting should be very loose, with airy sts for best felting results)
12 sts and 16 rows = 4 inches/10cm in St st with larger needles and 2 strands of A held tog
Felted: Approx 14 sts and 26 rows = 4 inches/10cm
To save time, take time to check gauge.

Special Abbreviation
M1 (make 1): Inc by making a backward lp over right needle.

Stripe Pattern
Rows 1 and 2: Work with 1 strand each A and B held tog.
Rows 3–6: Work with 2 strands of A held tog.
Rep Rows 1–6 for Stripe pat.

Pattern Note
Tote front, bottom and back are knit in 1 piece; side gussets are knit separately and sewn tog.

Tote
Front
With smaller needles and 2 strands of A held tog, cast on 26 sts. Knit 2 rows for garter st border.
Working in St st throughout, beg Stripe pat and work even for 16 rows.
Inc row (RS): K1, M1, knit to last st, M1, k1. (28 sts)
Continue to work in established pat, and rep inc row [every 6th row] 3 times. (34 sts)
Work even for 1 row, ending Stripe pat.

Bottom
With 2 strands A held tog, work 20 rows in St st.

Back
Dec row (RS): Work Stripe Pat in reverse order, beg with Rows 3–6, k1, ssk, knit to last 3 sts, k2tog, k1. (32 sts)

Continue to work in established pat, and rep dec row [every 6th row] 3 times. (26 sts)
Work even for 17 rows, ending Stripe Pat.
Next row (RS): With 2 strands A held tog, knit 2 rows for garter st border. Bind off all sts.

Side Gusset
Make 2
With 2 strands A held tog, cast on 17 sts.
Rows 1–8: Beg with a RS row, work even in St st.
Dec row (RS): K1, ssk, knit to last 3 sts, k2tog, k1. (15 sts)
Continue in St st, rep dec row [every 4th row] 5 times. (5 sts)
Work 8 rows even.
Next row (WS): P2tog, p1, p2tog. Sl rem 3 sts to a holder.

Assembly
Sew cast-on edge of each gusset to side edges of bottom. Fold front of tote up and sew sides to edges of gusset. Rep for back. Weave in yarn ends before felting.

Strap
Sl 3 sts from holder to dpn, attach 2 strands of A, *slide sts to other end of needle, pull yarn across back, k3, rep from * until I-cord measures approx 12 inches. Place sts on holder. Rep for other side. Slide sts from holders to needles, and work 3-needle bind off.

Bow

With smaller needles and 1 strand
A, cast on 80 sts.
Row 1 (WS): Knit across.
Row 2: K1, M1, knit to last 3 sts,
k2tog, k1.
Rows 3–10: Rep Rows 1 and 2.
 Bind off all sts.

Felting

Follow basic felting instructions
until tote is desired size.
 Sew snap inside, tie bow
and attach to center front after
felting. ◆

Basic Felting Instructions

 As with any project, you
should knit a gauge swatch
using the stitch pattern
indicated. Make a note of the
total measurements of the
swatch, then felt it to get your
felted gauge. This will also
help determine the amount
of felting time necessary to
achieve the size and look
you desire.
 Place piece in a zippered
pillow protector to protect
your washer from the felted
"fuzz" or yarn fibers that
accumulate during the felting
process, and place in washer.
Set the machine for the
smallest load size and hot-
water setting. To achieve the
best results, you want strong
agitation, so add an old pair of
blue jeans to make the load a
bit heavier. Add a small amount
(a teaspoon or less) of a clear
liquid dishwashing soap, start
your washer and timer.
 Felting can take place
instantly or not, so be vigilant
in watching over your project.
In approximately 4–5 minutes,
stop the washer to check the
progress of the felting. Remove
the piece from the bag, taking
care not to burn yourself,
squeeze the water out, stretch
this way and that, and check
the size. Repeat every 4–5
minutes, resetting the machine
to agitate. DO NOT allow
machine to drain and spin until
the piece is the desired size.

 Remove the now-felted piece
from its bag and rinse under
lukewarm water from your sink
faucet, until water runs clear.
Squeeze out excess water by
rolling in a thirsty towel.

Blocking & Drying
 Shape your purse using short
straws, knitting needles or even
chopsticks to form the bottom
and sides, making sure the
edges are straight and even.
When you have achieved the
desired size and look, leave the
pieces to dry in an airy place,
away from the sun and direct
heat. DO NOT dry in a clothes
dryer. It may take several hours,
or a day or two for the pieces
to dry completely.

NIFTY PLAID BAG

Three coordinating shades of wool yarn are knitted and felted for take along style.

DESIGN FROM SVETLANA AVRAKH

Finished Size
Approx 14 inches high x 8 inches wide.

Materials
- Patons Classic Merino Wool 100 percent wool worsted weight yarn (223 yds/100g per ball): 2 balls paprika (MC) #238, 3 balls russet #206 (A), 2 balls chestnut brown (B) #231
- Size 8 (5mm) straight and set of 4 double-pointed needles (dpn) or size needed to obtain gauge
- 1 cord lock

Gauge
19 sts and 25 rows = 4 inches/10 cm in St st
To save time, take time to check gauge.

Pattern Notes
Patons Design Studio has done a number of tests and can only assure results with the indicated yarn.

Plaid pattern is worked using the intarsia method. Use a separate strand of yarn for each block.

Bag Top
With straight needles and MC, cast on 156 sts.
Row 1 (RS): K12 MC, *k12 A, k12 MC; rep from * across.
Row 2: P12 MC, *p12 A, p12 MC; rep from * across.
Rows 3–20: Rep Rows 1 and 2.

Row 21: K12 A, *k12 B, k12 A; rep from * across.
Row 22: P12 A, *p12 B, p12 A; rep from * across.
Rows 23–40: Rep Rows 21 and 22.
Rows 41–120: [Rep Rows 1–40] twice.
Rows 121–140: Rep Rows 1–20.
With MC, bind off all sts.

Base
With straight needles and B, cast on 43 sts.

Work in garter st (knit every row) until base measures 10 inches from beg, ending with a WS row.
Bind off.

Handle
Make 1
With B and set of dpn, cast on 13 sts. Join without twisting and work in rnds, dividing sts among 3 needles, and placing a marker on first st. Knit in rnds until handle measures 45 inches from beg. Bind off.

Assembly

Felt all pieces (see Basic Felting Instructions on page 34).

Referring to Figs. 1 and 2, cut top 23 inches wide by 14 inches high; cut oval base 6 inches wide by 8 inches long.

Referring to stitch diagrams, fold top into a tube (Fig. 3) and with B sew back seam, keeping seam flat. Pin base to top (Fig. 4). With B and working on outside of bag, blanket stitch (see page 301) base to top. With B, blanket stitch around top of bag.

Trim handle to 32 inches long. Referring to photo, sew handle in place.

Twisted Cord

Cut 2 strands of B, each approx 3 yds long. Fold in half, tie a knot approx 1 inch from cut ends. Secure 1 end to doorknob or hook. Insert a pencil in other end and twist until yarn kinks back on itself when relaxed. Hold yarn at center of twisted strand, remove from doorknob and allow yarn to twist on itself. ·

Holes for cord

Fold top edge of bag as shown in Fig. 5 and poke ends of double-pointed knitting needles through all layers to mark position for cord holes. Cut little holes at marked places.

Beg at center front, thread twisted cord through eyelets as shown in diagram. Thread both ends of cord through cord lock. Tie a knot approx 1 inch from each end of cord, trim ends even. ◆

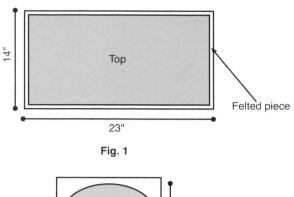

Fig. 1

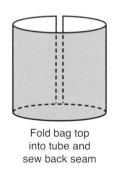

Fig. 2

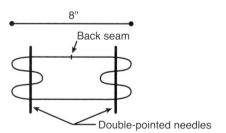

Fold bag top into tube and sew back seam

Fig. 3

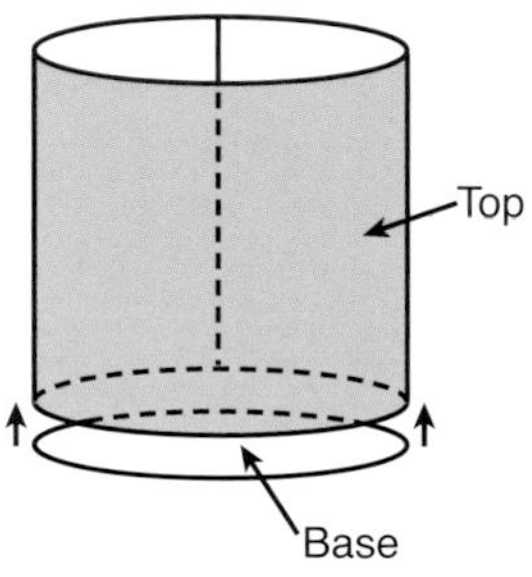

Top

Base

Fig. 4

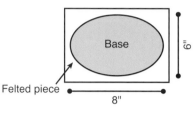

8"

Back seam

Double-pointed needles

Fold top of bag and insert double-pointed needles to mark eyelet holes.

Fig. 5

FELTED ROSE BAGS

Rose blossoms border the edge of this roomy bag that will go everywhere you go!

DESIGN BY SUE MORGAN FOR SOUTH WEST TRADING CO.

Finished Size
Approx 24-inch circumference x 12 inches high

Materials
- South West Trading Co. Karaoke 50 percent soy silk/50 percent wool worsted weight yarn (110 yds/100g per skein): 3 skeins desired color for bag, small amounts for flowers
- Size 6 (4mm) straight or double-pointed needles
- Size 10½ (6.5mm) circular needle or size needed to obtain gauge
- Stitch markers

Gauge
15 sts and 20 rows = 4 inches/10cm in St st with larger needles and 1 strand of yarn (before felting)
To save time, take time to check gauge.

Base
Using larger circular needle and 2 strands of yarn, cast on 40 sts, work 40 rows garter st.

Bag
Continue rest of bag using 1 strand only.
Foundation row: Place marker for beg of rnd (as this marker indicates beg of rnd, it is advisable to use a special color), k40, place marker, pick up and knit 20 sts along side of base, place marker, pick up and knit 40 sts across cast-on edge of base, place marker, pick up and knit 20 sts along rem side of base. (120 sts)

Work 68 rnds in St st, then work 6 rnds in garter st (knit 1 rnd, purl 1 rnd). Bind off, marking corners of bag.

Handles
Make 2
Option 1
Using smaller dpn, work a 5-st I-cord for approx 23 inches. Cast on 5 sts, *slide sts to other end of dpn, pull yarn across back, k5; rep from * for desired length. Bind off.

Option 2
Using smaller needles, cast on 5 sts. Work in St st until for approx 23 inches. Let sts curl around to form a tube and secure at regular intervals.

Tabs
Make 14
Using larger needles, cast on 5 sts. Work in St st for 10 rows. Bind off.

Roses
Make 10
Using larger needles, cast on 72 sts.
Rows 1 and 2: Knit across.
Row 3: [K2tog] across. (36 sts)
Row 4: Knit across.
Row 5: [K2tog] across. (18 sts)
Row 6: Knit across.
  Cut yarn, thread through sts and tighten. Wind rose around itself to form flower shape, using ends to secure.

Assembly
Tabs
Find center point of bag top, fold 1 tab in half and attach securely. Rep for opposite side. Space rem tabs evenly around top of bag, using corner markers and photo as a guide, attach securely. Remember that each handle will be threaded through 7 tabs so tabs need to be placed evenly so bag hangs correctly.

Attach roses evenly around bag as desired.

Thread handle through 7 tabs and attach cast-on and bound-off edges tog. Rep for 2nd handle.

Felting
Now for the fun bit! Don't worry about the size of your bag; it is about to shrink—big time!

Place finished bag in washing machine with a small amount of detergent and a pair of jeans (important for agitation) and run a hot wash/cold rinse. You may prefer a more felted look or a slightly smaller bag. If you do, then just repeat the wash process!

Bags pictured were washed twice. Adjust bag and flowers to shape and leave to dry thoroughly, away from a direct heat source. ◆

FUN & FASHIONABLE

You don't have to be over 50 to enjoy this felted hat & chenille purse!

HAT & SCARFLETTE DESIGNS BY ANNETTE MCRELL & JOANNE TURCOTTE FOR PLYMOUTH YARN CO.
PURSE DESIGN BY PATSY LEATHERBURY

INTERMEDIATE
4
MEDIUM

Hat Size
Finished size is determined by amount of felting

Materials
- Plymouth Galway 100 percent wool worsted weight yarn (210 yds/100g per ball): 2 balls red #16 (MC); for 2-color hat, 1 additional ball purple #13 (CC)
- Size 11 (8mm) double-pointed (dpn) and 24-inch circular needles or size needed to obtain gauge

Scarflette (optional)
- Plymouth Adriafil Stars 50 percent rayon/50 percent nylon bulky weight eyelash yarn (71 yds/50g per ball): 1 ball purple #81
- Size 10 (6mm) needles

Gauge
Hat: 12 sts = 4 inches/10cm before felting
To save time, take time to check gauge.

Special Abbreviation
M1 (make 1): Insert left needle from front to back under horizontal strand between st on left needle and st just worked, forming a lp on needle; k1-tbl.

Pattern Notes
These instructions were written for Galway yarn; results cannot be guaranteed with another yarn.

Project is worked with 2 strands of yarn held tog throughout. Knitting must be loose to felt properly.

HAT
Loosely cast on 90 sts. Join without twisting and knit 2 rnds.
Inc rnd: *K9, M1; rep from * around. (100 sts)

Continue to knit in rnds until hat measures 3 inches.
Dec rnd: *K8, k2tog; rep from * around. (90 sts)

Knit 1 inch more (4 inches total). Mark this point as beg of crown.

Crown
Note: Change to CC at this point if desired for 2-color hat.
Rnd 1: *[K2tog] 4 times, k1; rep from * around. (50 sts)
Rnds 2 and 3: Knit.
Rnd 4: *K2, M1, k3, M1; rep from * around. (70 sts)

Continue to knit on 70 sts until

total length from beg is 8 inches.
Note: If making 2-color hat, when hat measures 2½ inches from beg of crown, cut CC, join MC and continue to knit as above.

Shape top
Note: Change to dpn as needed.
Rnd 1: *K5, k2tog; rep from * around. (60 sts)
Rnd 2 and all even-numbered rnds: Knit.
Rnd 3: *K4, k2tog; rep from * around. (50 sts)
Rnd 5: *K3, k2tog; rep from * around. (40 sts)
Rnd 7: *K2, k2tog; rep from * around. (30 sts)
Rnd 9: *K1, k2tog; rep from * around. (20 sts)
Rnd 11: [K2tog] around. (10 sts)
Rnd 12: [K2tog] around. (5 sts)

Cut yarn, pull it through rem sts, pull tightly and fasten off. Weave in all ends before felting.

Felting
See Basic Felting Instructions on page 34. For blocking and drying, stretch hat over a bowl with a circumference that is slightly larger than your head. Curl up brim if desired. Brush to remove excess lint. Let dry in an airy place away from the sun and direct heat. It may take up to 2 days for hat to dry completely.

SCARFLETTE

Gauge

Gauge is not critical to scarf.

Scarflette

Loosely cast on 10 sts. Work in garter st until length fits around base of brim when slightly stretched. Bind off all sts. Sew cast-on edge to bound-off edge. Place around brim as shown in photo. This scarflette is removable.

PURSE

Finished Size

Approx 9 inches high

Materials

- Lion Brand Lion Chenille 100 percent acrylic worsted weight yarn (174 yds/85g per skein): 1 skein garnet #113
- Size 3 (3.25mm) 16-inch circular needle or size needed to obtain gauge
- Stitch marker
- Red drapery cord: 2 yds
- Red Hat pin or trim
- Purple silk flowers
- Pins or fabric glue
- 6-inch-square cardboard or red art board

Gauge

14 sts = 4 inches/10cm in St st
To save time, take time to check gauge.

Purse

Cast on 60 sts. Join without twisting, place marker at beg of rnd.
Rnd 1: Knit.
Rnd 2: Purl.

Rnds 3–10: [Rep Rnds 1 and 2] 4 more times for garter st top.
Rnds 11–14: Knit.
Rnd 15: K3, [yo, k2tog, k4) 9 times, yo, k2tog, k1.
Rnds 16–19: Knit.

Beg pat

Rnd 1: *K1, p1; rep from * to end of rnd.
Rnd 2: *P1, k1; rep from * to end of rnd.
Rep Rnds 1 and 2 for seed st until purse measures 9 inches.

Shape bottom

Rnd 1: [K8, k2tog] 6 times. (54 sts)
Rnds 2–6: Beg with a purl rnd, work in garter st.
Rnd 7: [K7, k2tog] 6 times. (48 sts)
Rnds 8–12: Rep Rnds 2–6.
Rnd 13: [K6, k2tog] 6 times. (42 sts)
Rnds 14–16: Beg with a purl rnd, work in garter st.
Rnd 17: [K5, k2tog] 6 times. (36 sts)
Rnds 18–20: Rep Rnds 14–16.
Rnd 21: [K4, k2tog] 6 times. (30 sts)
Rnd 22: Purl.
Rnd 23: [K3, k2tog] 6 times. (24 sts)
Rnd 24: Purl.
Rnd 25: [K2, k2tog] 6 times. (18 sts)
Rnd 26: [K1, k2tog] 6 times. (12 sts)
Rnd 27: [K2tog] 6 times. (6 sts)
Cut yarn, leaving a 6-inch tail. Run yarn end through rem sts, pull tight, and fasten off.

Finishing

Cut drapery cord in half. Thread 1 piece of cord through yo holes to make drawstring, beg at first hole of rnd, and knotting cord on inside of purse. Rep with other piece cord, beg at opposite side of purse. A small amount of fabric glue on knots will prevent raveling.

Cut a 5½-inch circle from cardboard and place in bottom of purse to shape bottom. Referring to photo, glue or pin purple flowers and trim to purse below drawstring. ◆

WRAPAROUND PURSE COVER

Add fresh life to a beloved purse with an innovative cover using some fun, novelty yarns.

DESIGN BY ELLEN EDWARDS DRECHSLER

Size
To fit over a purse measuring
10 x 12 x 3 inches

Finished Measurements
Height: 12 inches
Diameter: 30 inches

Materials
- Plymouth Encore Worsted 75 percent acrylic/25 percent wool worsted weight yarn (200 yds/100g per ball): 2 balls black #217 (MC)
- Plymouth Colorlash 100 percent polyester novelty eyelash yarn (220 yds/50g per ball): 1 ball each blue #32 (A) and raspberry #215 (B)
- Plymouth Dazzlelash 78 percent polyester/22 percent rayon novelty eyelash yarn (220 yds/ 50g per ball): 1 ball black #107 (C)
- Size 9 (5.5mm) double-pointed and 24-inch circular needles or size needed to obtain gauge
- Stitch markers
- Purchased purse
- Hot glue gun
- 1 yd black elastic thread
- Tapestry needle

Gauge
14 sts and 20 rnds = 4 inches/10cm in St st
To save time, take time to check gauge.

Pattern Note

Multiple strands of yarn are held tog for entire purse cover.

Cover

Beg at top with 2 strands of MC held tog, cast on 80 sts. Join without twisting, place marker between first and last st. Place 2nd marker after 40th st.

Work even in St st for 2 inches.

Add 1 strand each of MC, B and C. (5 strands held tog)

Work even until cover measures 12 inches, or 1 inch less than height of purse.

Cut all CC, knit 2 rnds with MC only.

Place marker 10 sts to the left and 10 sts to the right of original markers. Remove original markers. (20 sts between each marker)

Shape bottom

K 10 sts, mark this as new beg of round.

Dec rnd: [Ssk, k to 2 sts before marker, k2tog, k20] twice.

[Rep dec rnd] 8 times more, changing to dpn when necessary. There will be 20 sts on each of the longer sides and 2 sts between markers on the short ends.

Next rnd: [K2tog, k20] twice. (42 sts)

Divide sts evenly onto 2 needles.

Decide which side of cover you want as the 'public' side.

If you bind off with knit sts held tog, the purl side will become the RS of the cover and you will have

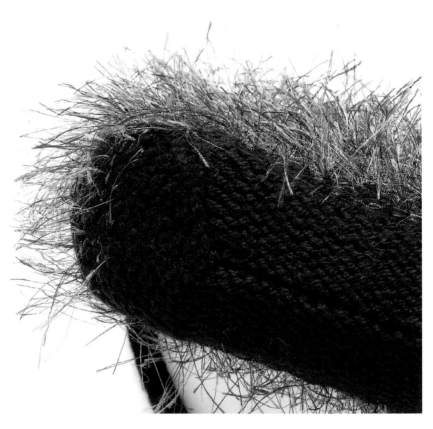

more eyelash showing. If you want less eyelash, bind off with the purl sts held tog.

Join bottom of cover using 3-needle bind off.

Handles

With 2 strands of MC held tog, cast on 6 sts leaving a long end for later use in attaching handle.

Work in I-cord for desired length of handle.

Bind off.

Cut yarn, leaving a 12-inch length for attaching handle.

Finishing

Pull cover over purse.

With double strand of elastic thread, sew a row of running sts directly below MC band. Pull elastic tightly and fasten. MC band will curl naturally.

With first rnd of CC at top edge of purse, spread glue in a bead along top edge and secure cover firmly to purse.

Sew handles to cover at outer corners. Reinforce handles by sewing top edge of cover to inside edge of handles. ◆

GARTER RIDGE BAG

Here is a quick purse that will delight young and old alike. Make several to diversify your wardrobe.

DESIGN BY LOIS S. YOUNG

Finished Size
Approx 9 inches wide x 10 inches high

Materials
- Plymouth Fantasy Naturale 100 percent mercerized cotton worsted weight yarn: (140 yds/100g per ball): 2 balls lime #5228 (A)
- Plymouth Eros 100 percent nylon novelty eyelash yarn (165 yds/50g per ball): 2 balls green variegated #1924 (B)
- Size 9 (5.5mm) 16-inch circular needle or size needed to obtain gauge
- Stitch markers

Gauge
15 sts and 25 rnds = 4 inches/10cm in Garter Ridge pat
To save time, take time to check gauge.

Pattern Stitch
Garter Ridge
Rnd 1: K1, p35; rep from * around.
Rnds 2, 4, 8 and 10: P1, k35; rep from * around.
Rnds 3, 5, 7 and 9: Knit.
Rnd 6: Purl.
Rep Rnds 1–10 for pat.

Pattern Note
One strand of each yarn is held tog for entire purse.

Bag
Cast on 36 sts, place marker, cast on 36 sts. (72 sts)
Join without twisting, place marker between first and last st.
Work even in Garter Ridge pat for 50 rnds.
Rep Rnds 1 and 2, rep Rnd 1.
Eyelet rnd: *K2tog, yo; rep from * around.
[Work Rnds 1–2] 3 times.
Bind off purlwise.

Twisted Cord Ties
Make 2
Cut 2 4-yd strands each of A and B.
Loop yarn around a cup hook or doorknob, fold in half and hold all ends tog.
Holding yarn taut, twist until yarn begins to kink upon itself.
Grasp cut ends in one hand, hold middle of cord with other hand. Bring cut end to looped end.
Release middle, letting cord twist back on itself.
Remove loop from knob or hook, smooth any remaining kinks.
Knot each end loosely.

Finishing
Turn bag inside out and sew bottom tog, folding at garter st "seams."
Turn to right side.
Run 1 cord through each side of bag, leaving an end at each "seam."
Adjust cords evenly, and knot them together.
Trim ends. ◆

SAFARI TRAVELER BAG

This quick-to-knit bag is trimmed with short eyelash yarn for animal-friendly style.

DESIGN BY FRANCES HUGHES

Finished Size
Approx 9 x 10½ inches (not including handles)

Materials
- On Line Tondo 100 percent wool super bulky yarn (50 yds/50g per skein): 5 skeins #106 (MC)
- Knitting Fever Brazilia Fantasy Color 100 percent polyester eyelash novelty yarn (98 yds/50g per skein): 1 ball #388 (CC)
- Size 11 (8mm) 16-inch circular needle or size needed to obtain gauge
- 2 plastic tortoiseshell purse handles

Gauge
9 sts = 4 inches/10cm in St st
Exact gauge is not critical to this project.

Pattern Note
Base of purse is worked back and forth in garter st, then sts are picked up around the edges. Body of purse is worked in rnds of St st.

Purse
With MC, cast on 20 sts.

Rows 1–9: Knit.
Pick up and knit 4 sts across first narrow end of base, 20 sts along cast-on edge, 4 sts across other end, knit 20 sts on needle. (48 sts)

Rnds 11–28: Join and work in St st. Cut MC.

Rnds 29–34: Using 4 strands of CC held tog, knit.
Bind off.

Assembly
Fold purse in half, marking center of front and back. Sew handles to purse, centering on markers. ◆

SNAZZY STRIPED PURSES & SCARVES

Choose soothing earthy tones or glowing rainbow-color yarns for these super-quick purses with matching scarves.

DESIGN BY SUE CHILDRESS

Finished Measurements

Bag: Approx 14 inches square (not including handles)

Scarf: Approx 5 x 34 inches

Materials

Bright Colors Version

- On Line Tondo 100 percent wool super bulky yarn (50 yds/50g per skein): 1 skein purple #6 (A), 1 skein salmon #3 (B), 1 skein green #15 (C), 2 skeins cranberry #13 (D)
- Nomotta Brazilia Fantasy 100 percent polyester eyelash novelty yarn (99 yds/50g per skein): 1 skein green #382 (CC), 1 skein cranberry #385 (DD)
- Nomotta Salsa 100 percent polyester eyelash novelty yarn (99 yds/50g per skein): 1 skein #532 purple (AA)
- Sirdar Funky Fur 100 percent polyester eyelash novelty yarn (99 yds/50g per skein): 1 skein #86 salmon (BB)
- 2 (12-inch) brown wooden purse handles
- Size 10 (6mm) needles or size needed to obtain gauge

Cream Version

- On Line Tondo 100 percent wool super bulky yarn (50 yds/50g per skein): 5 skeins cream #1 (E)

- Berroco Sizzle 100 percent polyester eyelash novelty yarn (98 yds/50g per skein): 1 ball #1713 (EE)
- 2 (12-inch) natural wooden purse handles
- Size 10 (6mm) needles or size needed to obtain gauge

Gauge

11 sts = 4 inches/10cm in garter st Exact gauge is not critical to this project.

Special Abbreviation

M1 (make 1): Increase 1 by inserting LH from front to back under horizontal strand between last st worked and next st on LH needle. With RH needle, knit in back of this loop.

Pattern Notes

Bag is cast on at top of 1 side and worked to other side of top.

Yarn amounts given are sufficient for both purse and scarf.

Use 2 strands of novelty yarn held tog.

PURSE

With D (E), cast on 30 sts.

Rows 1–20: Knit.

Row 21 and 22: [K1, M1] twice, knit to last 2 sts, [M1, k1] twice. Cut yarn, marking each end of last row. (38 sts)

Rows 23–28: Attach 2 strands of DD (EE), knit across. Cut yarn.

Rows 29–40: With C (E), knit. Cut yarn.

Rows 41–46: Attach 2 strands of CC (EE), knit. Cut yarn.

Rows 47–58: With B (E), knit. Cut yarn.

Rows 59–64: Attach 2 strands of BB (EE), knit. Cut yarn.

Rows 65–76: With A (E), knit. Cut yarn.

Rows 77–82: Attach 2 strands of AA (EE) knit. Cut yarn.

Row 83: With D (E), *k1, p1; rep from * across.

Row 84: *P1, k1; rep from * across.

Row 85–90: [Rep Rows 83 and 84] twice. Cut yarn.

Rows 91–96: Rep Rows 77–82. Cut yarn.

Rows 97–108: Rep Rows 65–76. Cut yarn.

Rows 109–114: Rep Rows 59–64. Cut yarn.

Rows 115–126: Rep Rows 47–58. Cut yarn.

Rows 127–132: Rep rows 41–46. Cut yarn.

Rows 133–144: Rep Rows 29–40. Cut yarn.

Rows 145–150: Rep Rows 23–28. Cut yarn.
Rows 151 and 152: With D (E) bind off 2 sts, knit to last 4 sts, [k2tog] twice. (30 sts)
Knit 20 rows.
Bind off all sts.

Assembly

Sew side seams from bottom through Row 23 on each side. Pull end of purse through cutout on base of purse handle, lap over and sew in place on WS.

SCARF

Note: Use 2 strands of novelty yarn held tog.
With D (E), cast on 13 sts.
Rows 1–12: Knit 12 rows D (E).
Rows 13–18: Knit 6 rows DD (EE).
Rows 19–30: Knit 12 rows C (E).
Rows 31–36: Knit 6 rows CC (EE).
Rows 37–48: Knit 12 rows B (E).
Rows 49–54: Knit 6 rows BB (EE).
Rows 55–66: Knit 12 rows A (E).
Rows 67–72: Knit 6 rows AA (EE).
Rows 73–96: Knit 24 rows D (E).
Rows 97–102: Knit 6 rows AA (EE).
Rows 103–114: Knit 12 rows A (E).
Rows 115–120: Knit 6 rows BB (EE).
Rows 121–132: Knit 12 rows B (E).
Rows 133–138: Knit 6 rows CC (EE).
Rows 139–150: Knit 12 rows C (E).
Rows 151–156: Knit 6 rows DD (EE).
Rows 157–168: Knit 12 rows D (E).
Bind off all sts knitwise. ◆

TRENDY SUMMER KNITS

These flirty and feather-light wraps and trendsetting warm weather sweaters will have you knitting in no time!

GOSSAMER LACE

This shawl is the perfect accent for a formal outfit for that special summer evening out.

DESIGN BY JULIE GADDY

Finished Size
Approx 24 x 68 inches (after blocking and excluding fringe)

Materials
- Knit One, Crochet Too Douceur et Soie 70 percent baby mohair/30 percent silk fingering weight yarn (225 yds/25g per ball): 5 balls cantaloupe #8320
- Size 6 (4mm) circular knitting needle or size needed to obtain gauge
- Size C/2 (2.75mm) crochet hook

Gauge
21 sts = 4 inches/10cm in pat (after blocking)
To save time, take time to check gauge.

Pattern Stitch
Vertical Lace Trellis (multiple of 2 sts + 1)
Rows 1 and 3 (WS): Purl across.
Row 2: K1, *yo, k2tog; rep from * across.
Row 4: *Ssk, yo; rep from * to last st, end k1.
Rep Rows 1–4 for pat.

Pattern Notes
To change the size of the shawl, use the following guidelines:
For a longer shawl, add 1 more ball of yarn, which will make the shawl approx 17 inches longer.

For a wider shawl, cast on an additional 32 sts (total of 159 sts) and add 1 more ball of yarn, which will make the shawl approx 6 inches wider.
For a shawl that is both longer and wider, combine the 2 changes above, which will require 3 additional balls of yarn.

Shawl
Cast on 127 sts.
Rep Rows 1–4 of pat until 1 ball of yarn remains, ending with a WS row.

Bind off all sts knitwise.
Shawl will measure approximately 54 inches unblocked.

Finishing
Block shawl.

Fringe
Following Fringe instructions on page 303, make Triple Knot Fringe. Cut yarn in 24-inch strands; using 2 strands for each knot, fringe each short end of scarf, placing knots in every 3rd st.
Trim ends even. ◆

FLASH OF GOLD SHOULDER SHAWL

Three different carry-along yarns are combined in a trendy shawl styled after traditional smoke rings.

DESIGN BY ANITA CLOSIC

Size
One size fits most

Finished Measurements
12 x 30 inches

Materials
- Plymouth Electra 100 percent nylon novelty eyelash yarn (125 yds/50g per ball): 1 ball gold/copper #20
- Plymouth Eros 100 percent nylon novelty railroad yarn (165 yds/50g per ball): 1 ball black #3017
- Plymouth Flash 100 percent nylon novelty eyelash yarn (190 yds/50g per ball): 1 ball black #901
- Size 17 (12.75mm) 24-inch circular needle or size needed to obtain gauge
- Stitch marker

Gauge
8 sts and 8 rnds = 4 inches/10cm in pat st
To save time, take time to check gauge.

Pattern Note
Hold 1 strand of each yarn tog for entire shawl.

Shawl
With 1 strand of each yarn held tog, loosely cast on 64 sts. Join without twisting, pm between first and last st.
Rnd 1: Knit.
Rnds 2 and 3: *Yo, k2tog; rep from * around.
   Rep Rnds 1–3 until shawl measures approx 12 inches, ending with Rnd 1.
   Bind off loosely. ◆

FIESTA GRANDE SHAWL

Inspired by the brilliant colors of a south-western fiesta, this shawl is a great way to use small amounts of several colors!

▪ DESIGN BY PATSY LEATHERBURY

Finished Size

Approximately 34 x 84 inches (excluding fringe)

Materials

- Katia Siesta 50 percent viscose/50 percent acrylic sport weight yarn from KFI Inc. (126 yds/50g per ball): 4 balls black #820 (MC), 3 balls each aqua #815, lime #816, pink #814, 2 balls each purple #818, turquoise #817, yellow #811, orange #812, red #813
- Size 3 (3.25mm) 29-inch circular needle or size needed to obtain gauge

Gauge

Approximately 20 sts = 4 inches/10cm in garter st
Gauge is not critical to this project.

Pattern Notes

This project is a good way to use small amounts of different colors of the same yarn, or to combine many different yarns of the same weight.

The garter st stripe pattern is reversible, and the size can easily be adjusted by casting on more or less sts.

Shawl

Cut 2 (374-inch) pieces of MC, knot pieces tog 6 inches from 1 end and cast on 400 sts, using long tail cast on. At end, knot both pieces again, leaving 6-inch tails.

*Tie next strand to previous strand, knit across, cut yarn, leaving a 6-inch tail. Rep from * for 225 rows, changing colors as desired, cutting yarn at end of every row, and being sure to knot yarns securely each time.

Bind off all sts, leaving 6-inch ends and knotting as before. Trim fringe even.

Sample project was worked in the following color sequence:
Rows 1–3: Black (MC).
Rows 4–6: Red.
Rows 7–9: Pink.
Rows 10 and 11: Orange.
Rows 12 and 13: Black.
Rows 14–17: Purple.
Rows 18–20: Turquoise.
Rows 21 and 22: Yellow.
Rows 23–25: Aqua.
Rows 26–29: Black.
Rows 30–33: Red.
Rows 34–37: Yellow.
Rows 38–41: Turquoise.
Rows 42 and 43: Black.
Rows 44 and 45: Lime.
Rows 46 and 47: Black.
Rows 48–55: [Rep Rows 44–47] twice.
Rows 56–60: Pink.
Rows 61–64: Purple.

Rows 65–69: Aqua.
Rows 70 and 71: Black.
Rows 72–74: Red.
Rows 75–77: Pink.
Rows 78–80: Orange.
Rows 81–83: Yellow.
Rows 84–86: Lime.
Rows 87–89: Aqua.
Rows 90–92: Turquoise.
Rows 93–95: Purple.
Rows 96 and 97: Black.
Rows 98–100: Pink.
Rows 101 and 102: Lime.
Rows 103 and 104: Pink.
Rows 105–108: Rep Rows 101–104.
Rows 109 and 110: Lime.
Rows 111–113: Pink.
Row 114–116: Black.
Rows 117–119: Purple.
Row 120: Turquoise.
Rows 121 and 122: Purple.
Rows 123 and 124: Turquoise.
Row 125: Purple.
Rows 126–128: Turquoise.
Row 129: Aqua.
Rows 130 and 131: Turquoise.
Rows 132 and 133: Aqua.
Row 134: Turquoise.
Rows 135–137: Aqua.
Row 138: Lime.
Rows 139 and 140: Aqua.
Rows 141 and 142: Lime.
Row 143: Aqua.

Rows 144–146: Lime.
Row 147: Yellow.
Rows 148 and 149: Lime.
Rows 150 and 151: Yellow.
Row 152: Lime.
Rows 153–155: Yellow.
Row 156: Orange.
Rows 157 and 158: Yellow.
Rows 159 and 160: Orange.
Row 161: Yellow.
Rows 162–164: Orange.
Row 165: Pink.
Rows 166 and 167: Orange.
Rows 168 and 169: Pink.
Row 170: Orange.
Rows 171–173: Pink.
Row 174: Red.
Rows 175 and 176: Pink.
Rows 177 and 178: Red.
Row 179: Pink.
Rows 180–182: Red.
Rows 183 and 184: Black.
Rows 185 and 186: Aqua.
Rows 187 and 188: Black.
Rows 189 and 190: Aqua.
Rows 191 and 192: Black.
Rows 193 and 194: Aqua.
Rows 195 and 196: Black.
Rows 197–199: Pink.
Rows 200–202: Yellow.
Rows 203–205: Orange.
Rows 206–208: Red.
Rows 209 and 210: Black.
Rows 211–213: Lime.
Rows 214–216: Aqua.
Rows 217–219: Turquoise.
Rows 220–222: Purple.
Rows 223–225: Black.
　Bind off with black. ◆

LITTLE BOWS TOP & WRAP

Shimmering yarn and an interesting stitch add feminine appeal to this beautiful summer set.

DESIGN BY DARLA SIMS

TOP

Size

Woman's small (medium, large, extra-large) Instructions are given for smallest size, with large sizes in parentheses. When only 1 number is given, it applies to all sizes.

Finished Size

Chest: 36 (40, 44, 48) inches

Materials

- Crystal Palace Yarns Shimmer 86 percent acrylic/14 percent nylon bulky weight tape yarn (90 yds/50g per ball): 5 (6, 7, 8) balls strawberry #2846
- Size 8 (5mm) needles
- Size 10½ (6.5mm) needles or size needed to obtain gauge
- Brooch back (optional)

Gauge

16 sts and 20 rows = 4 inches/10cm in Little Bows Pat with larger needles
To save time, take time to check gauge.

Pattern Stitch

Slipped Rib Pattern (odd number of sts)
Row 1 (WS): K1, *p1, k1; rep from * across.
Row 2: P1, *sl 1p wyif, p1; rep from * across.
Rep Rows 1 and 2 for pat.

Pattern Note

Sl all sts purlwise wyif, being careful not to pull yarn too tight.

Back

With smaller needles, cast on 63 (73, 83, 97) sts.

Work in Slipped Rib Pat until back measures 2 inches, ending with Row 2.

Next row: Purl across, inc 9 sts evenly. (72, 82, 92, 106 sts)

Change to larger needles.

Beg pat

Rows 1, 3 and 5: K1, *sl 5 sts wyif, k5; rep from * to last 11 (11, 11, 6) sts, end sl 5 wyif, k6 (6, 6, 1).

Row 2, 4 and 6: Purl.

Row 7: K3, *insert tip of RH needle from below under 3 loose strands, k1 in next st catching strands, k9; rep from * to last 9 (9, 9, 4) sts, end insert tip of RH needle from below under 3 loose strands, k1 in next st catching strands, k8 (8, 8, 3).

Row 8: Purl.

Rows 9, 11 and 13: K6, *sl 5 sts wyif, k5; rep from * to last 6 (6, 6, 11) sts, end sl 5 wyif, k1 (1, 1, 6).

Rows 10, 12 and 14: Purl.

Row 15: K8, *insert tip of RH needle from below under 3 loose strands, k1 in next st catching strands, k9; rep from * to last 4 (4, 4, 9) sts, end insert tip of RH needle from below under 3 loose strands, k1 in next st catching strands, k3 (3, 3, 8).

Row 16: Purl.

Rep Rows 1–16 until back measures approx 12 inches from beg, ending with Row 7 or 15. Purl next row, dec 1 st. (71, 81, 91, 105 sts)

Work 14 rows in Slipped Rib pat.

Bind off all sts.

Front

Work same as back.

Straps

With smaller needles, cast on 7 sts and work in Slipped Rib Pat until strap measures 16 inches or desired length. Bind off.

Finishing

Sew side seams. Sew on straps approx 3½ inches in from side seams.

Flower

With smaller needles, [cast on 7 sts, bind off 7 sts] 7 times. [Cast on 9 sts, bind off 8 sts] 7 times. Fasten off.

Beg at start of fringe, roll into circular shape with longer strands on outside and sew tog on WS.

If desired, sew to brooch back. Pin to 1 strap.

WRAP

Finished Size

Approx 12 x 52 inches (excluding fringe)

Materials

• Crystal Palace Yarns Shimmer 86 percent acrylic/14 percent nylon bulky weight tape yarn (90 yds/50g per ball): 9 balls strawberry #2846
• Size 8 (5mm) needles
• Size 11 (8mm) needles

Gauge

19 sts = 4 inches/10cm in Slipped Rib Pat with larger needles

To save time, take time to check gauge.

Wrap

With larger needles, cast on 57 sts. Work Rows 1 and 2 of Slipped Rib Pat until wrap measures approx 52 inches, ending with a WS row.

Bind off all sts.

Fringe border
Make 2

With smaller needles, cast on 35 sts, bind off 34 sts. [Turn, cast on 34 sts, bind off 34 sts] 21 times, fasten off last st.

Sew fringe borders to ends of wrap. ◆

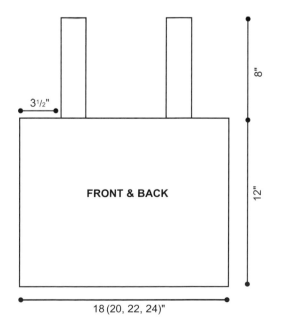

3½"

8"

12"

FRONT & BACK

18 (20, 22, 24)"

SILK CABLED SHELL

A dramatic cable and wide ribs highlight a classic shell. Wear it everywhere, from casual to elegant affairs.

DESIGN BY KENNITA TULLY

Size

Woman's small (medium, large, extra-large) Instructions are given for smallest size, with larger sizes in parentheses. When only 1 number is given, it applies to all sizes.

Finished Measurements

Chest: 36 (40, 44, 48) inches
Length: 20 (21, 22, 23) inches

Materials

- Brown Sheep Prairie Silks 72 percent wool/18 percent mohair/ 10 percent silk worsted weight yarn (88 yds/50g per skein): 7 (8, 9, 10) skeins dough #PS100
- Size 8 (5mm) needles or size needed to obtain gauge
- Cable needle
- Stitch markers
- Size G/6 (4mm) crochet hook

Gauge

18 sts and 20 rows = 4 inches/10cm in rib pat
To save time, take time to check gauge.

Special Abbreviations

BC (Back Cross): Sl 1 st to cn and hold in back, k2, k2 from cn.
FC (Front Cross): Sl 2 sts to cn and hold in front, k2, k2 from cn.

Pattern Stitch

Staghorn Cable (panel of 16 sts)
Rows 1, 3 and 5 (WS): Purl.
Row 2: K4, BC, FC, k4.
Row 4: K2, BC, k4, FC, k2.
Row 6: BC, k8, FC.
Rep Rows 1–6 for pat.

Pattern Notes

All decs for underarm and neck shaping are worked 1 st in from each edge.

First and last 2 sts at armhole and neck edge are kept in St st to ease later working of crochet trim.

Back

Cast on 82 (90, 98, 106) sts.

Set up pat (WS): P4, [k2, p2] 1 (2, 3, 4) times, k2, p3, k2, [p4, k2] 3 times, pm, work Staghorn Cable pat over next 16 sts, pm, [k2, p4] 3 times, k2, p3, k2, [p2, k2] 1 (2, 3, 4) times, p4.

Keeping sts between markers in Staghorn Cable pat, and rem in established rib pat, *at the same time* work side shaping by dec 1 st each end [every 4th row] 4 times. (74, 82, 94, 98 sts)

Inc 1 st each end [every 8th row] 4 times. (82, 90, 98, 106 sts)

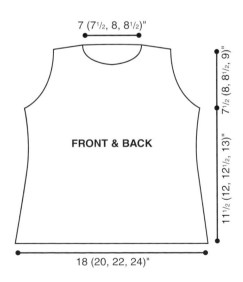

7 (7½, 8, 8½)"

7½ (8, 8½, 9)"

11½ (12, 12½, 13)"

FRONT & BACK

18 (20, 22, 24)"

Work even until back measures 11½ (12, 12½, 13) inches, ending with a WS row.

Shape armhole

Bind off 5 (6, 7, 8) sts at beg of next 2 rows. (72, 78, 84, 90 sts)

Dec 1 st each end [every RS row] 6 times. (60, 66, 72, 78 sts)

Work even until armhole measures 7½ (8, 8½, 9) inches, ending with a WS row.

Shoulder shaping

Bind off 5 (5, 6, 7) sts at beg of next 4 rows, then 4 (6, 6, 6) sts at beg of following 2 rows.

Bind off rem 32 (34, 36, 38) sts.

Front

Work as for back until armhole measures 5½ (5¾, 6, 6½) inches, ending with a WS row.

Shape neck

Work across 22 (25, 28, 31) sts, join 2nd ball of yarn and bind off center 16 sts, work to end of row.

Working on both sides of neck with separate balls of yarn, bind off at each neck edge [2 sts] 2 (2, 3, 3) times.

Dec 1 st at each neck edge [every other row] 4 (5, 4, 5) times. (14, 16, 18, 20 sts)

At the same time, when armhole measures same as for back, work shoulder shaping as for back.

Assembly

Sew shoulder seams.

Sew side seams.

Neck Trim

Beg at center back neck and working from left to right, with crochet hook work 1 row sc around entire neck line.

Fasten off.

Rep for armholes, beg at underarm. ◆

ALL OCCASION SHELL

No one will know how easy this Broken Garter Stitch pattern is to do!

DESIGN BY MARY MARIK

Size

Woman's extra-small (small, medium, large) Instructions are given for smallest size, with larger sizes in parentheses. When only 1 number is given, it applies to all sizes.

Finished Measurements

Chest: 33 (36, 40, 42) inches
Length: 18 (19, 20½, 21½) inches

Materials

- Lion Brand Microspun 100 percent microfiber acrylic sport weight yarn (168 yds/70g per ball): 3 (3, 4, 4) balls ebony #153 (A), 2 (3, 3, 3) balls French vanilla #98 (B)
- Size 3 (3.25mm) straight and 16-inch circular needles
- Size 5 (3.75mm) needles or size needed to obtain gauge
- Stitch markers
- Stitch holders

Gauge

24 sts and 42 rows = 4 inches/10cm pat with larger needles
To save time, take time to check gauge.

Pattern Stitch

Broken Garter Stitch (multiple of 10 sts + 6)
Row 1 (RS): With A, knit.
Row 2: With B, *k1, p4, k5; rep from * to last 6 sts, end k1, p4, k1.
Row 3: With B, knit.
Row 4: With A, *k6, p4; rep from * to last 6 sts, end k6.
Rep Rows 1–4 for pat.

Pattern Notes

Pattern is created on WS rows; color changes occur at the beginning of WS rows.

Color not in use is carried along edge of garment. At the beginning of Rows 2 and 4, where color change occurs, bring new color around old color to create a half-twist along the border.

There is a selvage stitch on each edge of garment, including armhole edges; these one-stitch borders are worked as knit stitches at the beginning and end of every row, and they are not included in the Broken Garter pattern stitch instructions. The selvage stitches make it easier to sew side seams and pick up stitches around armholes and neck edge.

Back

With smaller needles and A, cast on 98 (108, 118, 128) sts.

Bottom Border

Knit every row until piece measures 2 inches, ending with a WS row.
Change to larger needles.

Beg pat

Row 1: K1 (selvage st), work Row 1 of pat across to last st, k1 (selvage st).
Row 2: With B, k1, work Row 2 of pat, end k1.
Row 3: With B, k1, work Row 3 of pat, end k1.
Row 4: With A, k1, work Row 4 of pat, end k1.
Rep Rows 1–4 until back measures 10 (11, 12, 12½) inches from beg, including bottom border,

or desired length to underarm, ending with a Row 2.

Shape armhole
Bind off 6 (8, 8, 10) sts at beg of next 2 rows. (86, 92, 102, 108 sts)
Next row (dec row): K1, ssk, work to last 3 sts, k2tog, k1.

Maintain selvage sts and pat (markers placed between pat reps make this easier) while dec 1 st at each end as above every RS row until 58 (62, 66, 72) sts rem. (56, 60, 64, 70 sts in pat and 2 selvage sts)

Work even in pat until armhole measures 6½ (6½, 7, 7) inches, ending with a WS row.

Shape back neck
Next row (RS): K1, work in pat across next 12 (13, 14, 16) sts and place on holder; bind off center 32 (34, 36, 38) sts; work in pat to end of row.

Right shoulder
Bind off at neck edge [3 sts] once, then [2 sts] once. (8, 9, 10, 12 sts)

Work even until piece measures 18 (19, 20½, 21½) from beg.
Bind off.

Left shoulder
With WS facing join appropriate color at neck edge.

Bind off at neck edge [3 sts] once,

then [2 sts] once. (8, 9, 10, 12 sts)
Work even until piece measures 18 (19, 20½, 21½) from beg.
Bind off.

Front
Work as for back until piece measures 5½ (5½, 6, 6) inches above underarm, ending with a WS row.

Shape front neck
Next row (RS): K1, work in pat across 23 (20, 21, 23) sts and place sts on holder, bind off center 18 (20, 22, 24) sts; work in pat to end of row.

Right shoulder
Bind off at neck edge, [4 sts] once, then [3 sts] once.

Maintaining a 1-st selvage at neckline edge, ssk in 2nd and 3rd sts from edge every RS row until 8 (9, 10, 12) sts rem.

Work even until piece measures same as back.
Bind off.

Left shoulder
With WS facing, join appropriate color at neck edge.

Bind off at neck edge, [4 sts] once, then [3 sts] once.

Maintaining a 1-st selvage at neckline edge; knit next 2 sts tog

on every RS row until 8 (9, 10, 12) sts rem.

Work even until piece measures same as back.
Bind off.

Assembly
Sew shoulder seams.

Neck band
Hold with RS facing and beg at left shoulder, with A and smaller circular needle, pick up and knit 60 (62, 64, 66) sts around front and 50 (52, 54, 56) across back. (110, 114, 118, 122 sts)

Join, mark beg of rnd.

Work garter st in rnds, purl next rnd. Alternate knit and purl rnds until neckband measures approx ½ inch.
Bind off.

Armband
Hold with RS facing, with A and smaller straight needles, beg at underarm, pick up and knit 1 st in each color change of body (1 st for every 2 rows; work into selvage sts when picking up).

Work in garter st (knit every row) until armband measures approx ½ inch.
Bind off.
Rep for other armhole.

Finishing
Sew side seams. ◆

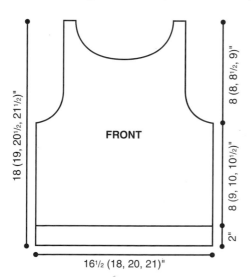

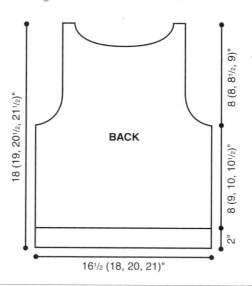

SMARTLY FITTED TOP

This refined, fitted shape features side ribbing continuing into the straps.

DESIGN BY SANDI PROSSER FOR S.R. KERTZER

Size

Woman's small (medium, large, extra-large) Instructions are given for smallest size, with larger sizes in parentheses. When only 1 number is given, it applies to all sizes.

Finished Measurements
Chest: 35½ (37, 39, 41) inches
Length: 22½ (22½, 23, 23) inches

Materials
- S.R. Kertzer Butterfly Super 10 100 percent mercerized cotton D.K. weight yarn (250 yds/125g per skein): 3 (3, 3, 4) skeins peony #3459
- Size 5 (3.75mm) needles
- Size 6 (4mm) needles or size needed to obtain gauge
- Stitch markers

Gauge
22 sts and 28 rows=4 inches/10cm in St st with larger needles
To save time, take time to check gauge.

Special Abbreviation
M1 (Make 1): Inc 1 by making a backward lp over right needle.

Back
With smaller needles, cast on 98 (102, 106, 110) sts. Work in k2, p2 rib for 2 inches, ending with a WS row.
Change to larger needles.
Row 1 (RS): [K2, p2] 5 times, knit to last 20 sts, [p2, k2] 5 times.
Row 2: [P2, k2] 5 times, purl to last 20 sts, [k2, p2] 5 times.
Rows 3 and 4: Rep Rows 1 and 2.
Row 5 (RS): [K2, p2] 5 times, k2tog, knit to last 22 sts, ssk, [p2, k2] 5 times.
Rows 6–8: Work even in established pat.
Rep [Rows 5–8] 5 times more. (86, 90, 94, 98 sts)
Work even until back measures 6½ inches from beg.
Next row: [K2, p2] 5 times, k1, M1, knit to last 21 sts, M1, k1, [p2, k2] 5 times. Work 5 rows even.
[Rep last 6 rows] 5 (5, 6, 6) times more. (98, 102, 108, 112 sts)
Work even until back measures 13½ inches from beg, ending with a WS row and placing marker at beg and end of last row worked.

Shape armhole
Row 1 (RS): [K2, p2] 5 times, k2tog, knit to last 22 sts, ssk, [p2, k2] 5 times.
Row 2: [P2, k2] 5 times, p2tog tbl, purl to last 22 sts, p2tog, [k2, p2] 5 times.
Rows 3 and 4: Rep Rows 1 and 2.
Row 5: [K2, p2] 5 times, k2tog, knit to last 22 sts, ssk, [p2, k2] 5 times.
Row 6: Work even.
Rep [Rows 5 and 6] 5 (5, 6, 6) times more. (78, 82, 86, 90 sts)

Work even until piece measures 15¾ inches from beg, ending with a WS row.
Work all sts in k2, p2 rib until piece measures 17 inches from beg, ending with a WS row.

Shape neck
Next row (RS): Rib 20 sts, join 2nd ball of yarn and bind off center 38 (42, 46, 50) sts, rib 20 sts.
Working both sides at once, continue in rib until back measures 22½ (22½, 23, 23) inches from beg. Bind off in rib.

Front
Work same as back.

Assembly
Sew shoulder seams. Sew side seams up to markers. ◆

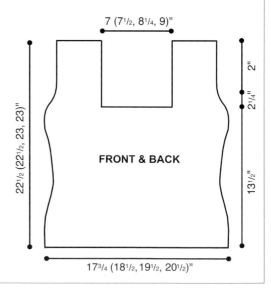

7 (7½, 8¼, 9)"

2"

2¼"

13½"

22½ (22½, 23, 23)"

FRONT & BACK

17¾ (18½, 19½, 20½)"

COUNTERPANE YOKE SWEATER

Squares in an antique counterpane were the inspiration for this summery top.

DESIGN BY UYVONNE BIGHAM

Size

Woman's small (medium, large) Instructions are given for smallest size, with larger sizes in parentheses. When only 1 number is given, it applies to all sizes.

Finished Measurements

Chest: 35½ (37½, 40) inches
Length: 20 inches

Materials

- Plymouth Fantasy Naturale 100 percent mercerized cotton worsted weight yarn (140 yds/ 100g per skein): 6 (6, 7) skeins light coral #4548
- Size 6 (4mm) or 7 (4.5mm) 29-inch circular needles for ribbing
- Size 7 (4.5mm), 8 (5mm) or 9 (5.5mm) set of 5 double-pointed and 29-inch circular needles or size needed to obtain gauge for body and yoke motifs

Gauge

For size small only: 18 sts and 25 rows = 4 inches/10cm in St st with size 7 needles
For size medium only: 17 sts and 24 rows = 4 inches/10cm in St st with size 8 needles
For size large only: 16 sts and 22 rows = 4 inches/10cm in St st with size 9 needles
To save time, take time to check gauge.

Pattern Notes

All sizes are worked in the same way; differences in size come from needle size and gauge difference.

Motifs for yoke are worked separately, then sewn together to form yoke.

It may be necessary to use a larger needle when binding off motifs.

Counterpane Motif
Make 20

With size 7 (8, 9) dpn, make a sl knot.

Working in center of knot, [draw up a st, yo] 4 times. (8 sts)

Divide sts onto 4 needles. Join without twisting, place marker between first and last st.

Rnd 1 and all odd-numbered rnds: Knit.

Rnd 2: *K1, yo; rep from * around. (16 sts)

Rnd 4: *K1, yo, k3, yo; rep from * around. (24 sts)

Rnd 6: *K1, yo, k5, yo; rep from * around. (32 sts)

Rnd 8: *[K1, yo] twice, k2tog, k1, ssk, yo, k1, yo; rep from * around. (40 sts)

Rnd 10: *K1, yo, k3, yo, k3tog, yo, k3, yo; rep from * around. (48 sts) Bind off loosely.

If necessary, tighten or sew center of motif closed.

Yoke

Sew 5 motifs tog to form a long strip, allowing bound-off edges of motif to fall to RS of work.

Rep for second strip. Sew both strips tog along 1 long edge.

Make 2nd yoke the same.

Join both yokes by sewing 1½ motifs tog along top edges to form shoulder seam.

Neck Edging

With size 6 (7, 7) circular needle, pick up and knit 16 sts along each full motif and 8 sts along each half-motif. Sts are picked up behind bound-off edge, allowing bound-off sts to fall to RS of work. (64 sts)

Join, place marker between first and last st.

Purl 1 rnd, work in k1, p1 rib for 1 rnd.

Bind off in rib.

Body

With RS facing and size 7 (8, 9)

circular needle, pick up and knit 16 sts along each motif at lower edge of yoke. Sts are picked up behind bound-off edge, allowing bound-off sts to fall to RS of work. (160 sts)

Join, place marker between first and last st.

Purl 1 rnd.

Work even in St st until body measures 11½ inches or desired

length from yoke.

Change to size 6 (7, 7) circular needle.

Work even in k1, p1 ribbing for 1½ inches more.

Bind off in rib.

Arm Edging

Work as for neck edging; you will have 64 sts around armhole. ◆

FUN IN THE SUN

Vertical stripes add a youthful look to a tank top just meant for a fun summer day.

DESIGN BY LOIS S. YOUNG

Size

Woman's small (medium, large) Instructions are given for smallest size, with larger sizes in parentheses. When only 1 number is given, it applies to all sizes.

Finished Measurements

Chest: 31 (36½, 43) inches
Length: 17 (18½, 20) inches

Materials

- Brown Sheep Cotton Fleece 80 percent Pima cotton/20 percent Merino wool worsted weight yarn (215 yds/100g per skein): 2 skeins raging purple #CW730 (MC), 1 (1, 2) skeins cotton ball # CW100 (A)
- Brown Sheep Cotton Fine 80 percent Pima cotton/20 percent Merino wool sport weight yarn (222 yds/50g per skein): 1 (1, 2) skeins each cotton ball #CW100, my blue heaven #CW560, raging purple #CW730
- Size 8 (5mm) double-pointed (2 only) and straight needles or size needed to obtain gauge
- 3 (⁹⁄₁₆-inch) buttons, La Mode #4521

Gauge

20 sts and 32 rows = 4 inches/10cm in Stripe pat
To save time, take time to check gauge.

Pattern Stitch
Stripe Sequence
Rows 1, 3 and 5 (RS): With B, knit.
Rows 2, 4 and 6: With B, purl.
Rows 7–10: With MC, knit.
Rows 11 and 13: With A, knit.
Rows 12 and 14: With A, purl.
Rows 15–18: With MC, knit.
Rep Rows 1–18 for pat.

Pattern Notes
Color B is comprised of 1 strand each color of Cotton Fine held tog.

Pat is worked sideways from seam to seam and stretches slightly. Take this into consideration when choosing size.

Ratios for picking up sts for I-cord Borders are 2 sts for every 4 rows on MC stripes, 3 sts for every 4 rows on A stripes, and 4 sts for every 6 rows on B stripes.

On curves at neck and underarms, work at rate of [pick up and knit 1 st, skip 1 st] 5 times.

Beg armhole and bottom borders at side seam, neck border at right shoulder seam.

Back
With B and straight needles, cast on 44 (49, 54) sts.

Beg with Row 1 (9, 15) of Stripe pat, work even for 8 (10, 12) rows, ending with Row 8 (18, 8) of pat.

Shape armhole
Inc 1 st [at end of every RS row] 5 times, end with Row 18 (10, 18) of pat. (45, 54, 59 sts)

Beg shoulder strap
Next row (RS): Work across row, cast on 32 (34, 37) sts. (81, 88, 96 sts)

Work even for 22 (30, 30) rows, end with Row 5 (5, 13) of pat.
Next row (WS): Bind off 16 (18, 21) sts, work to end of row. (65, 70, 75 sts)

Beg neck shaping
Dec 1 st [at end of every RS row] 5 times. (60, 65, 70 sts)

Work even for 38 (38, 40) rows, end with Row 8 (8, 18) of pat.

Inc 1 st [at end of every RS row] 5 times, end with Row 18 (18, 10) of pat. (65, 70, 75 sts)

Begin second shoulder strap
Next row (RS): Work across row, cast on 16 (18, 21) sts. (81, 88, 96 sts)

Work even for 22 (30, 30) rows, end with Row 5 (13, 5) of pat.

Next row (WS): Bind off 32 (34, 37) sts, work to end of row. (49, 54, 59 sts)

Shape armhole and underarm
Dec 1 st [at end of every RS row] 5 times, end with row 16 (6, 16). (44, 49, 54 sts)

Work even for 8 (10, 12) rows. Bind off all sts.

Front
Work as for back.

Assembly
Sew shoulder and side seams.

I-cord Borders
Beg as noted with RS facing, using MC and dpn, cast on 3 sts, pick up and knit 1 st from edge of garment.

All rows: *Slide sts to other end of needle, bring yarn around back of work to create a tube, k2, ssk, pick up and knit next st from edge of garment. Rep from * until entire opening is worked.

Sew final sts to cast-on edge of border.

Sew buttons to center front stripe, starting ½ inch below border. ◆

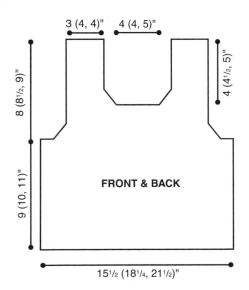

EBONY CAMISOLE

This striking fitted style can be layered or worn on its own for a special occasion.

DESIGN BY JOANNE TURCOTTE FOR PLYMOUTH YARNS

Size

Woman's extra-small (small, medium, large, extra-large) Instructions are given for smallest size, with larger sizes in parentheses. When only 1 number is given, it applies to all sizes.

Finished Measurements

Chest: 28 (31, 35, 39, 43) inches
Length: 20 (20½, 21, 22, 22) inches

Materials

- Plymouth Eros 100 percent nylon worsted weight novelty yarn (165 yds/50g per ball): 4 (4, 5, 5, 6) balls black #3017
- Size 6 (4mm) needles
- Size 7 (4.5mm) needles or size needed to obtain gauge

Gauge

20 sts = 4 inches/10cm in St st with larger needles
To save time, take time to check gauge.

Pattern Note

Garment is designed to be very close-fitting.

Back

With smaller needles, cast on 70 (78, 88, 98, 108) sts, work in garter st for 6 rows.

Change to larger needles and work in St st throughout until back measures 13 (13, 13, 13½, 13½) inches, ending with a WS row.

Shape armholes

Bind off 4 sts at beg of next 2 rows. (62, 70, 80, 90, 100 sts)

Beg on next row, dec 1 st at each end [every RS row] 8 (9, 10, 11, 13) times. (46, 52, 60, 68, 74 sts rem)

Work even until armholes measures 2½ (3, 3½, 4, 4) inches, ending on a WS row.

Neck band

Change to smaller needles and work in garter st for 5 rows. Bind off all sts.

Front

Work as for back.

Armbands

With smaller needles, RS facing, beg at left armhole edge seam, pick up and knit 16 (18, 20, 22, 22) sts along front armhole edge; cast on 40 (46, 52, 58, 64) sts for left shoulder strap; pick up and knit 16 (18, 20, 22, 22) sts along back armhole from neck edge to underarm. (72, 82, 92, 102, 108 sts)

Work in garter st for 4 rows. Bind off all sts.

Rep for other side, beg at back armhole edge, casting on for right shoulder strap, and ending at front armhole edge.

Assembly

Join side seams. ◆

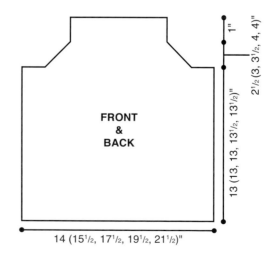

FRONT & BACK

1"

2½ (3, 3½, 4, 4)"

13 (13, 13, 13½, 13½)"

14 (15½, 17½, 19½, 21½)"

SASSY RUFFLED SKIRT

Ruffles flow from the eyelet-and-seed-stitch border of this spirited design.

DESIGN BY WHITNEY CHRISTMAS

Size

Woman's small (medium, large, extra-large, 2X-large, 3X-large) Instructions are given for smallest size, with larger sizes in parentheses. When only 1 number is given, it applies to all sizes.

Finished Measurements

Hip: 36 (40, 44, 48, 51, 56) inches
Length: 15 (15½, 16, 16½, 17, 17½) inches

Materials

- Lion Brand Microspun 100 percent microfiber sport weight yarn (168 yards/70g per ball): 4 (5, 6, 7, 8, 9) skeins lilac #144
- Size 7 (4.5mm) 24-inch and 36- and 60-inch circular needles or size needed to obtain gauge
- Stitch marker
- ¾-inch nonroll elastic: 36 (40, 44, 48, 52, 56) inches
- Large safety pin
- Sewing needle and thread

Gauge

20 sts and 25 rows = 4 inches/10cm in St st in rnds with larger needles To save time, take time to check gauge.

Pattern Note

Skirt is meant to be worn at hip.

In Rnds 17–31, it may be necessary to move marker 1 st left or right in order to maintain continuity of st pats.

The longer needle is necessary in order to accommodate all cast-on sts. Change to shorter needle as needed.

Skirt

With longer needle, cast on 540 (594, 666, 720, 774, 846) sts. Join without twisting, and mark beg of rnd.

Rnds 1 and 2: *P5, k13; rep from * around.
Rnd 3: *P5, ssk, k9, k2tog; rep from * around. (480, 528, 592, 640, 688, 752 sts)
Rnd 4: *P5, k11; rep from * around.
Rnd 5: *P5, ssk, k7, k2tog; rep from * around. (420, 462, 518, 560, 602, 658 ts)
Rnd 6: *P5, k9; rep from * around.
Rnd 7: *P5, ssk, k5, k2tog; rep from * around. (360, 396, 444, 480, 516, 564 sts)
Rnd 8: *P5, k7; rep from * around.
Rnd 9: *P5, ssk, k3, k2tog; rep from * around. (300, 330, 370, 400, 430, 470 sts)
Rnd 10: *P5, k5; rep from * around.
Rnd 11: *P5, ssk, k1, k2tog; rep from * around. (240, 264, 296, 320, 344, 376 sts)
Rnd 12: *P5, k3; rep from * around.
Rnd 13: *P5, sl 1, k2tog, psso; rep from * around. (180, 198, 222, 240, 258, 282 sts)
Rnd 14: *P5, k1; rep from * around.
Rnd 15: Purl.
Rnd 16: Knit to within 2 sts of marker, k2tog. (179, 197, 221, 239, 257, 281 sts)
Rnds 17–19: *K1, p1; rep from * around, taking care to purl into knit sts and knit into purl sts for seed st.
Rnd 20: Knit.
Rnd 21: Purl.
Rnds 22–24: *Yo, k2tog; rep from * around.
Rnd 25: Purl.
Rnd 26: Knit.
Rnds 27–31: Rep Rnds 17–21.

Work even in St st (knit every rnd) until skirt measures 16 (16½, 17, 17½, 18, 18½) inches from beg. Bind off loosely.

Finishing

Fold upper 1¼ inch edge to inside. Loosely sew bound-off edge to skirt to form casing, leaving 2-inch opening. Insert elastic and try on skirt. Tighten elastic as needed for a comfortable fit. Overlap elastic and make sure it isn't twisted; hand-sew to secure. Sew casing closed. ◆

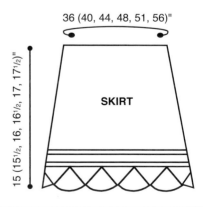

HOMESPUN JACKET

Bulky yarn and unique band construction combine in this quick-to-knit jacket.

DESIGN BY EDIE ECKMAN

INTERMEDIATE

5 BULKY

Size

Women's small (medium, large, extra-large) Instructions are given for smallest size, with larger sizes in parentheses. When only 1 number is given, it applies to all sizes.

Finished Measurements

Chest: 41 (44, 48½, 52) inches
Length: 24 (25½, 26, 27½) inches

Materials

- Berroco Pronto 50 percent cotton/50 percent acrylic bulky weight yarn (55yds/50g per skein): 18 (20, 23, 25) skeins beach beige #4405
- Size 10½ (6.5mm) 29-inch circular needles or size needed to obtain gauge
- 5 (⅞-inch) buttons: #MAR 155-32 Fossil Beige Marble from One World Button Co.
- Smooth waste yarn for stitch holder
- Tapestry needle

Gauge

13½ sts and 19 rows = 4 inches/10cm in pat.
To save time, take time to check gauge.

Pattern Notes

All pieces are worked back and forth on circular needles as if they were straight.

Circular needle is needed because of length of neck and front bands, which are worked as 1 piece.

Special Abbreviations

Make 1 (M1): Insert RH needle under horizontal bar after last st on RH needle and place loop onto LH needle; knit in back of this loop.
I-cord Bind-Off: *K2, sl 1 as to knit, k1, psso, sl these 3 sts back to LH needle. Do not turn work, rep from * until no sts rem on LH needle.

Pattern Stitch

Rows 1, 3, 5, 13, 15 and 17 (RS): Knit.
Row 2 and all WS rows: Purl.
Rows 7, 9 and 11: K1, *k3, p3, rep from *, k4.
Rows 19, 21 and 23: K1, *p3, k3, rep from *, p3, k1.
Row 24: Purl.
Rep Rows 1–24 for pat.

Back

Using provisional cast-on, cast on 71 (77, 83, 89) sts. Purl 1 row. Beg pat st on Row 1 and work even until 12½ (13, 13, 13½) inches from beg, end with a WS row.

Armhole shaping

Maintaining in established pat, bind off [2 sts] at beg of next 10 (12, 14, 14) rows, and [1 st] at beg of following 2 (2, 2, 3) rows. (49, 51, 53, 55 sts)

Work even until piece measures 20 (21½, 22, 23½) inches from beg, end with a WS row.

Back neck shaping

Maintaining established pat, k17 (18, 18, 19) sts, join new yarn and bind off next 15 (15, 17, 17) sts, knit to end. Working both sides at once, bind off [2 sts] at each neck edge 3 times. (11, 12, 12, 13 sts rem each side)

Shoulder shaping

Bind off [6 sts] at beg of next 2 rows, and [5 (6, 6, 7) sts] at beg of following 2 rows.

Left Front

Using provisional cast-on, cast on 35 (35, 41, 41) sts. Purl 1 row.

Beg pat st on Row 13 and work even until 12½ (13, 13, 13½) inches from beg, end with a WS row.

Armhole and neck shaping

Small and medium: Bind off 2 sts at armhole edge [every RS row] 5 times and [1 st] 2 (1) times and at the same time, bind off 1 st at neck edge [every 4th row] 12 times.
Large and X-large: Bind off 2 sts at armhole edge [every RS row] 8 times and, when 2 sets of armhole decs have been made, bind off 1 st at neck edge [every 4th row] 13 (12) times. (11, 12, 12, 13 sts rem)

Work even until same length as back to shoulder shaping, end with a WS row.

Shoulder shaping
Bind off 6 sts at beg of next row and 5 (6, 6, 7) sts at beg of following RS row.

Right Front
Work as for left front, reversing shaping.

Sleeves
Using Provision cast on, cast on 27 (33, 33, 39) sts. Purl 1 row.

Knit, inc 1 st each edge this and [every 4th row] 13 (14, 16, 14) times, then every 6th row 5 (4, 3, 4) times, bringing new sts into pat on Row 7 as follows: K1, M1, work Row 7 of pat st to last 2 sts, M1, k1. Continue working in established pat until all incs are made. (63, 69, 71, 75 sts)

Bind off [0 (0, 2, 2) sts] at beg of next 2 rows and [1 st] at beg of next 16 (18, 20, 22) rows. Bind off rem 47 (51, 47, 49) sts.

Finishing

Sleeve bands
Put sts from cast-on edge of sleeve back on needle, making sure that right leg of each st is on front of needle. Knit 1 row, dec 3 sts evenly spaced. Knit 5 rows. Cast on 3 sts at end of row. Turn. Work I-cord bind-off across row. Rep for 2nd sleeve.

Bottom bands
Sew shoulders and underarm seams. Mark places for 5 buttonholes evenly spaced along right front. Put sts from all cast-on edges on needle, making sure that right leg of each st is on front of needle. Knit 6 rows, ending with a WS row. Place sts from left front on holder. Cast on 3 sts. Work I-cord Bind off on back and right front sts. Put rem 3 sts on separate holder.

Button and neck bands
With a separate ball of yarn, RS facing, pick up and knit 200 (204, 210, 220) sts up right front, around neck and down left front. Knit 1 row. *K to buttonhole mark, yo, k2tog; rep from * 4 times, k to end. Knit 3 rows. Leave these sts on needle. Cut yarn.

Put 3 sts from small st holder on needle. Using yarn left from I-cord bind off, knit applied I-cord: *K2, sl1 as to k, pick up and k 1 st from bottom edge of right front band, psso, sl these 3 sts back to LH needle. Do not turn work, rep from * twice. Knit unattached I-cord to turn corner: *K3, sl these 3 sts to LH

needle. Do not turn work, rep from * once. Continue working I-cord bind off up right front, around neck, and down left front.

Work 2 rows of unattached I-cord at bottom left corner, then 3 rows of attached I-cord along bottom edge of left front band. Put rem sts on needle. Continue I-cord bind off on rem sts. Graft final 3 sts to beg of I-cord.

Set in sleeves and sew sleeve seams. Sew buttons opposite buttonholes. ◆

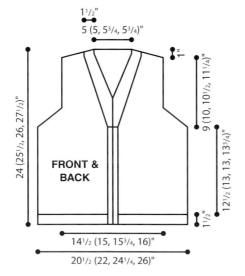

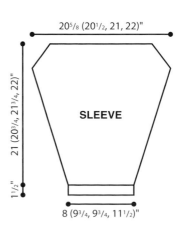

TANGERINE SMOOTHIE

Depend on this cardigan for chilly summer nights or to layer when the weather cools.

DESIGN BY SARA LOUISE HARPER

Size

Woman's small (medium, large, extra-large) Instructions are given for smallest size, with larger sizes in parentheses. When only 1 number is given, it applies to all sizes.

Finished Measurements

Chest: 36 (40, 44, 48) inches
Length: 22 (23, 23, 24) inches

Materials

- Class Elite Yarns Four Seasons 70 percent cotton/30 percent wool worsted weight yarn (87 yds/50g per skein): 11 (13, 14, 16) skeins orange peel #7655
- Size 7 (4.5mm) needles or size needed to obtain gauge
- Stitch holders
- 5 (11⁄16-inch/8mm) buttons from Dill-buttons #H-1084

Gauge

19 sts and 27 rows = 4 inches/10cm in pat
To save time, take time to check gauge.

Pattern Stitch

Moss Stitch Squares (multiple of 18 sts + 9)
Row 1 (RS): *K1, [p1, k1] 4 times, p9; rep from * to last 9 sts, end k1,

[p1, k1] 4 times.
Row 2: P1, [k1, p1] 4 times, *k9, p1 [k1, p1] 4 times; rep from * across.
Row 3: *P1, [k1, p1] 4 times, k9; rep from * to last 9 sts, end p1, [k1, p1] 4 times.
Row 4: K1, [p1, k1] 4 times, *p9, k1, [p1, k1] 4 times; rep from * across.
Rows 5–12: [Rep Rows 1–4] twice more.
Row 13: *P9, k1, [p1, k1] 4 times; rep from * to last 9 sts, end p9.
Row 14: K9, *p1, [p1, k1] 4 times, k9; rep from * across.
Row 15: *K9, p1, [p1, k1] 4 times; rep from * to last 9 sts, end k9.
Row 16: P9, *k1, [p1, k1] 4 times, p9; rep from * across.
Rows 17–24: [Rep Rows 13–16] twice more.
Rep Rows 1–24 for pat.

Pattern Notes

Cardigan is worked in one piece to armhole.

For those preferring to work from a chart, one is included on page 87 for Pattern Stitch.

Body

Cast on 171 (189, 207, 225) sts and work Rows 1–24 of pat until piece measures approx 14 (14½, 14, 15) inches, ending with a WS row.
Next row: Work 42 (47, 51, 56) sts and place on holder; work 87 (95,

105, 113) sts; place rem 42 (47, 51, 56) sts on 2nd holder.

Back

Continue to work in established pat until back measures 8 (8½, 9, 9) inches from armhole, ending with a WS row.

Shape back neck & shoulders

Row 1: At beg of row, bind off 9 (10, 11, 12) sts, work 19 (21, 23, 25) sts; bind off center 31 (33, 37, 39) back neck sts; work to end of row.
Row 2: Working both sides at once with separate balls, bind off 9 (10, 11, 12) sts at beg of next row, work across.
Rows 3 and 4: Bind off 9 (10, 11, 12) sts at beg of row, work across.
Rows 5 and 6: Bind off rem 10 (11, 12, 13) sts.

Right Front

Place right front sts on needles and continue to work in established pat until armhole measures 5 (5½, 6, 6) inches, ending with a WS row.

Shape neck

At neck edge, bind off 8 (9, 9, 10) sts, work 1 row even, bind off 2 sts [every other row] 3 (3, 4, 4) times, then [dec 1 st by ssk] 0 (1, 0, 1) times. (28, 31, 34, 37 sts)

Work until piece measures same as back to shoulder shaping, ending with a RS row.

Shape Shoulder

Bind off at shoulder edge [9 (10, 11, 12) sts] twice, then 10 (11, 12, 13) sts once.

Left Front

Place left front sts on needles and work in established pat until armhole measures 5 (5½, 6, 6) inches, ending with a RS row.

Shape neck

At neck edge, bind off 8 (9, 9, 10) sts, work 1 row even, bind off 2 sts [every other row] 3 (3, 4, 4) times, then [dec 1 st by k2tog] 0 (1, 0, 1) times. (28, 31, 34, 37 sts)

Work until piece measures same as back to shoulder shaping, ending with a RS row.

Shape Shoulder

Bind off at shoulder edge [9 (10, 11, 12) sts] twice, then 10 (11, 12, 13) sts once.

Sleeves

Cast on 37 (37, 41, 47) sts.

Set up pat

P5 (5, 7, 10), place marker, work Row 1 of pat across 27 sts, place marker, p5 (5, 7, 10).

Work pat Rows 2–12.

Beg on next row, inc 1 st at each edge [every 4th (4th, 5th, 5th) row] 8 (10, 10, 8) times, then [every 7th (6th, 6th, 8th) row] 10 (11, 11, 10) times, working inc into pat. Work even on 73 (79, 83, 83) sts until sleeve measures 17 (18, 19, 20) inches from cast-on edge. Bind off all sts in pat.

Assembly

Sew shoulder seams. Sew sleeve seam, then pin into armhole and sew in place.

Button band

Pick up and knit 88 (92, 92, 98) sts along left front. Knit 5 rows. Bind off all sts.

Buttonhole band

Pick up and knit 88 (92, 92, 98) sts along right front and knit 2 rows.

On next row, work buttonholes as follows: k2 (2, 2, 3), [yo, k2tog, k18 (19, 19, 20)] 4 times, end yo, k2tog, k4 (4, 4, 5).

Knit 2 rows. Bind off all sts.

Neck band

With RS facing and beg at button band edge, pick up and knit 72 (74, 76, 78) sts evenly around neck. Knit 2 rows. Bind off all sts.

Finishing

Sew buttons opposite buttonholes. Block gently. ◆

STITCH KEY

☐	Knit on RS, purl on WS
⊟	Purl on on RS, knit on WS

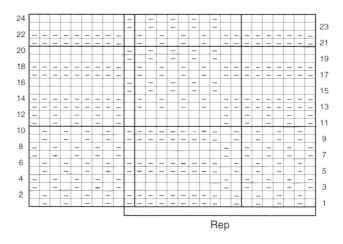

Rep

TANGERINE SMOOTHIE CHART

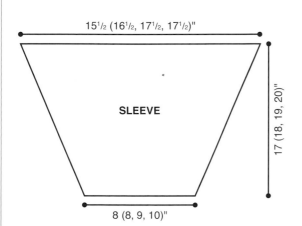

SLEEVE

15½ (16½, 17½, 17½)"

8 (8, 9, 10)"

17 (18, 19, 20)"

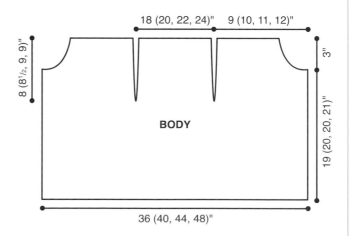

BODY

18 (20, 22, 24)"   9 (10, 11, 12)"

8 (8½, 9, 9)"

3"

19 (20, 20, 21)"

36 (40, 44, 48)"

ISLAND SENSATION

Made in vibrant shaded yarn, this pullover is reminiscent of a tropical island.

DESIGN BY N.Y. YARNS

Size

Woman's small (medium, large) Instructions are given for smallest size, with larger sizes in parentheses. When only 1 number is given, it applies to all sizes.

Finished Measurements

Chest: 34 (37, 39½) inches
Length: 17 (17½, 18) inches

Materials

- N.Y. Yarns Caprice 70 percent acrylic/20 percent cotton/8 percent viscose/2 percent acetate bulky weight yarn from Tahki/Stacy Charles (92yds/50g per ball): 8 (9, 9) balls lime/blues #4
- Size 10½ (6.5mm) needles or size needed to obtain gauge

Gauge

13 sts and 18 rows = 4 inches/10cm in St st
To save time, take time to check gauge.

Back & Front

Make 2 alike
Cast on 56 (60, 64) sts.
Row 1 (RS): *K2, p2; rep from * across.
Rep Row 1 until piece measures 2 inches from beg, ending with a WS row.
Work even in St st until piece measures 10 inches from beg, ending with a WS row.

Shape armhole

At beg of row, bind off [4 sts] twice then [2 sts] twice. Dec 1 st at each edge by k1, ssk, knit to last 3 sts, k2tog, k1 [every other row] 2 (3, 4) times. (40, 42, 44 sts)
Work even for 5 (5½, 6) inches, ending with a WS row.
Work in k2, p2 rib for 2 inches. Bind off in rib.

Sleeves

Cast on 26 (28, 30) sts and work in k2, p2 rib until piece measures 2 inches from beg, ending with a WS row.
Work in St st, inc 1 st at each edge [every 2 inches] 5 times. (36, 38, 40 sts)

Continue to work even in St st until sleeve measures 16 inches from beg, ending with a WS row.

Shape cap

Bind off 4 sts at beg of next 2 rows, then dec 1 st at each edge [every other row] 10 (11, 12) times. (8 sts)
Bind off rem sts.

Assembly

Block pieces to measurements. Sew 2¾ (3, 3¼)-inch shoulder seams, leaving 7-inch neck opening. Set in sleeves. Sew side and sleeve seams. ◆

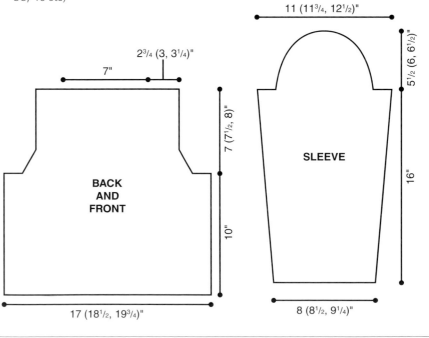

BACK AND FRONT

7"

2¾ (3, 3¼)"

7 (7½, 8)"

10"

17 (18½, 19¾)"

SLEEVE

11 (11¾, 12½)"

5½ (6, 6½)"

16"

8 (8½, 9¼)"

CAT'S EYE TOPPER

What's not to love with this simple design with I-cord ties, knit in alpaca-blend yarn?

DESIGN BY KENNITA TULLY

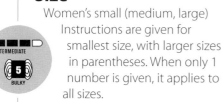

Size
Women's small (medium, large) Instructions are given for smallest size, with larger sizes in parentheses. When only 1 number is given, it applies to all sizes.

Finished Measurements
Chest: 36 (40, 44) inches
Length: 20 (21, 22) inches

Materials
- Plymouth Indecita Baby Alpaca Brush 80 percent baby alpaca/20 percent acrylic bulky weight yarn (110 yds/50g per ball): 5 (6, 7) balls celadon #1477
- Size 6 (4mm) double-pointed needles for I-cord ties
- Size 9 (5.5 mm) needles or size needed to obtain gauge
- Size H/8/5mm crochet hook (for trim)
- Stitch markers

Gauge
12 sts and 18½ rows = 4 inches/10cm in Cat's Eye pat with larger needles
To save time, take time to check gauge.

Special Abbreviations
M1 (Make 1): Inc 1 by making a backward loop over right needle.
2yo (Double yo): Wrap yarn twice around needle. On next row, [p1, k1] in lps.

Stitch Pattern
Cat's Eye (multiple of 4 sts)
Row 1 (RS): K4, *2yo, k4; rep from * across.
Row 2: P2, *p2 tog, [p1, k1] in 2yo of previous row, p2 tog; rep from *, to last 2 sts, p2.
Row 3: K2, yo, *k4, 2yo; rep from *, to last 6 sts, k4, yo, k2.
Row 4: P3, *[p2 tog] twice, [p1, k1] in 2yo of previous row; rep from * to last 7 sts, [p2 tog] twice, p3.
Rep Rows 1–4 for pat.

Pattern Notes
When shaping sleeves, work incs 1 st in from each edge, being careful to maintain pat, and working added sts in St st until there are enough sts for a full pat rep.

Back
Cast on 56 (60, 64) sts. Purl 1 row, then work in pat until back measures approx 12 (12½, 13) inches. Place marker at each end of row for armhole. Work even until back measures 20 (21, 22) inches, bind off all sts loosely. Place markers approx 6 (6½, 6¾) inches from each edge for shoulder seaming.

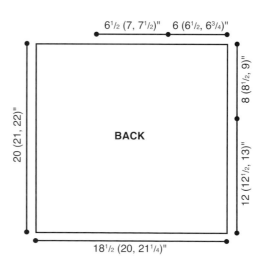

6½ (7, 7½)"   6 (6½, 6¾)"

8 (8½, 9)"

20 (21, 22)"

BACK

12 (12½, 13)"

18½ (20, 21¼)"

Left/Right Front
Make 2 alike

Working as for back, cast on 28 (32, 36) sts and work even until front measures 12 (12½, 13) inches, place marker at armhole edge. Work even until front measures 20 (21, 22) inches, bind off all sts loosely.

Sleeves

Cast on 28 (28, 32) sts. Purl 1 row, then work in pat, beg on Row 3, inc 1 st by M1 at each side [every 4th row] 0 (8, 11) times, then [every 6th row] 10 (4, 0) times. (48, 52, 54 sts)

Work even until sleeve measures 13 inches, bind off all sts.

Assembly

Block all pieces. Sew shoulder seams to markers. Sew sleeves between armhole markers. Sew sleeve and side seams. Fold back collar and mark bottom of collar for trim.

Trim

With crochet hook and RS facing and beg at center back, work reverse single crochet across bottom edge of sweater and up center front to bottom of collar; fasten off yarn. Join yarn at shoulder and work across back neck to other shoulder; fasten off yarn. Join yarn below collar marker and work rem of center front and bottom edge of sweater; join in first single crochet.

Work collar trim on WS of work in same manner.

I-Cord Ties
Make 2

With double-pointed needles, pick up and knit 3 sts at base of collar, *slide sts to opposite end of needle, k3; rep from * for approx 12-14 inches, slide sts to opposite end of needle, k3tog, fasten off.

Rep for tie on other front.

Tack down corners of collar. ◆

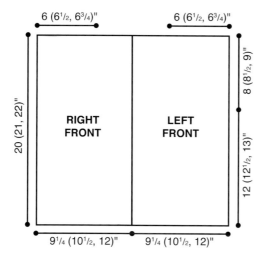

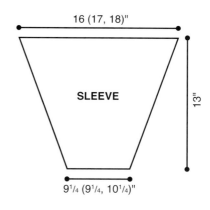

SWEATERS RICH WITH STYLE

Ultra-chic sweaters and flirty skirts for her,
classic sweaters for him and fun sweaters
for dog give lots of knitting pleasure!

DAY & NIGHT ENSEMBLE

Pair this ''little black skirt'' with the comfortable sweater for a wardrobe essential you'll wear from 9 to 5 and later!

DESIGNS BY SCARLET TAYLOR

Size

Woman's extra-small (small, medium, large) Instructions are given for smallest size, with larger sizes in parentheses. When only 1 number is given, it applies to all sizes.

Finished Measurements
Pullover
Chest: 35 (40½, 44, 48) inches
Length: 22½ (23, 23½, 24) inches
Skirt
Hip: 35 (37, 39, 41) inches
Waist (without elastic): 25 (27, 29, 31) inches

Materials
Pullover
- Brown Sheep Lamb's Pride Worsted 85 percent wool/15 percent mohair worsted weight yarn (190 yds/4 oz per skein): 5 (6, 6, 7) skeins sable #M07
- Size 6 (4mm) straight and 16-inch circular needles
- Size 8 (5mm) needles or size needed to obtain gauge
Skirt
- Brown Sheep Lamb's Pride Worsted 85 percent wool/15 percent mohair worsted weight yarn (190 yds/4 oz per skein): 4 (4, 5, 5) skeins onyx #M05

- Size 8 (5mm) 24-inch circular needle or size needed to obtain gauge
- 1 yd (1½-inch-wide) noncurling elastic
- Stitch markers

Gauge
Pullover
17 sts and 24 rows = 4 inches/10cm in St st with larger needles
Skirt
16 sts and 22 rnds = 4 inches/10cm in St st with smaller circular needle
To save time, take time to check gauge.

Special Abbreviation
M1 (Make 1): Insert LH needle under horizontal thread between st just worked and next st, knit through the back. This inc is used for sleeve shaping.

Pattern Note
Shorten or lengthen skirt as desired before placing dec markers.

PULLOVER

Back
With smaller needles, cast on 74 (86, 94, 102) sts.

Work in k2, p2 rib for 2 inches, ending with a WS row.
Change to larger needles and St st.
Work even until back measures 13½ inches, ending with a WS row.

Shape armholes
Next 2 rows: Bind off 2 (4, 3, 4) sts, work to end of row.
Dec row: K2, ssk, knit to last 4 sts, k2tog, k2.
P 1 row.
[Rep these 2 rows] 0 (1, 1, 2) times more. (68, 74, 84, 88 sts)
Work even until armhole measures 8 (8½, 9, 9½) inches, ending with a WS row.

Shape neck
Next row (RS): K20 (23, 28, 28), join 2nd ball of yarn and bind off center 28 (28, 28, 32) sts, knit to end of row.
Working on both sides of neck with separate balls of yarn, dec 1 st at each neck edge on next row. (19, 22, 27, 27 sts rem each side)

Shape shoulders
At each arm edge, bind off 6 (7, 9, 9) sts twice, then 7 (8, 9, 9) sts once.

Front

Work as for back until front measures 6¼ (6¾, 7¼, 7¾) inches, ending with a WS row.

Shape neck

Next row (RS): K26 (29, 34, 35), join 2nd ball of yarn and bind off center 16 (16, 16, 18) sts, knit to end of row.

Working on both sides of neck with separate balls of yarn, bind off at each neck edge [3 sts] 1 (1, 1, 2) times, then [2 sts] 1 (1, 1, 0) times. (21, 24, 27, 27 sts)

Dec row (RS): Knit to last 4 sts of left neck, k2tog, k2; drop yarn, pick up yarn for right side of neck, k2, ssk, knit to end of row.

Purl 1 row, rep dec row. (19 (22, 27, 27) sts rem each side)

Work even until armhole measures same as for back.

Shape shoulders as for back.

Sew shoulder seams.

Sleeves

With smaller needles, cast on 38 (38, 42, 42) sts.

Work in k2, p2 rib for 2 inches, ending with a WS row.

Change to larger needles.

Working in St st, inc 1 st each end [every 4th row] 0 (4, 3, 12) times, then [every 6th row] 15 (13, 14, 8) times. (68, 72, 76, 82 sts)

Work even until sleeve measures 19 (18½, 18½, 19) inches, ending with a WS row.

Shape cap

Next 2 rows: Bind off 2 (4, 3, 4) sts, work to end of row.

Dec row: K2, ssk, knit to last 4 sts, k2tog, k2.

Purl 1 row.

[Rep these 2 rows] 0 (1, 1, 2) times more. (62, 60, 66, 68 sts)

Neck Band

Beg at right shoulder seam with circular needle, pick up and knit 72 (72, 72, 76) sts around neck opening. Join, place marker between first and last st.

Work even in k2, p2 ribbing for 3½ inches.

Bind off in pat.

Assembly

Sew in sleeves.

Sew sleeve and side seams.

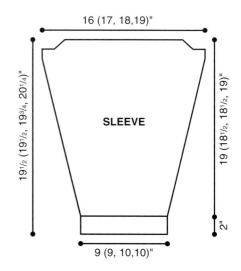

16 (17, 18, 19)"

SLEEVE

19½ (19½, 19¾, 20¼)"

19 (18½, 18½, 19)"

2"

9 (9, 10, 10)"

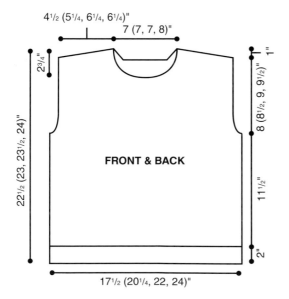

4½ (5¼, 6¼, 6¼)"

7 (7, 7, 8)"

2¾"

1"

8 (8½, 9, 9½)"

22½ (23, 23½, 24)"

FRONT & BACK

11½"

2"

17½ (20¼, 22, 24)"

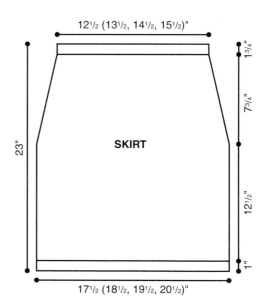

12½ (13½, 14½, 15½)"

1¾"

7¾"

23"

SKIRT

12½"

1"

17½ (18½, 19½, 20½)"

SKIRT

Beg at hem with circular needle, cast on 176 (184, 196, 204) sts.

Join without twisting, place marker between first and last st.

Work even in k2, p2 rib for 1 inch.

Dec rnd—size extra-small and medium only: [K2tog, k3, k2tog, k2] 4 times, [k2tog, k3] 28 (32) times. (140, 156 sts)

Sizes small and large only: [K2tog, k4, k2tog, k3] 3 times, [k2tog, k3] 29 (33) times, k2tog, k4. (148 164 sts)

All sizes: Work even until skirt measures 13½ inches or approx 9½ inches less than desired length.

Shape hips

Next rnd: K28 (29, 33, 34), pm, [k28 (30, 30, 32), place marker] 3 times, k28 (29, 33, 34). 5 markers on needle.

Dec rnd: [K2tog, knit to next marker, ssk, knit to next marker] twice, ssk, knit to end of rnd.

Knit 4 rnds.

[Rep last 5 rnds] 7 times more. (100, 108, 116, 124 sts)

Work even until skirt measures 21 inches or desired length.

Beg waistband

Work in k2, p2 rib for 1½ inches.

Purl 1 rnd for turning ridge.

Continue in established rib until waistband measures 3 inches.

Bind off in pat.

Finishing

Fold waistband to inside at turning ridge, forming casing.

Sew waistband in place leaving a 3-inch opening.

Cut elastic to comfortably fit waist when slightly stretched, plus a 1-inch overlap.

Thread elastic through casing. Overlap ends and sew tog securely.

Sew waistband opening. ◆

SATIN TWEED FITTED BLOUSE

This fitted blouse combines the luxury of alpaca with a unique novelty yarn that will give added pizzazz to any outfit.

DESIGN BY JEAN SCHAFER-ALBERS

Size
Woman's small (medium, large, extra-large) Instructions are given for smallest size, with larger sizes in parentheses. When only 1 number is given, it applies to all sizes.

Finished Measurements
Chest: 34 (37¾, 41½, 45) inches
Waist: 25½ (28¼, 33, 33¾) inches
Length: 23 (23½, 24, 25) inches

Materials
- Plymouth Indiecita Baby Alpaca D.K. 100 percent baby alpaca DK weight yarn (126 yds/50g per ball): 6 (7, 8, 8) balls royal blue #2115 (MC)
- Plymouth Eros 100 percent nylon novelty yarn (165 yds/50g per ball): 5 (6, 6, 7) balls primary multi #4789 (CC)
- Size 7 (4.5mm) double-pointed, 16- and 29-inch circular needles or size needed to obtain gauge
- Stitch markers
- Stitch holders
- Tapestry needle

Gauge
17 sts and 24 rows = 4 inches/10cm

in St st with 1 strand of each yarn held tog
To save time, take time to check gauge.

Special Abbreviations
CDD (Centered Double Decrease): Sl next 2 sts as if to k2tog, k1, pass 2 slipped sts over knit st. Center stitch will lie on top.
M1 (Make 1): With LH needle, lift running strand between last st worked and next st on LH needle and knit into back of it.

Pattern Stitch
Seed Stitch
Rnd 1: *K1, p1; rep from * to end of rnd.
Rnd 2: Knit the purl sts, purl the knit sts.
Rep Rnds 1–2 for pat.

Pattern Notes
Blouse is worked with 1 strand of each yarn held tog throughout.
Blouse is worked circular to armhole, where it is divided and worked in rows.
Sleeves are worked circular on double-pointed needles to sleeve cap, which is worked flat.

Body
With longer circular needle and 1 strand of each yarn held tog, cast on 180 (192, 204, 216) sts. Join without twisting, place marker between first and last st.
[Work in Seed St over 30 (32, 34, 36) sts, pm] 6 times.
Work 1 more rnd of Seed St.
Change to St st and work even for 3 rnds.
Dec rnd: [Knit to 1 st before marker, CDD, reposition marker] 6 times. (168, 180, 192, 204 sts)
[Knit 5 rnds, rep dec rnd] 3 times. (132, 144, 156, 168 sts)
[Knit 7 rnds, rep dec rnd] twice. (108, 120, 132, 144 sts)
Removing extra markers, place marker at beg of rnd and after 54th (60th, 66th, 72nd) st to mark side seams.

Begin body shaping
Knit 3 (3, 1, 1) rnds.
Next rnd: Inc by working M1 before and after each marker. (4 sts inc)
[Rep inc rnd every 4th (4th, 4th, 2nd) rnd] 7 (9, 10, 3) times, then [every 6th (0, 0, 4th) rnd] 1 (0, 0, 4) times. (144, 160, 176, 192 sts)
Work even until body measures 15 (15½, 16, 16) inches.

Divide for front and back

Work in rows from this point.
Next row: K 72 (80, 88, 96) sts, place rem sts on hold for front.

Back
Shape armhole

Bind off 6 (7, 7, 7) sts at beg of next 2 rows. (60, 66, 78, 82 sts)
Dec row (RS): K1, skp, knit to last 3 sts, k2tog, k1.
Next row: Purl.
[Rep last 2 rows] 1 (3, 5, 7) times. (56, 58, 62, 66 sts)
Work even until armhole measures 8 (8, 8, 9) inches.
Place sts on 3 holders, having 15 (15, 16, 17) sts for each shoulder and 26 (28, 30, 32) sts for back neck.

Front

Work as for back until armhole measures 4 (4, 4, 5) inches, ending with a WS row.

Begin neck shaping

K 22 (23, 25, 27) sts, join 2nd ball of yarn and bind off next 12 sts, knit to end of row.
Working both sides of neck

with separate balls of yarn, bind off at each neck edge [2 sts] 2 (3, 4, 5) times.
[Dec 1 st each side of neck every other row] 3 (2, 1, 0) times.
Work even on rem 15 (15, 16, 17) sts until armhole measures same as for back.
Join front and back shoulders with 3-needle bind-off.

Sleeves

Beg at cuff with dpn and 1 strand of each yarn held tog, cast on 48 (48, 54, 54) sts. Join without twisting, place marker between first and last st.
Next rnd: Working in Seed St, place marker after every 8th (8th, 9th, 9th) st.
Work 1 more rnd Seed St, then knit 7 rnds.
Dec rnd: [Knit to 1 st before marker, CDD, reposition marker] 6 times.
Knit 7 rnds, rep dec rnd. (24, 24, 30, 30 sts)
Remove all markers except one designating end of rnd.
Knit 5 (3, 5, 3) rnds.
Working in St st, [inc 1 st each side of marker every 6th (6th, 6th,

4th) rnd] 10 (15, 6, 2) times, then [every 8th (0, 8th, 6th) rnd] 3 (0, 7, 14) times.
Working in St st, k 5 (3, 5, 3) rnds even. (50, 54, 56, 62 sts)
Work even until sleeve measures 19 (19¾, 20¼, 20¼) inches.

Shape sleeve cap

Work in rows from this point.
Bind off 6 (7, 7, 7) sts at beg of next 2 rows.
[Dec 1 st each end every other row] 2 (4, 6, 8) times, then [every 4th row] 7 (5, 4, 6) times, and finally [every 6th row] 0 (1, 1, 0) times. (20 sts)
Purl 1 row.
Bind off 2 sts at beg of next 4 rows.
Bind off rem 12 sts.

Neck Edging

With shorter circular needle, pick up and knit 2 sts for every 3 rows and 1 st for every st around neck edge. Join, place marker between first and last st.
Knit 5 rnds.
Bind off loosely.
Sew sleeves into armholes. ◆

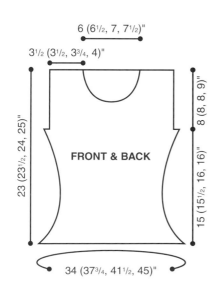

6 (6½, 7, 7½)"
3½ (3½, 3¾, 4)"
23 (23½, 24, 25)"
8 (8, 8, 9)"
15 (15½, 16, 16)"
FRONT & BACK
34 (37¾, 41½, 45)"

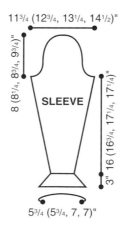

11¾ (12¾, 13¼, 14½)"
8 (8¼, 8¾, 9¾)"
16 (16¾, 17¼, 17¼)"
3"
SLEEVE
5¾ (5¾, 7, 7)"

YUKON PULLOVER

With big needles and chunky yarn, you will have a sporty pullover to wear in no time.

DESIGN BY KENNITA TULLY

Size

Adult's small (medium, large, extra-large) Instructions are given for smallest size, with larger sizes in parentheses. When only 1 number is given, it applies to all sizes.

Finished Measurements

Chest: 37¾ (41½, 45, 49) inches
Length: 23 (24, 25, 26) inches

Materials

- Plymouth Yukon Print 35 percent mohair/35 percent wool/30 percent acrylic bulky yarn (60 yds/100g per ball): 8 (9, 10, 11) balls purple multi #2004
- Size 15 (10mm) double-pointed, 16- and 29-inch circular needles or size needed to obtain gauge
- Stitch markers
- Stitch holders

Gauge

8½ sts and 12 rnds = 4 inches/10cm in St st
To save time, take time to check gauge.

Body

With longer circular needle, cast on 40 (44, 48, 52) sts, place marker, cast on 40 (44, 48, 52) more sts. (80, 88, 96, 104 sts)

Join without twisting, place marker between first and last st.

Work in k1, p1 rib for 4 rnds.

Change to St st and work even until body measures 13 (13½, 14, 14½) inches.

Removing markers, place 6 (6, 8, 8) sts at each underarm on separate holders, and 34 (38, 40, 44) sts on each of 2 more separate holders for front and back.

Sleeves

With dpn, cast on 18 (20, 20, 20) sts. Join without twisting, place marker between first and last st.

Work in k1, p1 rib for 4 rnds, change to St st.

Changing to circular needle when needed, [inc 1 st each side of marker every 6th (5th, 4th, 4th) rnd] 7 (4, 1, 6) times, then every 0 (6th, 5th, 5th) rnd 0 (4, 8, 4) times. (32, 36, 38, 40 sts)

Work even until sleeve measures 16¾ (17½, 17½, 18) inches, ending last rnd 3 (3, 4, 4) sts before marker. Removing marker, place next 6 (6, 8, 8) sts on

holder for underarm. Place rem sts on 2nd holder.

Join sleeves and body

Place marker between each section, k 34 (38, 40, 44) sts for front, 26 (30, 30, 32) sts for right sleeve, 34 (38, 40, 44) sts for back, 26 (30, 30, 32) sts for left sleeve. Place marker to denote end of rnd. (120, 136, 140, 152 sts)

Mark this last rnd at center front. Work even for 1½ inches above marker.

Beg raglan yoke shaping

Dec rnd: [K2, k2tog, knit to marker, ssk, k2] 4 times.

[Rep dec rnd every 2nd (3rd, 3rd, 3rd) rnd] 10 (1, 4, 1) times, then every 0 (2nd, 2nd, 2nd) rnd 0 (11, 8, 12) times.

At the same time, when yoke measures 5½ (6, 6½, 7) inches above center front marker, begin front neck shaping.

Neck shaping

Work to center 6 (6, 8, 8) sts, place

center 6 (6, 8, 8) sts on hold, turn.

Working in rows from this point, [dec 1 st at each side of neck every other row] 3 times.

Work until raglan decs are complete. (32, 32, 36, 40 sts)

Piece should measure approx 23 (24, 25, 26) inches. Leave rem sts on needle and cut yarn.

Collar

With 16-inch circular needle and RS facing, pick up and k 5 (6, 6, 6) sts along left neck edge, k 6 (6, 8, 8) sts from front neck holder, pick up and k 5 (6, 6, 6) sts along right neck edge, knit rem sts from needle. (48, 50, 56, 60 sts)

Join, place marker between first and last st.

Work even in St st for 2 (2, 3, 3) inches, then work 4 rnds in k1, p1 rib.

Bind off in ribbing.

Finishing

Sew underarm sleeve sts to underarm body sts, using Kitchener method. ◆

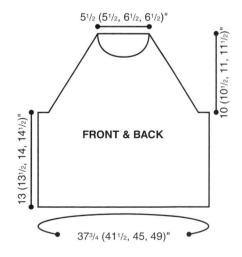

5½ (5½, 6½, 6½)"

10 (10½, 11, 11½)"

FRONT & BACK

13 (13½, 14, 14½)"

37¾ (41½, 45, 49)"

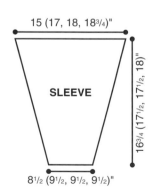

15 (17, 18, 18¾)"

SLEEVE

16¾ (17½, 17½, 18)"

8½ (9½, 9½, 9½)"

ENJOY THE FESTIVITIES

An interesting stitch pattern sets off the bodice and sleeves of this sparkling sweater.

DESIGN FROM SANDI PROSSER FOR S.R. KERTZER

Size

Woman's small (medium, large) Instructions are given for smallest size, with larger sizes in parentheses. When only 1 number is given, it applies to all sizes.

Finished Measurements

Chest: 35 (38½, 43½) inches
Length: 19½ (20, 20½) inches

Materials

- S.R. Kertzer Overture 50 percent mohair/25 percent viscose/10 percent nylon/10 percent acrylic/5 percent metallized polyester bulky weight yarn (84 yds/40g per ball): 10 (11, 12) balls forest #2165
- Size 8 (5mm) needles
- Size 9 (5.5mm) needles or size needed to obtain gauge

Gauge

15 sts and 20 rows = 4 inches/10cm in St st with larger needles
To save time, take time to check gauge.

Back

With larger needles, cast on 67 (76, 85) sts. Purl 1 row (WS).
Row 1 (RS): K3, *yo, k2, ssk, k2tog, k2, yo, k1; rep from * to last st, k1.

Row 2: Purl.
Row 3: K2, *yo, k2, ssk, k2tog, k2, yo, k1; rep from * to last 2 sts, k2.
Row 4: Purl.
Rep Rows 1–4 until back measures 8 inches from beg, ending with a WS row.
Next row: Knit, dec 1 (4, 3) sts evenly across row. (66, 72, 82 sts)
Continue to work even in St st until back measures 12½ inches from beg, ending with a WS row.

Shape armhole

At beg of row, bind off [3 sts] twice, [2 sts] twice, then dec 1 st at each edge [every other row] 2 (3, 4) times by k1, ssk, knit to last 3 sts, end k2tog, k1. (52, 56, 64 sts)
Continue to work even until armhole measures 7 (7½, 8) inches, ending with a WS row.

Shape neck & shoulders

Work first 15 (15, 17) sts, bind off center 22 (26, 30) sts, join 2nd ball of yarn and work to end.
Working both sides at once, dec 1 st at each neck edge [every row] 3 times. Bind off rem 12 (12, 14) sts.

Front

Work as for back until armhole

measures 4 (4½, 5) inches, ending with a WS row.

Shape neck & shoulders

K18 (20, 24), join 2nd ball of yarn and bind off center 16 (20, 24) sts, knit to end.
Working both sides at once with separate balls of yarn, bind off at each neck edge [2 sts] 3 times. Continue to work even until front measures same as back to shoulder, ending with a WS row. Bind off rem 12 (12, 14) sts.

Sleeves

With larger needles, cast on 51 sts. Purl 1 row (WS).
Row 1 (RS): K4, *yo, k2, ssk, k2tog, k2, yo, k1; rep from * to last 2 sts, k2.
Row 2: Purl.
Row 3: K3, *yo, k2, ssk, k2tog, k2, yo, k1; rep from * to last 3 sts, k3.
Row 4: Purl.
Rep Rows 1–4 for sleeve, *at the same time*, beg on Row 9 and maintaining pat, dec 1 st at each end [every 4th row] 5 times. (41 sts)
Continue to work even in pat until sleeve measures 7 inches from beg, ending with a WS row.
Beg on next row, inc 1 st at each edge [every 8th (8th, 6th) row] 6 (7, 9) times, working added sts in St st. (53, 55, 59 sts)
Work even in pat until sleeve

measures 17 (17½, 18) inches from beg, ending with a WS row.

Shape cap

At beg of row, bind off [3 sts] twice, then [2 sts] twice. Maintaining pat (be sure there is a dec for every yo, otherwise work sts in St st), dec 1 st at each end [every other row] 11 (12, 13) times. Bind off 3 sts at beg of next 4 rows. Bind off rem 9 (9, 11) sts.

Assembly

Block pieces to finished measurements. Sew right shoulder seam.

Neck band

With smaller needles, RS facing, pick up and knit 88 (92, 96) sts around neckline. Knit 2 rows. Bind off all sts knitwise.

Finishing

Sew left shoulder and neck band seam. Set in sleeves. Sew side and sleeve seams. ◆

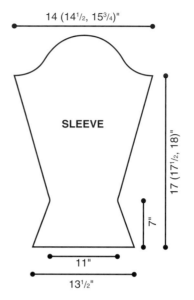

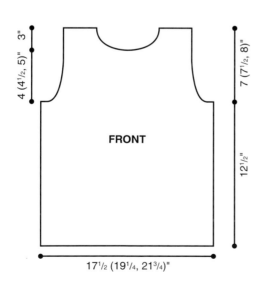

STYLISH TUNIC

Whether worn with silk or more casually with denim, you'll be in style.

DESIGN BY N.Y. YARNS

Size

Woman's small (medium, large) Instructions are given for smallest size, with larger sizes in parentheses. When only 1 number is given, it applies to all sizes.

Finished Measurements

Chest: 36 (38, 40) inches
Length: 22½ (23, 23½) inches

Materials

- N.Y. Yarns Wild Thing 48 percent acrylic/21 percent wool/31 percent nylon bulky weight yarn (64 yds/50g per ball): 9 (9, 11) balls #969 green
- Size 10 (6mm) needles or size needed to obtain gauge
- Size G/6/4mm crochet hook
- Stitch marker

Gauge

14 sts and 20 rows=4 inches/10cm in St st
To save time, take time to check gauge.

Back

Cast on 72 (76, 80) sts. Work in St st for 3 inches, ending with a WS row. Dec 1 st at each side by k1, ssk, knit to last 3 sts, ssk, k1, [every 10th row] 5 times. (62, 66, 70) sts)

Work even until back measures approx 15 inches from beg, ending with a WS row.

Shape armholes

Bind off 4 sts at beg of next 2 rows, then dec 1 st at each side [every other row] twice. (50, 54, 58 sts)

Work even until armholes measure approx 7½ (8, 8½) inches from beg of shaping, ending with a WS row.

Bind off all sts.

Front

Cast on 72 (76, 80) sts. Work as for back until front measures approx 15 inches from beg, ending with a WS row.

Shape armholes and V-neck

Bind off 4 sts at beg of next 2 rows. Dec 1 st at each side [every other row] twice, placing marker between center 2 sts. (50, 54, 58 sts)

Work to center marker, join 2nd ball of yarn, work to end. Working both sides at once, dec 1 st at each neck edge by knit across left front to last 3 sts, k2tog, k1; on right front, k1, ssk, knit to end, [every 4th row] 9 times. Work even until piece measures same as back. Bind off rem 16 (18, 20) sts on each side.

Sleeves

Cast on 32 (34, 36) sts. Work in St st, inc 1 st at each side [every other row] 7 times. (46, 48, 50 sts)

Work even until sleeve measures approx 17 inches from beg, ending with a WS row.

Shape cap

Bind off 4 sts at beg of next 2 rows, then dec 1 st at each side as for armhole shaping [every other row] 13 (14, 15) times. Bind off rem 12 sts.

Assembly

Block pieces to measurements. Sew shoulder seams. Set in sleeves; sew sleeve seams. Sew side seams leaving 4 inches open from lower edge on each side for side slits.

Using crochet hook and 1 strand each yarn, work 1 row sc around neck edge and around each side slit. ◆

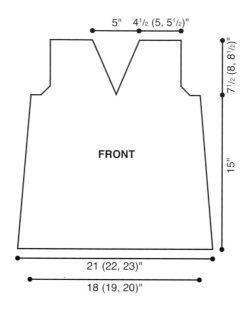

5"   4½ (5, 5½)"

7½ (8, 8½)"

15"

FRONT

21 (22, 23)"

18 (19, 20)"

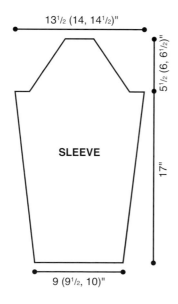

13½ (14, 14½)"

5½ (6, 6½)"

17"

SLEEVE

9 (9½, 10)"

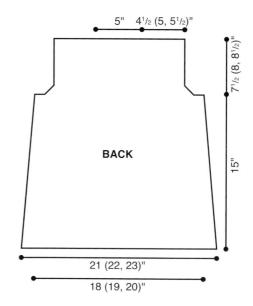

5"   4½ (5, 5½)"

7½ (8, 8½)"

15"

BACK

21 (22, 23)"

18 (19, 20)"

DIVA DARLING

You'll look divine, dahling! This basic silhouette becomes out-of-the-ordinary in a new lush sparkly yarn.

DESIGN BY LORNA MISER FOR SOUTH WEST TRADING CO.

Size

Woman's small (medium, large, extra-large) Instructions are given for smallest size, with larger sizes in parentheses. When only 1 number is given, it applies to all sizes.

Finished Measurements

Chest: 38 (42, 46, 50) inches
Length: 22 (23½, 24, 25) inches

Materials

- South West Trading Co. Diva 72 percent acrylic/28 percent nylon bulky weight yarn (56 yds/50g per skein): 11 (12, 14, 15) skeins vivacious
- Size 9 (5.5mm) straight and 24-inch circular needles
- Size 11 (8mm) straight and 24-inch circular needles or size needed to obtain gauge
- Stitch markers
- Stitch holders

Gauge

13 stitches and 19 rows = 4 inches (10cm) in rev St st with larger needles
To save time, take time to check gauge.

Back

With smaller needles, cast on 61 (67, 75, 81) sts.

Rows 1 and 3 (WS): P1, *k1, p1; rep from * across.
Rows 2 and 4: K1, *p1, k1; rep from * across.

Change to larger needles and work even in rev St st until body measures 13 (13½, 14, 14½) inches from beg.

Shape underarms

At beg of next 2 rows, bind off 9 sts. (43, 49, 57, 63 sts)

Work even until armhole measures 9 (9, 10, 10½) inches.

Bind off all sts.

Front

Work as for back until body measures 12 (12½, 13, 13½) inches from beg.

Divide for V-neck shaping

Work across 30 (33, 37, 40) sts, place center st on holder for neck edging; attach 2nd skein of yarn and continue across rem sts.

Continue each side separately while also working neck and armhole shaping. Work armhole shaping as for back, at the same time, dec 1 st at neck edge [every 4th row] 9 (9, 8, 9) times, then [every RS row] 2 (2, 5, 4) times. (10, 13, 15, 18 shoulder sts rem)

Work even until same length as back.

Bind off all sts.
Sew shoulder seams for stability.

Neck edging

With smaller circular needle, pick up and knit 23 (23, 27, 27) sts across back neck, 34 (36, 38, 39) sts along left front neck edge, knit center st and place open ring marker through it, pick up and knit 34 (36, 38, 39) sts along right front neck edge. Join.

Work k1, p1 ribbing around, working dec at center marked st as follows: Work to 1 st before marked st, sl next 2 sts tog as if to k2tog, sl next st knitwise, place LH needle through all 3 sts tog from left to right and knit these 3 sts tog. (This dec keeps center st on top.) Work 4 rnds of k1, p1 ribbing and dec at center each rnd.

Bind off.

Sleeves

With smaller needles, cast on 29 (29, 31, 33) sts. Work 4 rows of k1, p1 rib as for back.

Change to larger needles and work in rev St st, inc 1 st at each edge [every 4th row] 14 (14, 17, 18) times. (57, 57, 65, 69 sts)

Work even until sleeve measures 19 (18, 17, 16) inches from beg, or desired length, place marker at each edge of piece for underarm. Work even for 3 more inches.

Bind off all sts.

Assembly

Sew bound-off edge of sleeve to inside corners of body armhole shaping. Sew 3 inches of each sleeve edge to front and back bound-off underarm sts.

Sew sleeve and side seams. ◆

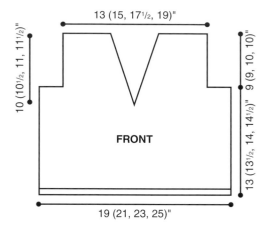

13 (15, 17½, 19)"

10 (10½, 11, 11½)"

9 (9, 10, 10)"

FRONT

13 (13½, 14, 14½)"

19 (21, 23, 25)"

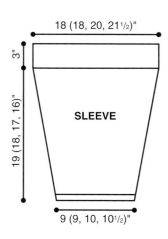

18 (18, 20, 21½)"

3"

19 (18, 17, 16)"

SLEEVE

9 (9, 10, 10½)"

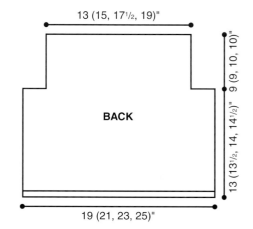

13 (15, 17½, 19)"

9 (9, 10, 10)"

BACK

13 (13½, 14, 14½)"

19 (21, 23, 25)"

DAPPLED FOREST GLEN

Flared sleeves add a unique touch to a basic pullover perfect for any occasion.

DESIGN BY MELISSA LEAPMAN

Size
Woman's small (medium, large, extra-large, 2X-large) Instructions are given for smallest size, with larger sizes in parentheses. When only 1 number is given, it applies to all sizes.

Finished Measurements
Chest: 37 (40, 43½, 47, 51) inches

Materials
- Brown Sheep Handpaint Originals 70 percent mohair/30 percent wool worsted weight yarn (88 yds/50g per hank): 11 (12, 13, 14, 15) hanks forest floor #HP70
- Size 8 (5mm) needles or size needed to obtain gauge

Gauge
18 sts and 24 rows = 4 inches/10cm in St st
To save time, take time to check gauge.

Special Abbreviation
M1 (Make 1): Make a backwards lp and place on RH needle.

Pattern Notes
In order to distribute color randomly, work two-row stripes, alternating from two different balls of yarn, and carrying yarn up side of work.

For fully fashioned dec, work as follows:

On RS rows: K3, ssk, work to last 5 sts, k2tog, k3.

On WS rows: P3, p2tog, work to last 5 sts, p2tog-tbl, p3.

For fully fashioned inc, work as follows:

On RS rows: K2, M1, work to last 2 sts, M1, k2.

Back

Cast on 75 (81, 88, 95, 102) sts. Work even in garter St for 1 inch, inc 9 (9, 10, 11, 12) sts evenly on last WS row. (84, 90, 98, 106, 114 sts)

Change to St st and work even until back measures 14 (14½, 14½, 15, 15) inches, ending with a WS row.

Shape armholes

Next 2 rows: Bind off 2 (3, 4, 6, 6) sts, work to end of row. (80, 84, 90, 94, 104 sts)

Work fully fashioned dec at each end [every row] 4 (5, 9, 9, 14) times, then [every other row] 6 (7, 5, 6, 4) times. (60, 62, 64, 64, 66 sts)

Work even until armhole measures 7 (7½, 7½, 8, 8½) inches, ending with a WS row.

Shape shoulders

Bind off 4 (4, 5, 5, 5) sts at beg of next 4 rows, then 5 (5, 4, 5, 6) sts at beg of following 2 rows.

Bind off rem 34 sts.

Front

Work as for back until armhole measures 4½ (5, 5, 5½, 6) inches, ending with a WS row.

Shape neck

Next row (RS): K 22 (22, 23, 24, 25) sts, join 2nd ball of yarn and bind off next 16 sts for front neck, knit to end of row.

Working on both sides of neck with separate balls of yarn, bind off at each neck edge [2 sts] twice.

Dec 1 st each side of neck [every row] twice, then [every other row] 3 times. (13, 13, 14, 15, 16) sts

Work even until armhole measures same as for back.

Shape shoulders

At each arm edge, bind off 4 (4, 5, 5, 5) sts twice, then 5 (5, 4, 5, 6) sts once.

Sleeves

Cast on 53 (55, 55, 56, 56) sts.

Work even in garter St for 1 inch, inc 6 (6, 6, 7, 7) sts evenly on last WS row. (59, 61, 61, 63, 63 sts)

Change to St st.

Shape sleeve flare

Work fully fashioned dec at each end [every 4th row] 9 times. (41, 43, 43, 45, 45 sts)

Work even until sleeve measures 9 (9, 9, 9½, 9½) inches, ending with a WS row.

Begin sleeve shaping

Work fully fashioned inc at each end [every 4th row] 0 (0, 0, 0, 3) times, [every 6th row] 6 (4, 4, 8, 6) times, and finally [every 8th row] 1 (3, 3, 0, 0) times. (55, 57, 57, 61, 63 sts)

Work even until sleeve measures 17½ (18, 18½, 19, 19) inches, ending with a WS row.

Shape sleeve cap

Next 2 rows: Bind off 2 (3, 4, 6, 6) sts, work to end of row. (51, 51, 49, 49, 51 sts)

Work fully fashioned dec at each end [every other row] 6 (9, 10, 13, 15) times, then [every row] 11 (8, 6, 3, 2) times. (17 sts)

Bind off 2 sts at beg of next 4 rows.

Bind off rem 9 sts.

Sew left shoulder seam.

Neck Band

With RS facing, pick up and k 84 sts around neckline.

Work even in garter st for ½ inch, ending with a WS row.

Next row (RS): Knit, dec 12 sts evenly. (72 sts)

Work even in garter st until neck band measures 1 inch, ending with a WS row.

Bind off loosely.

Assembly

Sew right shoulder seam, including side of neck band.

Sew in sleeves. Sew sleeve and side seams. ◆

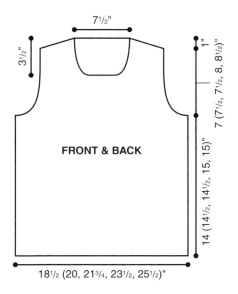

FRONT & BACK

7½"

3½"

1"

7 (7½, 7½, 8, 8½)"

14 (14½, 14½, 15, 15)"

18½ (20, 21¾, 23½, 25½)"

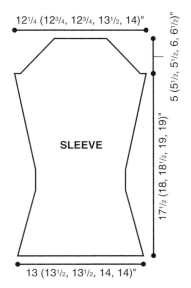

SLEEVE

12¼ (12¾, 12¾, 13½, 14)"

5 (5½, 5½, 6, 6½)"

17½ (18, 18½, 19, 19)"

13 (13½, 13½, 14, 14)"

RAZZLE DAZZLE SWEATER

Easy stitches and a special yarn give spectacular results for a first project.

DESIGN BY LAURA GEBHARDT

Size

Woman's small (medium, large) To fit a bust measurement of 34–36 (38–40, 42–46) inches. Instructions are given for smallest size, with larger sizes in parentheses. When only 1 number is given, it applies to all sizes.

Finished Measurements

Chest: 40 (46½, 54) inches
Length: 26 (27½, 28) inches

Materials

- Bernat Soft Boucle Glitter 76.3 percent acrylic/19 percent nylon/4.7 percent polyester bulky weight yarn (205 yds/4 oz per ball): 5 (5, 6) balls black #7006
- Size 8 (5mm) 29-inch circular needle or size needed to obtain gauge
- Tapestry needle

Gauge

15 sts and 22 rows = 4 inches/10cm in St st
To save time, take time to check gauge.

Special Abbreviation

M1 (Make 1): Make a backwards loop and place on RH needle.

Back

Cast on 75 (87, 101) sts.

Rib Pattern

Row 1: K2, *p1, k1, rep from * to last st, k1.
Row 2: K1, purl to last st, k1.
[Rep rows 1–2] 3 times. (8 rows)
Work even in St st until back measures 26 (27½, 28) inches from beg, ending with a WS row. Keep first and last st in garter st for selvage edge.
Bind off all sts.

Front

Work as for back until front measures 23 (24½, 25) inches, ending with a WS row.

Shape neck and shoulders

K28 (34, 41), attach 2nd ball of yarn and bind off next 19 sts for neck, knit to end of row.
Working on both sides of neck simultaneously with separate balls of yarn, [bind off 2 sts at each neck edge] twice.

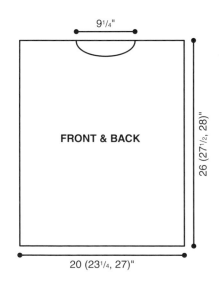

9¼"

FRONT & BACK

26 (27½, 28)"

20 (23¼, 27)"

   [Dec 1 st at each neck edge]
4 times.
   Work even for 4 rows on
remaining 20 (26, 33) sts.
   Bind off.

Sleeves

Cast on 33 (35, 35) sts.
[Rep Rows 1–2 of Rib Pat] 8 times.
Row 17: K1, *M1, k1, rep from * to
last st, k1. (64, 68, 68 sts)
   Work even in St st maintaining
garter st selvages until sleeve
measures 17 (17½, 18½) inches.
   Bind off.
   Sew shoulder seams.

Collar

Beg at center back neck, pick up
and knit 18 sts across back of neck,
16 sts down left side of neck, 19
sts across front of neck, 16 sts up
right front of neck, and 17 sts across
remaining back neck. (86 sts)
   Place marker between first and
last st.
   Work even in rnds of k1, p1 rib for
12 inches. Bind off in rib.

Finishing

Measure down and mark 8½ (9, 9)
inches from shoulder seam on front
and back.
   Sew sleeve into armhole
between markers, having center of
sleeve at shoulder seam.
   Sew sleeve and side seams. ◆

17 (18, 18)"

17 (17½, 18½)"

SLEEVE

CHUNKY TURTLENECK TUNIC

A touch of color adds spark to a chunky Aran-style pullover.

DESIGN BY BONNIE FRANZ

Size

Woman's extra-small (small, medium, large, extra-large) Instructions are given for smallest size, with larger sizes in parentheses. When only 1 number is given, it applies to all sizes.

Finished Measurements

Chest: 35 (39, 43, 47, 51) inches
Total length: 27½ (28, 28¼, 28¼, 29) inches
Sleeve length: 16½ (17, 17, 17, 17¼) inches

Materials

- Brown Sheep Burley Spun 100 percent wool super bulky yarn (132 yds/8 oz per hank): 4 (5, 5, 5, 6) hanks cream #BS10 (MC), 1 hank fuchsia #BS23 (CC)
- Size 13 (9mm) needles or size needed to obtain gauge
- Cable needle
- Stitch holders

Gauge

10 sts and 13 rows = 4 inches/10cm in Cable & Rib pat
9 sts and 12 rows= 4 inches/10cm in Sleeve Rib pat
To save time, take time to check gauge.

Pattern Stitches

A. Cable & Rib

Row 1 (RS): K1, *p2, k4; rep from * to last 3 sts, p2, k1.

Rows 2 and 4: P1, *k2, p4; rep from * to last 3 sts, k2, p1.

Row 3: K1, *p2, k4, p2, place next 2 sts on cn and hold in front, k2, k2 from cn; rep from * to last 3 sts, p2, k1.

Rep Rows 1–4 for pat.

B. Sleeve Rib

Row 1: P2, *k4, p2; rep from * across.

Row 2: K2, *p4, k2; rep from * across.

Rep Rows 1–2 for pat.

Back

With CC cast on 46 (52, 58, 64, 70) sts.

Change to MC and purl 1 row.

Work even in Cable & Rib pat until back measures 18 (18½, 18, 17, 18) inches, ending with a WS row.

Shape armhole

Next 2 rows: Bind off 2 (2, 3, 3, 3) sts, work in established pat to end of row. (42, 48, 52, 58, 64 sts)

Row 3: Ssk, work in pat to last 2 sts, k2tog.

Row 4: Work even in pat.

Rep [Rows 3 and 4] 2 (5, 5, 6, 8) times more. (36, 36, 40, 42, 46 sts)

Work even until armhole measures 8½ (8½, 9¼, 10, 10) inches, ending with a WS row.

Shape shoulders

Bind off 5 (5, 5, 6, 6) sts at beg of next 2 rows, then 6 (6, 6, 6, 7) sts at beg of following 2 rows.

Place rem 14 (14, 18, 18, 20) sts on holder for back neck.

Front

Work as for back until armhole measures 6½ (6½, 6½, 7, 7) inches, ending with a WS row.

Shape neck

Work across 15 (15, 16, 17, 18) sts, place next 6 (6, 8, 8, 10) sts on holder for front neck, join 2nd ball of yarn and work across rem 15 (15, 16, 17, 18) sts.

Working on both sides of neck with separate balls of yarn, dec [1 st at each neck edge every row] 4 (4, 5, 5, 5) times. (11, 11, 11, 12, 13 sts) on each side.

Work even until armhole measures same as for back.

Shape shoulders

At each arm edge, bind off 5 (5, 5, 6, 6) sts once, then 6 (6, 6, 6, 7) sts once.

Sleeves

With CC, cast on 20 (22, 22, 24, 26) sts.

Change to MC and purl 1 row.

Set up pat

Size extra-small and extra-large only (RS):
[P2, k4] 3 (4) times, p2.

Size small and medium only (RS): K1 [p2, k4] 3 times, p2, k1.

Size large only (RS): K2 [p2, k4] 3 times, p2, k2.

Work in established Sleeve Rib pat, inc 1 st each end [every 6th row] 0 (0, 3, 3, 8) times, every 7th row 5 (3, 3, 4, 0) times, then every 8th row 1 (3, 0, 0, 0) times. (32, 34, 34, 38, 42 sts)

Work added sts into pat.

Work even until sleeve measures 16½ (17, 17, 17, 17¼) inches ending with a WS row.

Shape sleeve cap

Next 2 rows: Bind off 2 (2, 2, 2, 3) sts, work to end of row. (28, 30, 30, 34, 36 sts)

Dec 1 st each end [every row] 2 (3, 1, 2, 2) times, [every other row] 6 (5, 8, 8, 8) times, and finally [every row] 2 (3, 1, 2, 2) times.

Bind off rem 8 (8, 10, 10, 12) sts.

Collar

Sew left shoulder seam.

With RS facing using MC, knit across 14 (14, 18, 20, 20) sts of back neck holder, pick up and knit 11 (14, 14, 15, 15) sts along left neck edge, knit across 6 (6, 8, 8, 10) sts of front neck holder, pick up and knit 11 (14, 14, 16, 15) sts along right neck edge. (42, 48, 54, 60, 60 sts)

Note: *Collar will fold over upon completion, therefore, WS of sweater will be facing you, but you will be working on RS of collar.*

Next row: K2 [p2, k4] 6 (7, 8, 9, 9) times, p2, k2.

Work even in established Sleeve Rib pat until collar measures 5 (5, 5½, 5½, 6) inches, ending with a WS row.

Change to CC and bind off very loosely in pat.

Assembly

Sew rem shoulder seam and collar seam.

Sew sleeves into armholes, easing to fit.

Sew side and sleeve seams. ◆

WARM-AS-TOAST SWEATER

Choose this sweater for comfort and coziness, but know that it looks just as wonderful as it feels!

DESIGN BY CARON INTERNATIONAL

Size

Woman's small (medium, large) Instructions are given for smallest size, with larger sizes in parentheses. When only 1 number is given, it applies to all sizes.

Finished Measurements

Chest: 39 (42, 45) inches
Length: 18½ (19½, 20½) inches

Materials

- Caron Cozi 79 percent acrylic/21 percent polyester bulky weight yarn (75 yds/2.5 oz per skein): 6 (7, 8) skeins toasted almond #0003
- Size 11 (8mm) straight and 16-inch circular needles or size needed to obtain gauge
- Size 13 (9mm) 16-inch circular needle
- Stitch holders
- Stitch markers

Gauge

12 sts and 12 rows = 4 inches/10cm in rev St st with smaller needles
To save time, take time to check gauge.

Back

With smaller needles, cast on 52 (58, 62) sts.
Row 1 (RS): Purl.
Row 2: Knit.

Rows 3 and 4: Purl.
Row 5: Purl.
Row 6: Knit.

Continue in rev St st (purl on RS, knit on WS), at the same time, inc 1 st each edge [every 12th row] 3 times. (58, 64, 68 sts)

Work even until piece measures approx 9 (9½, 10) inches from beg, ending with a WS row.

Shape armholes

Maintaining pat, dec 1 st (p2tog) at each end of next row, then [every other row] 8 (9, 10) times. (40, 44, 46 sts)

Work even in pat until piece measures approx 17½ (18½, 19½) inches from beg, ending with a WS row.

Shape shoulders

At beg of row, bind off [3 (4, 4) sts] 4 times, then [4 (4, 5) sts] twice. Place rem 20 sts on holder for back neck.

Front

Work as for back, including armhole shaping, until piece measures approx 15½ (16½, 17½) inches from beg, ending with a WS row.

Shape neck

Work across 13 (15, 16) sts, place center 14 sts on a holder for front neck, join 2nd skein of yarn and

work across rem 13 (15, 16) sts. Working both sides at once with separate skeins of yarn, dec 1 st at each neck edge [every other row] 3 times. (10, 12, 13 sts on each side)

Work even until piece measures same as back to shoulder shaping, ending with a WS row.

Shape shoulders

Bind off at each armhole edge 3 (4, 4) sts twice, then 4 (4, 5) sts once.

Sleeves

With larger needles, cast on 26 (28, 30) sts.
Row 1 (RS): Purl.
Row 2: Knit.
Rows 3 and 4: Purl.

Continue in rev St st, at the same time, inc 1 st at each edge [every 6th row] 10 (10, 11) times. (46, 48, 52 sts)

Work even until sleeve measures approx 17 (18, 19) inches from beg, ending with a WS row.

Shape sleeve cap

Beg on next row, dec 1 st at each edge [every other row] 8 (9, 10) times. (30, 30, 32 sts)
Work 1 row even.
Bind off all sts.

Collar

Sew shoulder seams.

Hold with RS facing, beg at left shoulder seam with smaller circular needle, pick up and knit 13 sts along left front neck edge, knit 14 sts from front holder, pick up and knit 13 sts along right neck edge, knit 20 sts from back neck holder. (60 sts)

Place marker and join. Knit in rnds until collar measures 3½ inches. Change to larger circular needle and knit until collar measures approx 7 inches from beg. Bind off all sts very loosely.

Assembly

Set in sleeves. Sew side and sleeve seams. Block lightly if desired. ◆

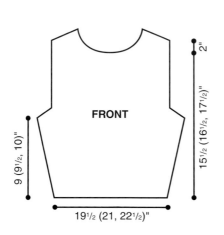

FRONT

9 (9½, 10)"

15½ (16½, 17½)"

2"

19½ (21, 22½)"

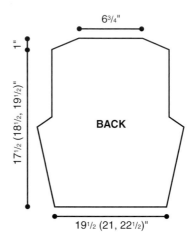

BACK

6¾"

1"

17½ (18½, 19½)"

19½ (21, 22½)"

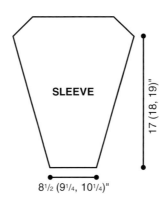

SLEEVE

17 (18, 19)"

8½ (9¼, 10¼)"

STARFLOWER SWEATER

Make an impression on the teen scene with this unique pullover.

DESIGN BY LAURA POLLEY

Size

To fit a 36 (38, 40, 42)-inch chest.
Instructions are given for smallest size, with larger sizes in parentheses. When only one number is given, it applies to all sizes.

Materials

- Plymouth Encore 75 percent acrylic/25 percent wool worsted weight yarn (200 yds/100g per ball): 4 (4, 5, 6) balls blue heather #1793 (A), 3 (3, 4, 5) balls dark pink heather #1794 (B)
- Size 7 (4.5mm) needles
- Size 9 (5.5mm) needles or size needed to obtain gauge
- Tapestry needle

Gauge

24 sts and 22 rows = 4 inches/10cm in star pat with larger needles
To save time, take time to check gauge.

Pattern Notes

Pat includes 1 st at each edge in St st for selvages. Work all incs and decs inside these selvage sts.

When working shaped portions of sweater, keep added sts in St st until there are enough to work into Star pat. Work all added sts into Star pat as soon as possible.

Special Abbreviation

Star St (SS): P3tog, leaving sts on needle, yo, p these 3 sts tog again, slip off needle.

Pattern Stitches
2/2 Rib

Row 1 (RS): K2, *p2, k2, rep from * to end.
Row 2: P2, *k2, p2, rep from * to end.
Rep Rows 1–2 for pat.

Star Pattern

Row 1 (RS): With A, knit.
Row 2: With A, p1, *SS, p1, rep from * to end.
Row 3: With B, knit.
Row 4: With B, p3, SS, *p1, SS, rep from * to last 3 sts, p3.
Rep Rows 1–4 for pat.

Back

With smaller needles and A, cast on 121 (129, 133, 141) sts. Change to larger needles.

Work in Star pat until back measures 9 (9, 10, 11) inches, ending with a WS row.

Shape armhole

Bind off 10 sts at beg of next 2 rows. (101, 109, 113, 121 sts)

Work even in pat until armhole measures 8 (9, 9, 9) inches, ending with a WS row.

Shape neck

Work across 31 (35, 35, 39) sts, join 2nd ball of yarn and bind off next 39 (39, 43, 43) sts for back neck, work to end of row.

Working in est pat on both sides of neck at same time with separate balls of yarn, [dec 1 st at each neck edge every other row] twice. (29, 33, 33, 37 sts each side)

Work even until armhole measures 9 (10, 10, 10) inches, ending with a WS row. Bind off.

Front

Work as for back until armhole measures 6 (7, 6½, 6½) inches, ending with a WS row.

Shape neck

Work across 36 (40, 40, 44) sts, join 2nd ball of yarn and bind off next 29 (29, 33, 33) sts for front neck, work to end of row. Bind off at each neck edge 3 sts once, then 2 sts once.

[Dec 1 st each side of neck every 4th row] twice. (29, 33, 33, 37 sts each side)

Work even in pat until armhole measures same as back, end with a WS row. Bind off.

Sleeves

With smaller needles and A, cast on 50 (54, 54, 54) sts.

Work in 2/2 rib for 1 inch, inc 3 sts on last WS row. (53, 57, 57, 57 sts) Change to larger needles.

Work in Star pat, [inc one st each side every 3rd row] 28 (32, 32, 32) times. (109, 121, 121, 121 sts)

Work even until sleeve measures 20 (21, 20, 19) inches from beg, ending with a WS row. Bind off.

Finishing

Sew one shoulder seam.

Neck Band

With RS facing using smaller needles and A, beg at open shoulder edge, pick up and knit 110 (110, 122, 122) sts around neck edge. Beg with Row 2, work 2/2 rib for 1 inch.

Bind off in rib.

Sew neck band and rem shoulder seam.

Sew sleeves into armhole, having top 1½ inch of sleeve edges against bound-off sts of underarm.

Sew side and sleeve seams. ◆

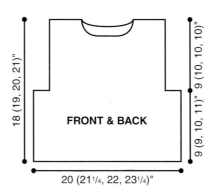

18 (19, 20, 21)"

9 (9, 10, 10)" 9 (10, 10, 10)"

FRONT & BACK

9 (9, 10, 11)"

20 (21¼, 22, 23¼)"

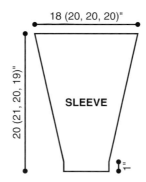

18 (20, 20, 20)"

20 (21, 20, 19)"

SLEEVE

MOOD-BOOSTING TUNIC

Our deceptively easy-to-knit, double-stranded tunic is accented with stripes and a slip-stitch border.

DESIGN BY JEAN SCHAFER-ALBERS

Size

Woman's small (medium, large, extra-large) Instructions are given for smallest size, with larger sizes in parentheses. When only 1 number is given it applies to all sizes.

Finished Measurements

Chest: 39 (42, 45½, 50) inches
Length: 23 (23, 23¾, 23¾) inches
Sleeve length: 18 (18½, 19¼, 19¼) inches

Materials

- Brown Sheep Nature Spun 100 percent wool worsted weight yarn (245 yds/100g per skein): 4 (5, 5, 6) skeins turquoise wonder #78 (A), 3 (4, 4, 5) skeins spring green #109 (B), 1 skein Peruvian pink #N85 (C)
- Size 10 (6mm) straight and 16-inch circular needles or size needed to obtain gauge
- Stitch holders

Gauge

14 sts and 20 rows = 4 inches/10cm in St st.
To save time take time to check gauge.

Pattern Stitch

Moss Slip Stitch (multiple of 2 sts + selvage)

Row 1 (RS): With A, k1, *k1, sl 1p; rep from *, end k1.
Row 2: With A, k1 *sl 1p, k1; rep from *, end k1.
Row 3: With B, k1, *sl 1p, k1; rep from *, end k1.
Row 4: With B, k1, *k1, sl 1p; rep from *, end k1.

Special Abbreviation

M1 (Make 1): Inc 1 st by making a backward loop over RH needle. Knit in back of loop on next row.

Pattern Notes

Sweater is worked throughout by stranding 2 yarns tog.

Moss Slip Stitch pat is used for bottom and sleeve edge borders. Slip all sts purlwise with yarn on WS of fabric.

Marbled look of yarn in main sections of sweater is achieved by stranding 2 different colors of yarn together.

Selvage stitches are included in pattern for ease in sewing seams.

Back
Border

With 2 strands of A, cast on 82 (90, 98, 106) sts (includes selvage sts).
Foundation row (WS): K1 (selvage st), *k1, p1; rep from * to last st, k1 (selvage st).

Row 1 (RS): K1, work Row 1 of Moss Slip Stitch pat to last st, end k1.
Row 2–4: Work Rows 2–4 of pat.
Rows 5–8: Rep Rows 1–4 of pat.
Dec row: With 2 strands of B, work first row of stripe and at the same time, dec 14 (16, 18, 18) sts evenly across. (68, 74, 80, 88 sts)

Work 3 more rows for stripe. Attach 2 strands of C and work 2 rows for next stripe. With 2 strands of A, work 4 rows for next stripe.

Body

With 1 strand each of A and B, work even in St st until back measures 15½ (15, 15½, 14½) inches, ending with a WS row.

Shape underarms

Bind off 5 (6, 7, 8) sts at beg of next 2 rows, then dec 1 st at each edge [every RS row] 4 (4, 5, 6) times by k1, ssk, knit to last 3 sts, end k2tog, k1. (50, 54, 56, 60 sts)

Continue to work even until back measures 23 (23, 23¾, 23¾) inches. Place 13 (14, 15, 16) sts for each shoulder and center 24 (26, 26, 28) sts for back neck on holders.

Front

Work as for back until front measures 19¾ (19¾, 20½, 20½) inches, ending with a WS row.

Shape neck

K20 (22, 23, 25) sts, join additional skeins of A and B, bind off center 10 sts; knit to end.

Working both sides at once with separate skeins of yarn, bind off at each neck edge [2 sts] 2 (3, 3, 4) times, then dec 1 st at neck edge [every RS row] 3 (2, 2, 1) times by k2tog on left side, ssk on right side. (13, 14, 15, 16 sts)

Work even until front measures same as back, place sts on holders.

Assembly

Join front and back shoulders using 3-needle bind off.

Sleeves
Border

With 2 strands of A, cast on 36 (36, 38, 40) sts (includes 2 selvage sts). Work as for Rows 1–8 of back border pat.

Body

Dec row: With 2 strands of B, work first row of stripe and at the same time, dec 6 (6, 4, 6) sts evenly across. (30, 30, 34, 34 sts)

Work rem stripe rows as for back and at the same time, inc 1 st by M1 at each edge [every 4th row] 0 (4, 2, 5) times, [every 6th row] 11 (10, 12, 10) times, [every 8th row] 1 (0, 0, 0) times. (54, 58, 62, 64 sts)

When stripes are completed, continue in St st with 1 strand each of A and B until all incs are made, then work even until sleeve measures 18 (18½, 19¼, 19¼) inches, end with a RS row.

Shape cap

Bind off 5 (6, 7, 8) sts at beg of next 2 rows, then dec 1 st at each edge as for underarms [every other row] 4 (4, 5, 6) times. (36, 38, 38, 36 sts)
Purl 1 row.
Bind off all sts.

Neck band

With 2 strands of A and 16-inch circular needle, knit across 24 (26, 26, 28) back neck sts, pick up and knit 4 sts for every 5 rows along left neck edge, pick up and knit 10 sts across front neck, pick up and knit 4 sts for every 5 rows along right edge of neck. (Needs to be an even number of sts) Join, placing a marker at beg of rnd.

Rnd 1: *K1, p1; rep from * around.
Rnd 2: With 2 strands of C, knit.
Rnd 3: Rep Rnd 1.
Rnd 4: With 2 strands of B, knit.
Rnd 5: Rep Rnd 1.
Bind off loosely in pat.

Finishing

Sew sleeves into armholes, matching underarms.
Sew sleeve and side seams. ◆

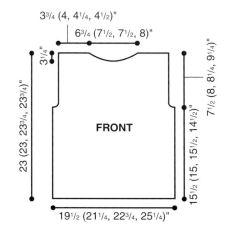

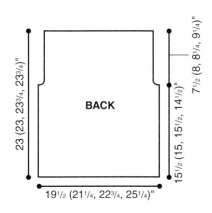

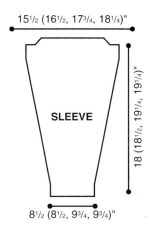

IT'S ALL ABOUT SHINE

This glimmering cropped hoodie is ready to shine!

DESIGN BY CARI CLEMENT FOR CARON INTERNATIONAL

Size

Woman's extra-small (small, medium, large, extra-large, 2X-large) Instructions are given for smallest size, with larger sizes in parentheses. When only 1 number is given, it applies to all sizes.

Finished Measurements

Chest: 34 (38, 42, 46, 50, 54) inches
Length: 17 (18, 19, 19½, 20, 20½) inches

Materials

- Caron Glimmer 85 percent acrylic/15 percent polyester bulky weight chenille yarn (55 yds/50g per skein): 9 (10, 11, 13, 15, 16) skeins willow #0009
- Size 10½ (6.5mm) needles or size needed to obtain gauge
- Size J/10 (6mm) crochet hook
- Separating jacket zipper: 11 (12, 13, 14, 14, 15) inches long
- 3-inch-wide piece of cardboard for loop pompoms

Gauge

12 sts and 21 rows = 4 inches/10cm in St st
To save time, take time to check gauge.

Back

Cast on 52 (58, 64, 70, 76, 82) sts.
Beg with a WS row, work even in St st until back measures approx 8½ (9, 9½, 10, 10½, 10½) inches from beg, ending with a WS row.

Shape armholes

Bind off 2 (3, 4, 5, 6, 7) sts at beg of next 2 rows. (48, 52, 56, 60, 64, 68 sts)
Dec 1 st at each side [every other row] 2 (3, 4, 5, 6, 7) times. (44, 46, 48, 50, 52, 54 sts)
Work even until armhole measures approx 8 (8½, 9, 9½, 10, 10½) inches from beg of shaping, ending with a WS row.

Shape shoulders & neck

At beg of row, bind off [6 (6, 7, 7, 7, 7) sts] twice, then [6 (6, 6, 6, 6, 7) sts] twice for shoulders. Bind off rem 20 (22, 22, 24, 26, 26) sts for back neck.

Left Front

Cast on 26 (29, 32, 35, 38, 41) sts.
Work as for back to underarm, ending with a WS row.

Shape armhole

Bind off 2 (3, 4, 5, 6, 7) sts at beg of next row, then dec 1 st at armhole edge [every other row] 2 (3, 4, 5, 6, 7) times. (22, 23, 24, 25, 26, 27 sts)
Work even until armhole measures approx 5 (5½, 6, 6½, 7, 7½) inches, ending with a RS row.

Shape neck

At neck edge, bind off 5 (6, 6, 7, 8, 8) sts, work to end. (17, 17, 18, 18, 18, 19 sts rem)
Work 1 row even, then dec 1 st [every WS row] 5 times. (12, 12, 13, 13, 13, 14 sts rem for shoulder)
Work even until armhole measures same as back to shoulder shaping, ending with a WS row.

Shape shoulders

At beg of RS row (armhole edge), bind off [6 (6, 7, 7, 7, 7) sts] once, then [6 (6, 6, 6, 6, 7) sts] once.

Right Front

Work as for left front to underarm, ending with a RS row.

Shape armhole

Bind off 2 (3, 4, 5, 6, 7) sts at beg of next row, then dec 1 st at armhole edge [every other row] 2 (3, 4, 5, 6, 7) times. (22, 23, 24, 25, 26, 27 sts)
Work even until armhole measures approx 5 (5½, 6, 6½, 7, 7½) inches, ending with a WS row.

Shape neck

At neck edge, bind off 5 (6, 6, 7, 8, 8) sts, work to end. (17, 17, 18, 18, 18, 19 sts rem)
Dec 1 st [every WS row] 5 times. (12, 12, 13, 13, 13, 14 sts rem for shoulder)
Work even until armhole measures same as back to shoulder shaping, ending with a RS row.

Shape shoulders

At beg of WS row (armhole edge), bind off [6 (6, 7, 7, 7, 7) sts] once, then [6 (6, 6, 6, 6, 7) sts] once.

Sleeves

Cast on 30 (30, 32, 34, 36, 38) sts.
Beg with a WS row, work even in St st for 3 rows.
Beg on next row, inc 1 st at each side on this row, then [every 8th row] 0 (0, 0, 0, 2, 2) times, [every 10th row] 0 (0, 6, 5, 7, 7) times, [every 12th row] 2 (7, 2, 3, 0, 0) times, [every 14th row] 4 (0, 0, 0, 0, 0) times. (44, 46, 50, 52, 56, 58 sts)

Work even until sleeve measures approx 17 (17½, 17½, 18, 18, 18) inches from beg, ending with a WS row.

Shape cap

At beg of row, [bind off 2 (3, 4, 5, 6, 7) sts] twice, then dec 1 st on each side [every other row] 12 (13, 13, 13, 14, 14) times. (16, 14, 16, 16, 16, 16 sts rem)

Bind off 3 (2, 3, 3, 3, 3) sts at beg of next 2 rows, then bind off rem 10 sts.

Hood
Left half

Cast on 38 (40, 40, 44, 48, 48) sts.

Beg with a WS row, work even in St st until piece measures approx 12 inches from beg, ending with a WS row.

Shape top

At center back, bind off every RS row [5 (5, 5, 5, 6, 6) sts] 4 (8, 8, 4, 8, 8) times, then [6 (0, 0, 6, 0, 0) sts] 3 (0, 0, 4, 0, 0) times.

Right half

Work as for left half until piece measures 12 inches from beg, ending with a RS row.

Shape top

At center back, bind off every WS row [5 (5, 5, 5, 6, 6) sts] 4 (8, 8, 4, 8, 8) times, then [6 (0, 0, 6, 0, 0) sts] 3 (0, 0, 4, 0, 0) times.

Assembly

Block pieces to measurements as needed, following instructions on ball band. Sew shoulder seams. Set in sleeves; sew sleeve and side seams. Sew hood pieces tog, then sew hood around neck shaping, easing to fit along back neck.

Lower Edge, Fronts & Hood Edging

With RS facing, using crochet hook, beg at side seam between right front and back, sc in back lps only across cast-on edge to center right front; work 3 sc in corner st, sc along right center front keeping edge flat, sc around hood opening, sc along left center front having same number of sc as right front, work 3 sc in corner, work in back lps only across lower edge to beg. Fasten off.

Sleeve Edging

Join with sc in sleeve seam, working back lps only of cast on sts, sc along lower edge of sleeve. Fasten off.

Sew zipper into center front opening inside crochet edge, beg approx 1 inch below neck shaping.

Ties
Make 2

With crochet hook, work a chain 14 inches long. Fasten off.

Sew 1 tie to each neck edge where hood joins neck shaping.

Loop Pompoms
Make 2

Note: Do not cut lps on pompoms.

Wrap yarn around a 3-inch piece of cardboard 20 times; using a 12-inch piece of yarn, tie through all strands at center of cardboard; slide lps off cardboard, tie rem strands with same piece of yarn. Attach one pompom to end of each tie. ◆

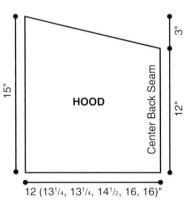

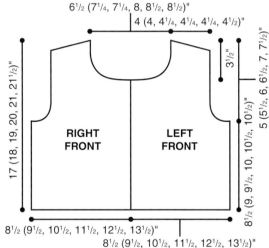

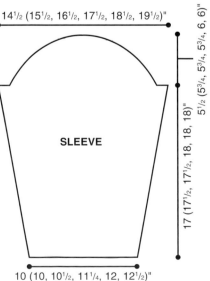

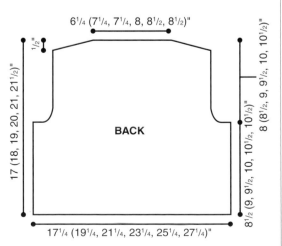

CASUAL HOODED PULLOVER

The cable panels give this hooded pullover a Celtic feeling, while letting you practice twist stitches and saddle shoulders.

DESIGN BY KATHARINE HUNT

Size

To fit 32 (36, 40, 44, 48)-inch chest. Instructions are given for smallest size, with larger sizes in parentheses. When only 1 number is given, it applies to all sizes.

Finished Measurements

Chest: 38 (42, 47, 51½, 56) inches
Length: 24½ (25½, 26, 26½, 27½) inches
Height of hood: 14½ (14½, 15¼, 15¼, 15¾) inches

Materials

- Lion Brand Wool-Ease 86 percent acrylic/10 percent wool/4 percent rayon yarn (197 yds/85g per ball): 8 (8, 9, 9, 10) balls wheat #402
- Size 7 (4.5mm) needles
- Size 9 (5.5mm) straight and 32-inch circular needles or size needed to obtain gauge.
- 7-inch neckline zipper
- Tapestry needle

Gauge

18 sts = 4 inches/10cm in St st with larger needles
To save time, take time to check gauge.

Special Abbreviations

Cable 4 Front (C4F): Sl next 2 sts to cn and hold in front, k2, k2 from cn.
Twist 4 Back (T4B): Sl next 2 sts to cn and hold in back, k2, p2 from cn.
Twist 4 Front (T4F): Sl next 2 sts to cn and hold in front, p2, k2 from cn.

Pattern Stitch

Cable (panel of 26 sts)
Row 1 (RS): P1, k2, p4, C4F, p4, C4F, p4, k2, p1.
Row 2 and all WS rows: K the knit sts and p the purl sts.
Row 3: P1, k2, p4, k4, p4, k4, p4, k2, p1.
Row 5: Rep Row 1.
Row 7: P1, k2, p2, [T4B, T4F] twice, p2, k2, p1.
Row 9: P1, k2, p2, k2, p4, C4F, p4, k2, p2, k2, p1.
Row 11: P1, k2, p2, k2, p4, k4, p4, k2, p2, k2, p1.
Row 13: Rep Row 9.
Rows 15–22: Rep Rows 11–14.
Row 23: P1, k2, p2, [T4F, T4B] twice, p2, k2, p1.
Row 24: Rep Row 2.
Rep Rows 1–24 for pat.

Back

With smaller ndls, cast on 108 (118, 128, 138, 148) sts, and

work in rib pat as follows:
Row 1 (RS): *K1, p1, k1, p2, rep from * to last 3 sts, end k1, p1, k1.
Row 2: Knit the knit sts and purl the purl sts.

Continue in rib pat for 1¾ (1¾, 2, 2, 2¼) inches, ending with a WS row.
Next row (RS): With larger needles, k16 (19, 23, 27, 31), work Row 1 of cable panel, k24 (28, 30, 32, 34), work Row 1 of cable panel, k16 (19, 23, 27, 31).
Next row: Knit the knit sts and purl the purl sts.

Continue in estabished cable panel until piece measures 15 (15½, 15½, 16, 16½) inches.

Shape armhole

At beg of next 2 rows, bind off 8 (8, 10, 12, 12) sts. (92, 102, 108, 114, 124 sts rem)

Continue to work even in established pat until piece measures 23 (24, 24½, 25, 26) inches from beg.

Shape shoulders

At beg of row, bind off [11 (12, 10, 12, 12) sts] twice, [9 (11, 8, 10, 10) sts] twice, [8 (9, 8, 8, 10) sts] twice, and [0 (0, 8, 7, 9) sts] twice. Bind off rem 36 (38, 40, 40, 42) sts across back neck, at the same time, dec 2 (3, 3, 4, 4) sts evenly across.

Front

Work as for back until piece measures 1 (1, 1½, 1, 2) inches past armhole shaping, ending with a WS row.

Work in pat across 41 (46, 49, 52, 57) sts, bind off center 10 sts, work across rem 41 (46, 49, 52, 57) sts.

Next row: Work to first neck edge, attach another ball of yarn at second neck edge and complete row.

Continue working both sides at once until neck opening measures 6 inches from bound-off sts, ending with a WS row.

Shape right neck

Work on right front sts only.

Row 1 (RS): Bind off 3 sts at neck edge, complete row.

Row 2: Work to last 2 sts, p2tog.

Rows 3 and 4: Rep Rows 1 and 2.

Row 5: Dec 2 sts, work to end of row.

Dec 1 st at neck edge [every row] 3 (4, 5, 5, 6) times. (28, 32, 34, 37, 41 shoulder sts rem)

At the same time, when front armhole length matches back, work shoulder shaping as for back.

Shape left neck

Work as for right neck, reversing shaping.

Sleeves

With smaller needles cast on 48 (48, 53, 53, 58) sts.

Work 1¾ (1¾, 2, 2, 2¼) inches in rib pat as for back, ending with a WS row, and inc 6 (6, 5, 5, 4) sts evenly across last row. Change to larger needles. (54, 54, 58, 58, 62 sts)

Beg pat

Row 1 (RS): K14 (14, 16, 16, 18) sts, work Row 1 of cable panel, k14 (14, 16, 16, 18).

Continue in established cable pat, at the same time, beg on Row 5, inc 1 st at each edge [every 4th row] 23 (25, 26, 26, 26) times. (100, 104, 110, 110, 114 sts)

Continue to work even until sleeve measures 19½ (20, 21, 22, 22½) inches from beg, ending with a WS row.

At beg of row [bind off 35 (37, 40, 40, 42) sts] twice. (30 sts rem)

Shoulder saddle

Continue working cable panel until work measures 2½ (3, 3½, 4, 4½) inches, ending with a WS row.

First dec row (RS): P2tog, work in pat to last 2 sts, p2tog. Maintaining pat, work 7 rows.

Second dec row (RS): P1, k2, p2tog, work in pat to last 5 sts, p2tog, k2, p1. Maintaining pat, work 5 rows.

Third dec row (RS): P1, k1, sl1, p1, psso, work in pat to last 4 sts, k2tog, k1, p1. Work 5 rows.

Fourth dec row (RS): Dec 4 sts across row by [p2tog] 4 times. (20 sts rem)

Check saddle shoulder edge against length of shoulder shaping on back, and work to same length. Bind off all sts.

Hood
Make 2 as mirror images

Left Side of Hood

With larger needles, cast on 4 sts. Working in St st, follow chart for hood shaping, reading RS rows from right to left on chart. (47, 48, 49, 50, 52 sts)

Work even for 47 (47, 51, 51, 53) rows, then follow chart for top

CHART A
Hood

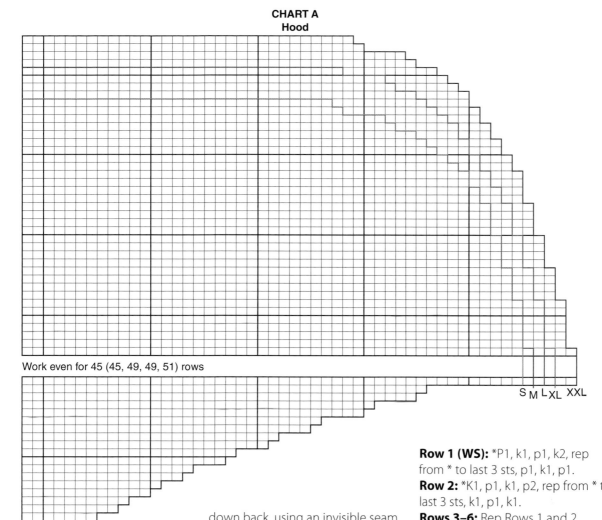

Work even for 45 (45, 49, 49, 51) rows

S M L XL XXL

shaping. Bind off rem 29 (29, 30, 30, 31) sts.

Right Side of Hood
Work as for left hood, reversing all shapings, reading RS rows from left to right on chart.

Finishing
Block pieces by pinning to size and covering with a damp cloth until dry. Do not press.

Insert sleeves into armholes, and sew edges of saddles to front and back shoulders. (Bound off edge of saddle forms part of neck edge.)

Beg at top front, with RS tog, sew hood pieces tog along top and down back, using an invisible seam. Turn hood right side out.

Pin hood in place, matching front edges with front neck opening, aligning back seam with center back of neck edge, and easing shaped edges to fit. Sew hood in place.

Hood and zipper band
With circular needle and RS facing, working from right to left, beg at right bottom of front opening, pick up and knit 38 sts to top of neck, 88 (88, 93, 93, 98) sts up right hood edge to top center, 1 st in seam, 88 (88, 93, 93, 98) sts down left hood edge to top of neck, then 38 sts to bottom of front opening. (253, 253, 263, 263, 273 sts)

Note: *Be careful not to stretch bottom of zipper opening as you work.*

Row 1 (WS): *P1, k1, p1, k2, rep from * to last 3 sts, p1, k1, p1.
Row 2: *K1, p1, k1, p2, rep from * to last 3 sts, k1, p1, k1.
Rows 3–6: Rep Rows 1 and 2.
Bind off in rib on WS.
Sew bottom edges of front band to bottom of opening, being careful to align ribbing on both sides.
Sew zipper in place, making sure that edges of bands meet to conceal zipper when zipped.
Sew body and sleeve seams. ◆

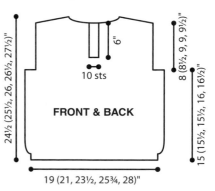

24½ (25½, 26, 26½, 27½)"

6"

10 sts

8 (8½, 9, 9, 9½)"

15 (15½, 15½, 16, 16½)"

FRONT & BACK

19 (21, 23½, 25¾, 28)"

FEELIN' GOOD BOLERO

This cardigan does double duty as a bolero for use over that little black dress, or as a bed jacket for chilly nights.

DESIGN BY SARA LOUISE HARPER

Size
Woman's extra-small (small, medium, large, extra-large)
Instructions are given for smallest size, with larger sizes in parentheses. When only 1 number is given, it applies to all sizes.

Finished Measurements
Chest: 36 (40, 44, 48, 52) inches
Length: 15 (16, 17, 18, 19) inches

Materials
- Lion Brand Suede 100 percent polyester bulky weight yarn (85 yds/122g per skein): 5 (6, 6, 7, 8) skeins desert #200
- Size 9 (5.5mm) needles or size needed to obtain gauge
- Stitch holders
- Safety pin
- 1 (1-inch) button

Gauge
13 sts and 24 rows = 4 inches/10cm in garter st
To save time, take time to check gauge.

Special Abbreviation
M1 (Make 1): Insert tip of needle under horizontal thread between st just worked and next st, k1 tbl.

Back
Cast on 52 (58, 64, 70, 78) sts and work in garter st until back measures 8 (9, 9½, 10, 10½) inches.

Shape armholes
Bind off 6 sts at beg of next 2 rows. (40, 46, 52, 58, 66 sts)
Work even until armhole measures 7 (7, 7½, 8, 8½) inches.

Shape neck and shoulders
Work first 11 (14, 16, 18, 20) sts, attach a 2nd skein of yarn and bind off center 18 (18, 20, 22, 26) sts; work 11 (14, 16, 18, 20) sts. Working both sides at once with separate skeins of yarn, work 2 rows more, then place all sts on holders.

Left Front
Cast on 2 sts.
Row 1 (WS): K1, yo, k1.
Row 2: K2, M1, k1.
Row 3: K1, M1, k3.
Row 4: K4, M1, k1.
Row 5: K1, M1, k5.
Mark RS of work with a safety pin, and continue to inc 1 st [every row] at end of RS rows and beg of WS rows until there are 30 (32, 36, 38, 42) sts on needle.
Buttonhole (RS): Knit to last 5 sts, k3tog, yo, k1, M1, k1.

At same edge as incs, beg to dec 1 st [every 3rd (3rd, 5th, 4th, 4th) row] 3 (2, 14, 6, 12) times, then [every 5th (6th, 0, 6th, 9th) row] 10 (10, 0, 8, 4) times. *At the same time*, when front measures 8 (9, 9½, 10, 10½) inches, bind off 6 sts at beg of RS row. Continue until front measures same as back, then place rem 11 (14, 16, 18, 20) sts on holder.

Right Front
Cast on 2 sts.
Row 1 (RS): K1, yo, k1.
Row 2: K2, M1, k1.
Row 3: K1, M1, k3.
Row 4: K4, M1, k1.
Row 5: K1, M1, k5.
Mark RS of work with a safety pin, and continue to inc 1 st [every row] at beg of RS rows and end of WS rows until there are 30 (32, 36, 38, 42) sts on needle.

At same edge as incs, beg to dec 1 st [every 3rd (3rd, 5th, 4th, 4th) row] 3 (2, 14, 6, 12) times, then [every 5th (6th, 0, 6th, 9th) row] 10 (10, 0, 8, 4) times. *At the same time*, when front measures 8 (9, 9½, 10, 10½) inches, bind off 6 sts at beg of WS row. Continue until front measures same as back, then place rem 11 (14, 16, 18, 20) sts on holder.

Sleeves

Cast on 22 (24, 26, 26, 28) sts and work in garter st, inc 1 st each end of needle [every 8th (9th, 9th, 8th, 8th) row] 12 (11, 9, 13, 11) times, then [every 0 (0, 13th, 0, 13th) row] 0 (0, 2, 0, 2) times. (46, 46, 48, 52, 54 sts)

Work even until sleeve measures 18 (19, 20, 20, 21) inches from beg. Bind off all sts loosely.

Assembly

Bind off front and back shoulders, using 3-needle bind off.

Sew sleeves into armholes, then sew sleeve and side seams. Sew button on right front to match buttonhole. ◆

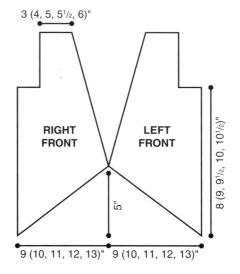

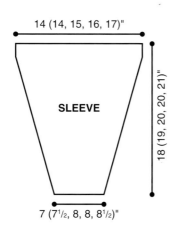

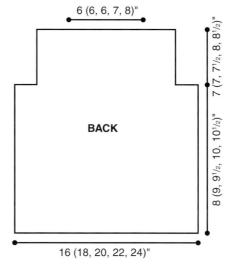

"THE BOMB" IN STRIPES

Designed for keeping out the cold, this jacket is knit with a double strand of self-striping yarn.

DESIGN BY COLLEEN SMITHERMAN

Size

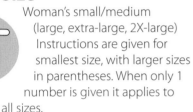

Woman's small/medium (large, extra-large, 2X-large) Instructions are given for smallest size, with larger sizes in parentheses. When only 1 number is given it applies to all sizes.

Finished Measurements

Chest: 39 (44, 48, 52) inches
Length: 21 (21½, 22, 22½) inches
Sleeve length from center back: 27¾ (30, 31, 31⅜) inches

Materials

- Moda Dea Sassy Stripes 100 percent acrylic light (DK) weight self-striping yarn (147 yds/50g per skein): 6 (7, 8, 9) skeins polo #6948 (A), 4 (4, 5, 5) skeins swish #6952 (B), 4 (4, 5, 5) skeins crush #6946 (C)
- Size 10 (6mm) straight and 16-inch circular needles or sizes needed to obtain gauge
- Size 10½ (6.5mm) 16-inch circular needle
- Size 11 (8mm) 16-inch circular needle
- Stitch markers
- Stitch holders
- 36 inches of scrap yarn in a contrasting color
- Size G/6 (4mm) crochet hook

- 18 (20, 20, 20)-inch lightweight separating zipper: navy blue
- Sewing needle with contrasting and matching sewing thread
- Row counter (optional)

Gauge

16 sts and 22 rows = 4 inches/10 cm in St st with size 10 needles and 2 strands of yarn held tog
To save time, take time to check gauge.
Note: *It is important for both st and row gauge to be accurate in this design.*

Special Abbreviation

M1 (make 1): Insert left needle from back of work under strand between last st worked and next st on left needle; knit into front of lp to form a new st.

Stripe Sequence

8 (20, 26, 28) rows with A
*7 rows with B
15 rows with C
7 rows with B
21 rows with A
   Rep stripe sequence from * until center back or center front is reached.

Pattern Notes

Jacket back is knit from cuff to cuff, and fronts from cuff to center front.

In order to make stripe pat symmetrical and matched on fronts and back, sequence is reversed when center back is reached.

When pat refers to left and right edges of work, it refers to left and right edges as seen from RS of work (knit side).

For best mingling of stripes, knit with 2 strands held tog with 1 strand coming from outside of skein and 1 strand from inside of skein.

Back

Beg at left cuff, with 2 strands of B and size 10 needles, cast on 19 (23, 23, 23) sts.
Row 1 (RS): K1, *p1, k1; rep from * across.
Row 2: P1, *k1, p1; rep from * across.   Rep Rows 1 and 2 until ribbing measures approx 1 inch from beg, ending with a WS row and inc 1 (0, 1, 1) st on last row. Cut B. (20, 23, 24, 24 sts)

Left sleeve back

With 2 strands of A and size 10 needles, beg stripe sequence and work 5 rows in St st. Inc 1 st on left edge of work as seen from RS (see Pattern Notes) on this row and [every 5th row] 15 (4, 9, 28) more times and then [every 6th row] 8 (19, 16, 0) times, and at the same time, when piece measures 11 (12, 12, 12½) inches, beg incs for underarm. On right edge of work, inc 1 st [every 5th (6th, 6th, 6th) row] 7 (6, 6, 5) times, then 1 st [every other row] 3 (2, 3, 3) times.

When piece measures 18⅛ (18⅝, 19, 18¼) inches, left sleeve back is complete.

Note: *Top of sleeve incs will not be completed at this point.*

Left shoulder
At end of next WS row, cast on 27 (28, 26, 26) sts on right edge of work. (74, 75, 76, 76 sts)

Work even on right edge, continuing rem inc for shoulder shaping on left edge until piece measures 25⅜ (26⅝, 27½, 27½) inches. (81, 83, 85, 87 sts)

Shape back neck
Rows 1, 3, 5 and 9: Dec 1 st at left edge of work.
Rows 2, 4 and 6–8: Work even.
Work next 7 (9, 11, 12) rows even. (77, 79, 81, 83 sts)
Center back reached; beg reverse stripe sequence.
Work next 8 (10, 11, 13) rows even, then beg inc for back neck edge.
Rows 1, 5, 7 and 9: Inc 1 st at left edge of work.
Rows 2–4, 6, 8 and 10: Work even. (81, 83, 85, 87 sts)

Right shoulder
Dec 1 st on left edge on next row, [every 6th (6th, 6th, 5th) row] 8 (19, 16, 29) times, then [every 5th row] 16 (5, 10, 0) times, and at the same time, when back measures 19⅝ (22⅛, 24⅛, 26⅛) inches, bind off 27 (28, 26, 26) sts on right edge and beg right sleeve back shaping.

Right sleeve back
Continue with sequence of dec on left edge and beg underarm shaping on next row. Dec at right

edge of sleeve 1 st [every other row] 3 (2, 3, 3) times, then every 5th (6th, 6th, 6th) row] 7 (6, 6, 5) times.

Continue with sleeve dec on left side of work until sleeve back measures 17⅛ (17⅝, 18, 17¼) inches, ending with a WS row and beg ribbing for cuff. (20, 23, 24, 24 sts)

Cuff
Row 1 (RS): K1, *p1, k1; rep from * across until 3 (2, 3, 3) sts rem, p2tog (p1, p2tog, p2tog), k1. (19, 23, 23, 23 sts)
Row 2: P1, *k1, p1; rep from * across.
Row 3: K1, *p1, k1; rep from * across.
Rep Rows 2 and 3 until rib measures approx 1 inch. Bind off in rib.

Bottom Band
With size 10 needles and 2 strands of A held tog, RS facing, pick up and knit 79 (89, 97, 105) sts across straight lower edge of body.
Row 1 (WS): P1, *k1, p1; rep from * across.
Row 2: K1, *p1, k1; rep from * across.
Rep Rows 1 and 2 until ribbing measures approx 1 inch. Bind off in rib.

Right Front
Beg at cuff, work in stripe sequence, shaping as for left back until front measures approx 2⅜ (3⅜, 3⅜, 4) inches after cast-on for body, ending with a WS row.

Pocket opening
K4, drop yarn; with contrasting scrap yarn, k20 (20, 22, 22); slide scrap yarn sts back to left needle and knit rest of row (including the scrap yarn sts) with original yarn.
Continue established stripe sequence and shaping as for back until piece measures 25¾ (26⅝, 27½, 27½) inches. (81, 83, 85, 87 sts)

Shape neck edge
Rows 1 and 3: Bind off 3 sts at left edge.
Rows 2, 4, 6, 8, 10 and 12–14: Work even.
Row 5: Bind off 2 (2, 3, 3) sts at left edge.
Rows 7, 9, 11 and 15: Dec 1 st at left edge. (69, 71, 72, 74 sts)
Work even until piece measures 28¾ (29¾, 30⅞, 31⅛) inches. Bind off.

Pocket Lining
Remove scrap yarn from pocket opening, catching all live sts on separate holders for each side. Transfer sts nearest side seam from holder to size 10 needle, being careful not to twist sts.
With 2 strands of A, work in St st until piece measures length needed to reach to center front: approx 6⅝ (7¾, 8½, 9) inches or approx 36 (43, 47, 49) rows. Bind off.

Pocket Band
Transfer sts from holder nearest center front to size 10 needle, being careful to not twist sts. With 2 strands of A held tog, work in k1, p1 ribbing for approx 1 inch. Bind off in rib.

Front Bottom Band
With size 10 needles and 2 strands of A held tog, RS facing, pick up and knit 39 (45, 51, 55) sts along straight lower edge of front. Work as for back band.

Left Front
Beg at cuff, with 2 strands of B and size 10 needles, cast on 19 (23, 23, 23) sts.
Row 1 (RS): K1, *p1, k1; rep from * across.
Row 2: P1, *k1, p1; rep from * across.
Rep Rows 1 and 2 until ribbing measures approx 1 inch from beg, ending with a WS row and inc 1 (0, 1, 1) st on last row. Cut B. (20, 23, 24, 24 sts)

Left sleeve back

With 2 strands of A and size 10 needles, beg stripe sequence and work 5 rows in St st. Inc 1 st on right edge of work as seen from RS (see Pattern Notes) on this row and [every 5th row] 15 (4, 9, 28) more times and then [every 6th row] 8 (19, 16, 0) times, and at the same time, when piece measures 11 (12, 12, 12½) inches, beg inc for underarm. On left edge of work, inc 1 st [every 5th (6th, 6th, 6th) row] 7 (6, 6, 5) times, then 1 st [every other row] 3 (2, 3, 3) times. (47, 47, 50, 50 sts)

When piece measures 18⅛ (18⅝, 19, 18¼) inches, sleeve back is complete.

Left shoulder

At end of next RS row, cast on 27 (28, 26, 26) sts on left edge of work. (74, 75, 76, 76 sts)

Continue established shaping and work until front measures approx 2⅜ (3⅜, 3⅜, 4) inches after cast-on for body, ending with a RS row.

Pocket opening

P4, drop yarn; with contrasting scrap yarn, p20 (20, 22, 22); slide scrap yarn sts back to left needle and complete of row with original yarn.

Continue established stripe sequence and shaping as for back until piece measures 25¾ (26⅝, 27½, 27½) inches. (81, 83, 85, 87 sts)

Shape neck edge

Rows 1 and 3: Bind off 3 sts at right edge.

Rows 2, 4, 6, 8, 10 and 12–14: Work even.

Row 5: Bind off 2 (2, 3, 3) sts at right edge.

Rows 7, 9, 11 and 15: Dec 1 st at right edge. (69, 71, 72, 74 sts)

Work even until piece measures 28¾ (29¾, 30⅞, 31⅛) inches.

Bind off.

Work pocket lining and band as for right front.

Zipper Placket

With 2 strands of A and crochet hook, RS facing, beg at bottom edge of right front, sl st along edge as follows; work approx 7 sl sts along bottom ribbing and 1 sl st between each column of knit sts along rest of center front. Fasten off yarn. From RS, with 2 strands of A, dc in each sl st. Center front should measure approx 18¼ (18¾, 19, 19½) inches. Beg at neck edge, rep for left center front.

Collar

Sew sleeve and side seams.

With size 10 circular needle and 2 strands of A, RS facing, pick up and knit 19 (19, 21, 21) sts along front neck edge, place marker, 13 (14, 15, 16) sts from right shoulder seam to center back, place marker, 14 (15, 16, 17) sts from center back to left shoulder seam, place marker, and 19 (19, 21, 21) sts along front neck edge. (65, 67, 73, 75 sts)

Rows 1 and 3: K2, *p1, k1; rep from * to last st, k1.

Rows 2 and 4: P2, *k1, p1; rep from * to last st, p1.

Change to size 10½ circular needle.

Row 5: *Work in established pat to next marker, M1, k1, M1; rep from * across, complete row in established pat. (71, 73, 79, 81 sts)

Row 6: P2, *k1, p1; rep from * across, removing markers, end p1.

Rows 7–10: Work in established pat.

Change to size 11 circular needle.

Rows 11–17: Continue in established pat.

Bind off loosely in rib.

Finishing

Sew pocket band and pocket linings in place on fronts.

Using sewing needle and contrasting thread, baste zipper in place with center fronts touching center of zipper tape and bottom of zipper aligned with bottom of center fronts, folding any excess zipper tape to inside at top. With matching thread, sew zipper in place. From inside, secure zipper tape along edges with whipstitch. Remove basting threads.

Gently steam collar to expand ribs at free edge to desired shape. ◆

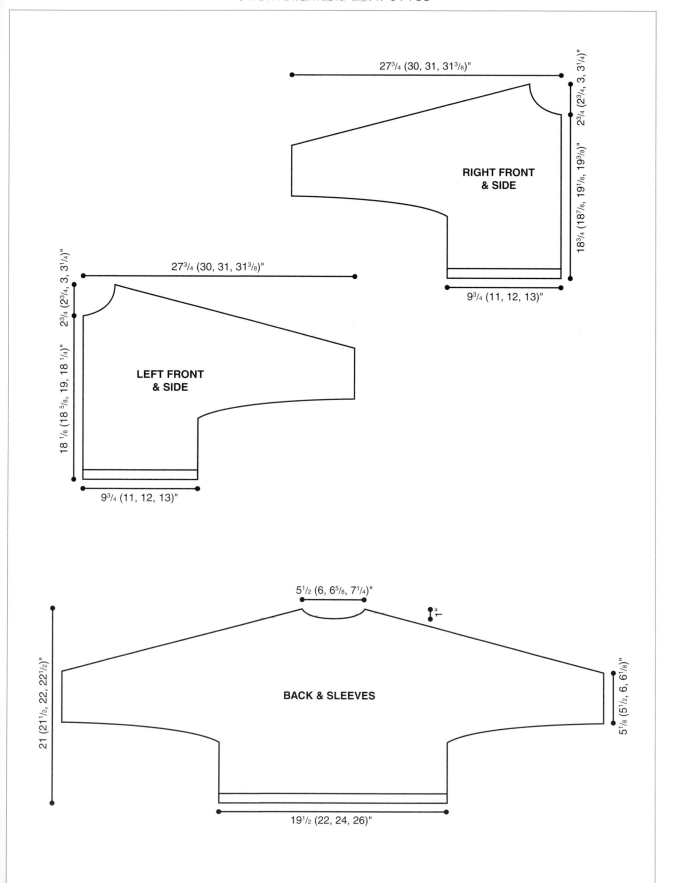

27³/₄ (30, 31, 31³/₈)"

2³/₄ (2³/₄, 3, 3¹/₄)"

RIGHT FRONT & SIDE

18³/₄ (18⁷/₈, 19¹/₈, 19³/₈)"

9³/₄ (11, 12, 13)"

27³/₄ (30, 31, 31³/₈)"

2³/₄ (2³/₄, 3, 3¹/₄)"

LEFT FRONT & SIDE

18¹/₈ (18⁵/₈, 19, 18¹/₄)"

9³/₄ (11, 12, 13)"

5¹/₂ (6, 6⁵/₈, 7¹/₄)"

1"

BACK & SLEEVES

21 (21¹/₂, 22, 22¹/₂)"

5¹/₈ (5¹/₂, 6, 6¹/₈)"

19¹/₂ (22, 24, 26)"

CONFIDENT ZIP JACKET

Alternating two rows of each yarn combined with using the seed stitch, results in a sweater with the confidence to go from office to evening events.

DESIGN BY DIANE ZANGL

Size

Woman's extra-small (small, medium, large) Instructions are given for smallest size, with larger sizes in parentheses. When only 1 number is given, it applies to all sizes.

Finished Measurements

Chest: 35 (39, 44, 48) inches
Side to underarm: 11 (11, 12, 12) inches
Sleeve length: 17½ (18, 18, 18½) inches

Materials

- Berroco Pleasure 66 percent angora/29 percent Merino wool/5 percent nylon worsted weight yarn (130 yds/50g per ball): 5 (6, 7, 8) balls Tokyo midnight #8663 (MC)
- Berroco Quest Colors 100 percent nylon worsted weight yarn (82 yds/50g per ball): 4 (5, 6, 7) balls Poiret #9934 (CC)
- Size 6 (4mm) needles
- Size 7 (4.5mm) 24-inch circular needle or size needed to obtain gauge
- Stitch holders
- 16 (16, 18, 18)-inch separating zipper

- 1¼-inch zipper pull Baronet #00520 from JHB International
- Matching sewing thread
- Size G/6/4mm crochet hook (optional)

Gauge

17 sts and 28 rows = 4 inches/10cm in Seed st with larger needles
To save time, take time to check gauge.

Special Abbreviation

M1 (make 1): Inc by making a backward lp over right needle.

Pattern Stitch

Seed St (odd number of sts)
All rows: K1, *p1, k1; rep from * across.
Work 2 rows of MC, then 2 rows CC for pat.

Pattern Notes

Keep track of rows. Whenever you see this symbol (#), stop and record the number of rows completed.

Carry yarn not in use up side of work.

For a proper fit, make sure row gauge is correct.

Right Half

Back

With MC, using larger needles and your favorite provisional method, cast on 61 (63, 65, 69) sts.

Work even in Seed pat for 24 (26,

28, 28) rows. Place sts on holder; do not cut yarns.

Front

With CC, using larger needles and your favorite provisional method, cast on 41 (41, 43, 45) sts.

Work even in Seed pat for 14 rows.

Shape neck

Next row (RS): K1, M1, work in pat across.
Next row: Work even in pat. [Rep last 2 rows] 3 (4, 5, 5) times more. (45, 46, 49, 51 sts)
Cut yarns and place sts on holder.

Join front and back

Work across back sts, cast on 15 (16, 15, 17) sts for side of neck, work across front sts. (121, 125, 129, 137 sts)

Work even in pat until body measures 8¾ (9¾, 11, 12) inches above cast-on sts of back, ending with a WS row. (#)

Beg sleeve

Bind off 30 sts at beg of next 2 rows. (61, 65, 69, 77 sts)

Work even for 2 (18, 18, 12) rows.

Beg on next row, dec 1 st at each end [every 8th (6th, 6th, 6th) row] 11 (13, 13, 15) times by ssk at beg of row and k2tog at end. (39, 39, 43, 47 sts)

Work even until sleeve measures 13½ (14, 14, 14½) inches, ending with a WS row. (#)

Beg cuff

Change to smaller needles and MC. Knit 1 row, dec 2 (2, 1, 0) sts. (37, 37, 42, 47 sts)

Row 1 (WS): P2, *k3, p2; rep from * across.

Row 2: K2, *p3, k2; rep from * across.

Rep Rows 1 and 2 until cuff measures 4 inches. (#)

Bind off.

Left Half
Back

Remove provisional cast-on sts at center back and place sts on larger needle. With RS facing, join CC and work as for right back.

Note: *Count first row of CC as Row 3.*

Front

With CC, using larger needles and provisional method, cast on 41 (41, 43, 45) sts.

Work even in Seed pat for 14 rows.

Shape neck

Next row (RS): Work in pat to last st, end M1, k1.

Next row: Work even in pat.

[Rep last 2 rows] 3 (4, 5, 5) times more. (45, 46, 49, 51 sts)

Join front and back

Work across front sts, cast on 15 (16, 15, 17) sts for side

of neck, work across back sts.

Complete body and sleeve as for right half.

Sew sleeve and side seams.

Collar

With MC and smaller needles, RS facing, pick up and knit 12 (13, 14, 14) sts along front and shaped edge of right neck, 10 (11, 11, 12) sts along cast-on side of right neck, 23 (24, 27, 30) sts along back neck, 10 (11, 11, 12) sts along cast-on sts of left neck, and 12 (13, 14, 14) sts along front and shaped edge of left neck. (67, 72, 77, 82 sts)

Work in ribbing as for cuff for 2½ inches.

Bind off in pat.

Bottom Rib

With MC and smaller needles, RS facing, pick up and knit 1 st in each color stripe across bottom edge. You must have a multiple of 5 sts + 2.

Work even in rib as for cuff until bottom rib measures 4 (4, 5, 5) inches.

Bind off in pat.

Right Front Band

Remove provisional cast-on and place resulting sts on larger circular needle.

With WS facing, join yarn at neck. Pick up and purl 1 st for every row along edge of collar, purl sts of front edge, pick up and purl 1 st for every row along bottom rib. Turn. Cast on 6 sts to LH needle.

Next row (RS): *Sl 1, k2, p2, p2tog, sl 1p wyif, turn, k2tog, k2, p3; rep from * until all picked-up sts have been worked.

Bind off rem 6 sts.

Left Front Band

Remove provisional cast-on and place resulting sts on larger circular needle.

With RS facing, pick up and knit 1 st for every row along edge of collar, knit sts of front edge, pick up and knit 1 st for every row along bottom rib. Cast on 6 sts to RH needle. Turn.

Next row (WS): *Sl 1, p2, k2, p2tog, sl 1p wyif, turn, k2tog, p2, k3; rep from * until all picked-up sts have been worked.

Bind off rem 6 sts.

Sew in zipper. If desired, attach zipper pull.

If desired, to stabilize neckline work 1 row of sl sts on inside where collar joins body. ◆

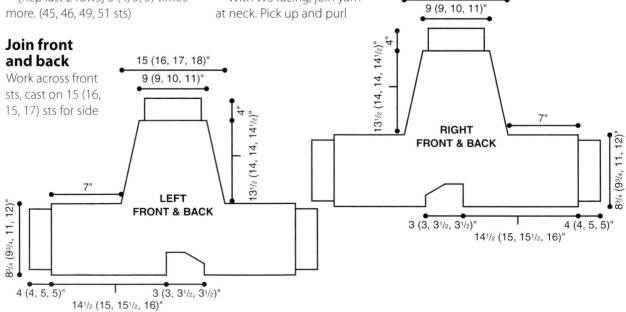

ZIP VEST

For elegant or casual wear, this zippered vest is a perfect match for cargo pants or to add pizzazz to a simple dress.

DESIGN BY DIANE ZANGL

Size

Woman's small (medium, large, extra-large) Instructions are given for smallest size, with larger sizes in parentheses. When only 1 number is given, it applies to all sizes.

Finished Measurements

Chest: 36 (40, 44, 48) inches
Armhole depth:
8½ (9, 9½, 10) inches
Side to underarm:
11 (11½, 11½, 12) inches

Materials

- Plymouth Alpaca Bouclé 90 percent alpaca/10 percent nylon bulky weight yarn (70 yds/50g per ball): 7 (8, 10, 12) balls burnt orange #17 (MC)
- Plymouth Indiecita Alpaca 100 percent Peruvian Alpaca worsted weight yarn (100 yds/50g per ball): 2 balls black #500 (CC)
- Size 4 (3.5mm) 29-inch circular needle
- Size 5 (3.75mm) 29-inch circular needle
- Size 6 (4mm) 29-inch circular needle or size needed to obtain gauge
- Stitch holders
- Stitch markers
- 16- (18-, 18-, 18-) inch separating zipper
- Matching sewing thread

Gauge

13 sts and 21 rows = 4 inches/10cm in rev St st with MC and larger needles
To save time, take time to check gauge.

Special Abbreviation

M1 (Make 1): Make a backward lp and place on RH needle.

Pattern Notes

Reverse Stockinette Stitch (Rev St st) is used for the body and collar of the vest. Front edges and collar are edged with I-cord. A casing and drawstring finish the lower edge.

As it is difficult to see the sts with this yarn, mark the purl side of the body and collar as the RS of your work. You may want to carry a waste strand of CC along the edges of body, armhole and collar. This will make it easier when picking up sts for the edgings.

Body

With CC and size 5 needles, cast on 154 (174, 190, 208) sts. Work even in St st for 1¾ inch, ending with a WS row.

Form casing

With size 4 needles, pick up each cast-on st at lower edge. Fold

casing in half, bringing needle with picked-up sts to back of work. Knit sts will be on outside.

With opposite end of size 5 needle, k2tog (1 st from each needle) across row.

Change to size 6 needles and MC.
Next row (WS): Purl, dec 38 (42, 46, 52) sts evenly. (116, 132, 144, 156 sts)

Work even in rev St st until body measures 11 (11½, 11½, 12) inches, ending with a WS row.

Divide for fronts and back

P 24 (26, 29, 30) sts and place on holder, bind off next 10 (14, 14, 18) sts for right underarm, p 48 (52, 58,

60) sts for back, bind off next 10 (14, 14, 14, 18) sts for left underarm, purl to end of row and sl front sts to holder. Mark last row of fronts and back. Keep track of rows from this point, as it is almost impossible to count them in your work.

Back

With WS facing, join yarn at left underarm. Working on back sts only, [dec 1 st at each end every other row] 3 (3, 4, 4) times. (42, 46, 50, 52 sts)

Work even in rev St st until armhole measures 8½ (9, 9½, 10) inches, ending with a WS row.

Shape shoulders

Short rows: Purl to last 3 (4, 4, 4) sts, turn, sl 1, knit to last 3 (4, 4, 4) sts, turn.

Sl 1, purl to last 6 (8, 8, 8) sts, turn, sl 1, knit to last 6 (8, 8, 8) sts turn.

Sl 1, purl to last 10 (11, 12, 13) sts, turn, sl 1, knit to last 10 (11, 12, 13) sts turn.

Place 10 (11, 12, 13) sts at each side on separate holders for shoulders.

Place rem 22 (24, 26, 26) sts on another holder for back neck.

Fronts

Sl sts of fronts to larger needle. With WS facing, join a separate ball of yarn to each front. Working on both fronts with separate balls of yarn, [dec 1 st at each arm edge every other row] 3 (3, 4, 4) times. (21, 23, 25, 26 sts)

Work even until armholes measure 6 (6½, 6½, 6½) inches, ending with a WS row.

Shape neckline

Next row (RS): Place 8 (9, 10, 10) sts at each neck edge on holders.

[Dec 1 st at each side of neck every row] 3 times. (10, 11, 12, 13 sts)

Work even until armhole measures same as for back.

Shape shoulders as for back, using short rows.

Join shoulders, using 3-needle bind-off method.

Collar

With RS facing using MC and size 6 needles, knit across 8 (9, 10, 10) sts of right front neck, pick up and knit 12 (12, 16, 18) sts along right neck edge, place marker, k 22 (24, 26, 26) sts of back neck, place marker, pick up and knit 12 (12, 16, 18) sts along left neck edge, k 8 (9, 10, 10) sts of left front neck. (62, 66, 78, 82 sts)

Shape back of collar

Purl to right shoulder marker, turn, sl 1, knit to left shoulder marker, turn.

Sl 1, purl to 3 sts beyond marker, turn, sl 1, knit to 3 sts beyond marker, turn.

Sl 1, purl to 6 sts beyond marker, turn, sl 1, knit to 6 sts beyond marker, turn.

Sl 1, purl to end of row. Remove markers.

Work even in rev St st until collar measures 2 inches at front edge.

[Dec 1 st each end every other row] 3 times. (56, 60, 72, 76 sts)

Place sts on holder.

Finishing
Front I-cord edging

With RS facing, beg at lower right front corner above casing using CC and size 5 needles, pick up and knit 1 st in each row along front edge, place marker and record number of sts, pick up and purl 1 st in each row along short edge of collar, place marker and record sts, [p3, M1] along long edge of collar, pick up and purl along short edge of collar same number of sts as on opposite edge, pick up and knit along left front edge same number of sts as for right front. Cut yarn.

Return to right front corner and cast on 4 sts to LH needle. *K3, ssk, sl sts back to LH needle. Rep from * until all picked-up sts have been worked.

Armhole edging

Beg at center of underarm with CC and size 5 needles, pick up and knit 1 st in each bound-off st of underarm and 1 st in each row of armhole. Do not cut yarn.

Cast on 4 sts to RH needle, sl these sts to LH needle.

Rep from * as for front edging until all picked-up sts have been worked. Cut yarn and sew last row of sts to cast-on sts.

Drawstring

Cast on 4 sts. *K4, replace sts to LH needle. Rep from * until cord measures approx 48 (52, 56, 60) inches long. Bind off.

Thread drawstring through casing. Tie an overhand knot in each end.

Sew in zipper. ◆

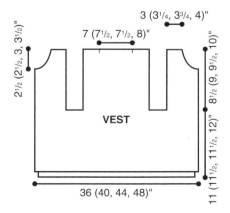

3 (3¼, 3¾, 4)"

7 (7½, 7½, 8)"

2½ (2½, 3, 3½)"

8½ (9, 9½, 10)"

11 (11½, 11½, 12)"

VEST

11 (11½, 11½, 12)"

36 (40, 44, 48)"

MY DOG & ME

For your morning walk, dress your dog in style with a sweater to match your pullover.

DESIGNS BY BONNIE FRANZ

Size

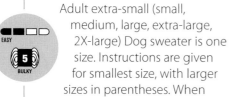

Adult extra-small (small, medium, large, extra-large, 2X-large) Dog sweater is one size. Instructions are given for smallest size, with larger sizes in parentheses. When only 1 number is given, it applies to all sizes.

Finished Measurements
Pullover
Chest: 32 (36½, 40, 43½, 48, 51½) inches
Length: 23 (24, 25, 26½, 27½, 28½) inches
Sleeve length: 16½ (17½, 17½, 18, 18½, 19½) inches
Dog Sweater
Around stomach: 17½ inches
Length: 14 inches

Materials
- Brown Sheep Lamb's Pride Superwash
  Bulky 100 percent wool bulky weight yarn (110 yds/100g per skein): 7 (7, 8, 9, 10, 11) amethyst #SW62 (MC), 2 (2, 3, 3, 4, 4) skeins blaze #SW145 (CC)
- Size 9 (5.5mm) 16-inch circular and double-pointed needles
- Size 10½ (6.5mm) 16-, 24- and 36-inch circular and double-pointed needles or size needed to obtain gauge
- Stitch markers
- Stitch holders
- 1 toggle button

Blocked Gauge
14 sts and 21 rows = 4 inches/10cm in St st with larger needles
To save time, take time to check gauge.

Stripe Sequence
Work in St st for 6 rnds/rows MC, 1 rnd each CC, MC, CC.
Rep these 9 rnds for pat.

Pattern Notes

Pullover is worked in the round on circular needles to the underarm.

Upper portion is worked back and forth in rows.

Sleeves are worked on double-pointed and circular needles in the round.

Dog sweater may be made larger by adding 4 sts for every added 1 inch of body girth. Add extra length after body band.

PULLOVER

Body

With MC and smaller needles, cast on 50 (58, 62, 68, 76, 80) sts, place marker, cast on 50 (58, 62, 68, 76, 80) sts.

Join without twisting, place marker between first and last st.

Work in k1, p1 ribbing for 2 inches, inc 12 (12, 16, 16, 16, 20) sts evenly on last rnd. (112, 128, 140, 152, 168, 180 sts)

Change to larger needles.

Work even in Stripe Sequence until body measures 14 (14½, 15, 15½, 16, 16) inches.

Divide for front and back

K 56 (64, 70, 76, 84, 90) sts and place on holder for front, knit to end of row.

Back

Work in rows from this point in established color sequence until armhole measures 9 (9½, 10, 11, 11½, 12½) inches.

Bind off all sts.

Front

Sl sts from holder to needle.

Work as for back until armhole measures 6 (6½, 7, 8, 8, 9) inches, ending with a WS row.

Shape neck

Next row: K 22 (25, 28, 30, 34, 37) sts, place center 12 (14, 14, 16, 16, 16) sts on holder, join 2nd ball of yarn and k 22 (25, 28, 30, 34, 37) sts.

Working on both sides of neck with separate balls of yarn, dec 1 st at each neck edge [every other row] 4 (4, 5, 5, 5, 6) times. (18, 21, 23, 25, 29, 31 sts)

Work even until armhole measures same as for back.

Bind off all sts.

Sleeves

Using MC and dpn, cast on 24 (26, 30, 32, 32, 36) sts.

Join without twisting, place marker between first and last st.

Work even in k1, p1 ribbing for 2 inches, inc 2 (2, 2, 2, 4, 4) sts evenly on last rnd. (26, 28, 32, 34, 36, 40 sts)

Change to larger needles.

Working in Stripe Sequence, inc 1 st each side of marker [every 3rd rnd] 12 (12, 8, 18, 16, 16) times, then [every 4th round] 5 (6, 9, 2, 4, 5) times. (60, 64, 66, 74, 76, 82 sts)

Change to longer needles as necessary.

Work even until sleeve measures 16½ (17½, 17½, 18, 18½, 19½) inches. Bind off all sts.

Sew shoulder seams.

Neck Band

With MC and smaller circular needle, pick up and knit 58 (62, 64, 68, 72, 74) sts around neck edge including sts on holder.

Join, place marker between first and last st.

Work in k1, p1 ribbing for 6 rnds. Bind off loosely in pat.

Assembly

Sew sleeves into armholes.

DOG SWEATER

Body

Beg at tail, with MC and smaller needles, cast on 46 sts.

Work even in k1, p1 ribbing for 6 rows.

Change to larger needles.

Work even in Stripe Sequence until body measures 6 inches, ending with a RS row.

Cast on 15 sts at end of last row. (61 sts)

Beg stomach band

Join, pm between first and last st. Work in rnds until band measures 3 inches, ending 15 sts before marker on last rnd.

Next row: Bind off 15 sts, remove marker work to end of row.

Work even in rows from this point until sweater measures 13 inches.

Change to smaller needles.

With MC only, work even in k1, p1 ribbing for 6 rows.

Beg neck strap

Next row: Bind off 40 sts, work to end of row.

Work even in garter st on rem 6 sts until strap measures 6½ inches or desired length.

Buttonhole row: K2, k2tog, yo, k2.

Work even in garter st for ½ inch more.

Bind off all sts.

Sew on button opposite strap. ◆

MOSS STITCH DIAMONDS

This wonderful unisex sweater will be a favorite among teens and adults alike.

DESIGN BY KATHARINE HUNT

Size

To fit adult medium (large, extra-large, 2X-large, 3X-large) Instructions are given for smallest size, with larger sizes in parentheses. When only 1 number is given, it applies to all sizes.

Finished Measurements

Chest: 40 (44½, 49, 53, 57½) inches

Materials

- Patons Canadiana Colours 100 percent acrylic worsted weight yarn from Spinrite Yarns (205 yds/85g per ball): 9 (10, 10, 11, 11) balls mood indigo #7369 (A)
- Patons Canadiana 100 percent acrylic worsted weight yarn from Spinrite Yarns (241 yds/100g per ball): 1 ball navy #34 (B)
- Size 5 (3.75mm) needles
- Size 7 (4.5mm) needles or size needed to obtain gauge
- Tapestry needle

Gauge

20 sts and 32 rows = 4 inches/10cm in pat with larger needles
To save time, take time to check gauge.

Pattern Note

Pat st requires a little extra attention, especially when worked in a dark color. To help keep your place in pat, the designer suggests using yarn markers of a contrasting color between reps.

Back

With smaller needles and B, cast on 98 (110, 122, 130, 142) sts.
Row 1 (RS): P2, *k2, p2, rep from * across.
Row 2 (WS): K2, *p2, k2, rep from * across.
Continue in established rib pat, working Rows 3 and 4 with A, Rows 5 and 6 with B. Continue in rib with A until 16 (16, 18, 20, 20) rows from beg, ending on a WS row, inc 2 (1, 0, 3, 2) sts evenly across last row. (100, 111, 122, 133, 144 sts)
Following Chart A, work in Moss St Diamond pat, beg and ending as indicated for chosen size.
Continue in pat until piece measures 5¾ (16, 16, 16, 16½) inches from beg, ending with RS facing for next row.

Shape armhole

Bind off 10 sts at beg of next 2 rows. (80, 91, 102, 113, 124 sts)
Maintaining established pat, and working 1 armhole edge st on each side in garter st, work even until armhole measures 9¼ (9½, 10, 10½, 11) inches, ending with RS facing for next row.

Shape shoulders

At beg of row, dec [8 (10, 10, 12, 12) sts] twice, [7 (9, 8, 9, 12) sts] twice, then [7 (8, 8, 9, 10) sts] twice.
Sizes M(L): Bind off rem 36 (37) sts.
Sizes XL(2XL, 3XL): Bind off 6 (7, 8) sts at beg of next 2 rows, then bind off rem 38 (39, 40) sts.

Front

Work as for back until armhole measures 6¾ (6¾, 7¼, 7½, 8) inches, ending with RS facing for next row.

Shape neck

Work in established pat across 1 (36, 41, 46, 51) sts to neck edge, turn. Leave rem sts on holder or spare needle.
Maintaining established pat, dec 1 st at neck edge [every row] 6 times, then [every other row] 3 times. (22, 27, 32, 37, 42 sts rem)
Work 7 (9, 9, 11, 11) rows even, ending with RS facing for next row.
Shape left shoulder as for back.
With RS facing, join yarn to rem sts, and bind off 18 (19, 20, 21, 22) sts for front neck, work in pat to end of row. Maintaining est pat, dec 1 st at neck edge [every row] 6 times, then [every other row] 3 times. (22, 27, 32, 37, 42 sts)
Work 8 (10, 10, 12, 12) rows even, ending with WS facing for next row.
Shape right shoulder as for back.

Sleeves
Make 2

With smaller needles and B, cast on 42 (46, 50, 50, 54) sts and work in rib pat and color sequence as for back, ending with a WS row, and inc 11 (7, 5, 7, 3) sts evenly across last row. (53, 53, 55, 57, 57 sts)

Change to larger needles and work following Chart B, beg and ending as indicated for chosen size.

Working new sts into pat, beg on 5th row, inc 1 st at each end of needle [every 4th row] 17 (18, 19, 20, 22) times (87, 89, 93, 97, 101 sts), then [every 6th row] 4 (4, 5, 5, 6) times. (95, 97, 103, 107, 113 sts)

Continue to work even until sleeve measures 19 (20, 20½, 21½, 22) inches from beg, with RS facing for next row. Bind off all sts.

Finishing

Pin pieces to measurements, cover with a damp cloth and allow to dry.

Neck band

Sew right shoulder seam. With A and smaller needles, RS facing, pick up and knit 21 (23, 23, 25, 25) sts along left front neck edge, 18 (19, 19, 19, 22) sts across front, 21 (23, 23, 25, 25) sts along right front neck edge, and 34 (37, 37, 37, 38) sts across back neck. (94, 102, 102, 106, 110 sts)

Row 1 (WS): Knit.

Row 2: P2, *k2, p2, rep from * across.

Row 3: K2, *p2, k2, rep from * across.

Work 1 (1, 3, 3, 3) more rows in A. Work 2 rows in B, 2 in A and 2 in B. Bind off in rib with B on WS.

Sew left shoulder and neck band seam. Sew sleeves into armholes. Sew side and sleeve seams. Do not press. ◆

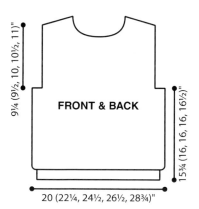

9¼ (9½, 10, 10½, 11)"

FRONT & BACK

15¾ (16, 16, 16, 16½)"

20 (22¼, 24½, 26½, 28¾)"

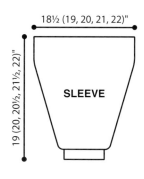

18½ (19, 20, 21, 22)"

19 (20, 20½, 21½, 22)"

SLEEVE

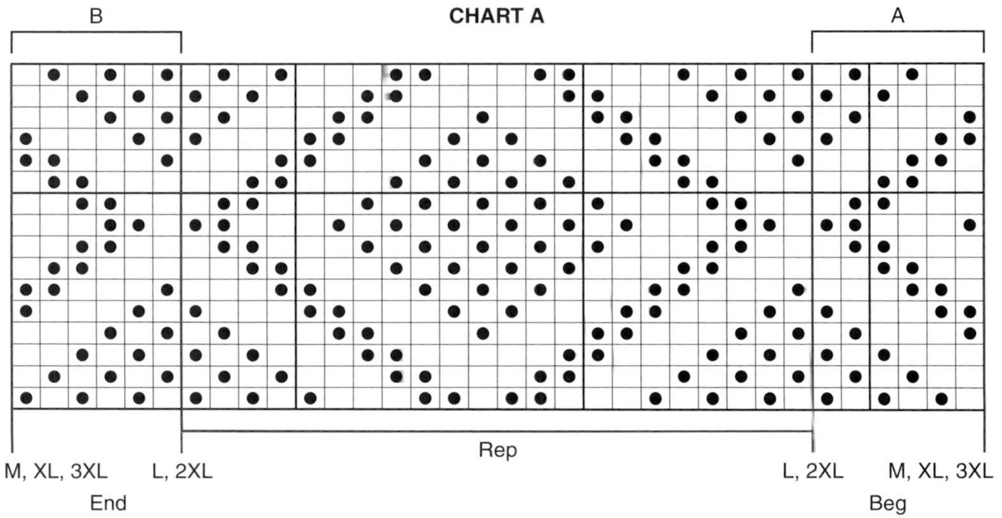

STITCH KEY

□ K on RS, p on WS
● P on RS, k on WS

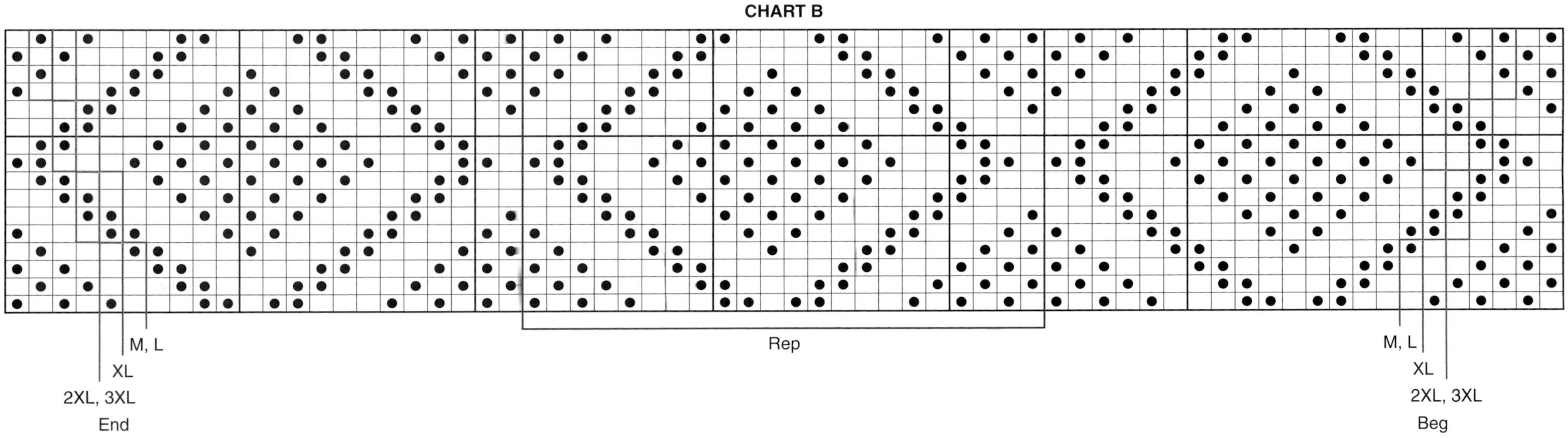

CHART A

A

B

Rep

Beg · M, XL, 3XL
L, 2XL

L, 2XL
End · M, XL, 3XL

CHART B

Rep

Beg
2XL, 3XL
XL
M, L

M, L
XL
2XL, 3XL
End

RELAXED V-NECK

Great rugged looks are sure to please the contemporary male.

DESIGN BY SCARLET TAYLOR

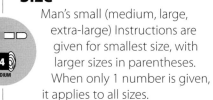

Size

Man's small (medium, large, extra-large) Instructions are given for smallest size, with larger sizes in parentheses. When only 1 number is given, it applies to all sizes.

Finished Measurements

Chest: 42½ (45, 48½, 51½) inches
Length: 25 (25, 26, 26) inches

Materials

- Brown Sheep Lamb's Pride 85 percent wool/15 percent mohair worsted weight yarn (190 yds/4 oz per skein): 9 (9, 10, 11) skeins prairie fire #M-181
- Size 8 (5mm) needles, or size needed to obtain gauge

Gauge

21 sts and 28 rows = 4 inches/10cm in Broken Rib pat
To save time, take time to check gauge.

Special Abbreviation

M1 (Make 1): Insert LH needle under the horizontal thread which is between st just worked and the next st, and knit into the back of it.

Pattern Stitch

Broken Rib (odd number of sts)
Row 1 (RS): K1, *p1, k1; rep from * across.
Row 2: Purl.
Rep Rows 1 and 2 for pat.

Special Technique

Fully fashioned dec for front neck
On RS rows: Work across left front in pat to last 4 sts, k2tog, k2; at beg of right front, k2, ssk, complete row in pat.

Fully fashioned inc for sleeve
On RS rows: Work 2 sts, M1, work across to last 2 sts, M1, work last 2 sts.

Back

Cast on 111 (119, 127, 135) sts.
Next row (RS): Beg Broken Rib pat, and work even until back measures approx 15 (14½, 15, 14½) inches from beg, ending with a WS row.

Shape armholes

Bind off 7 (7, 7, 8) sts at beg of next 2 rows. (97, 105, 113, 119 sts)
Continue to work even in established pat until back measures approx 24 (24, 25, 25) inches from beg, ending with a WS row.

Shape shoulders

Bind off at beg of row [11 (13, 12, 13) sts] twice, then [11 (12, 13, 14) sts] 4 times. Bind off rem 31 (31, 37, 37) sts in pat for back neck.

Front

Work same as back until front measures approx 19 (19, 19½, 19½) inches from beg, ending with a WS row.

Shape V-neck

Next row (RS): Work across first 44 (48, 52, 55) sts, k2 tog, k2; join 2nd skein of yarn and bind off 1 st; k1, ssk, work across rem 44 (48, 52, 55) sts. (47, 51, 55, 58 sts each side)
Working both sides at once with separate skeins of yarn, work fully fashioned dec at each neck edge [every other row] 10 (10, 14, 14) times, then [every 4th row] 4 (4, 3, 3) times. (33, 37, 38, 41 sts each side)
Continue to work even in pat until front measures same as back to shoulders, ending with a WS row.

Shape shoulders

Bind off at each shoulder edge [11 (13, 12, 13) sts] once, then [11 (12, 13, 14) sts] twice.

Sleeves

Cast on 51 (55, 57, 61) sts.
Next row (RS): Beg Broken Rib pat and *at the same time,* work fully fashioned inc at each side [every 6th row] 17 (19, 22, 25) times, then [every 8th row] 5 (4, 2, 0) times, working added sts into pat. (95, 101, 105, 111 sts)
Continue to work even until sleeve measures approx 22¾ (23¼, 23¾, 24) inches from beg, ending with a WS row.
Bind off in pat.

Assembly

Sew shoulder seams. Set in sleeves. Sew sleeve and side seams. ◆

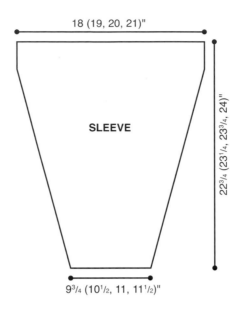

18 (19, 20, 21)"

SLEEVE

22³/₄ (23¹/₄, 23³/₄, 24)"

9³/₄ (10¹/₂, 11, 11¹/₂)"

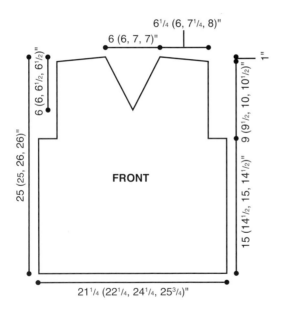

6¹/₄ (6, 7¹/₄, 8)"

6 (6, 7, 7)"

6 (6, 6¹/₂, 6¹/₂)"

1"

9 (9¹/₂, 10, 10¹/₂)"

FRONT

25 (25, 26, 26)"

15 (14¹/₂, 15, 14¹/₂)"

21¹/₄ (22¹/₄, 24¹/₄, 25³/₄)"

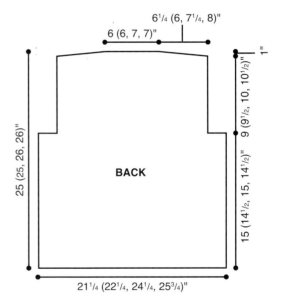

6¹/₄ (6, 7¹/₄, 8)"

6 (6, 7, 7)"

1"

9 (9¹/₂, 10, 10¹/₂)"

BACK

25 (25, 26, 26)"

15 (14¹/₂, 15, 14¹/₂)"

21¹/₄ (22¹/₄, 24¹/₄, 25³/₄)"

HEATHERED DENIM PULLOVER

This versatile worsted weight cotton sweater is suitable for all sizes and shapes.

DESIGN BY EDIE ECKMAN

Sizes

Unisex small (medium, large, extra-large) Instructions are given for smallest size, with larger sizes in parentheses. When only 1 number is given it applies to all sizes.

Finished Measurements

Chest: 42 (48, 52½, 58) inches
Length: 25 (26, 27, 28) inches

Materials

- Coats & Clark Aunt Lydia's 75 percent cotton/25 percent acrylic worsted weight yarn* (400 yds/8 oz per ball): 4 (4, 5, 5) balls denim chambray #1056
- 3 mm Rainbow Elastic thread from K¹C₂ Solutions (25 yds/card): 1 card grey #20
- Size 5 (3.5 mm) needles and 16-inch circular needle
- Size 7 (4.5 mm) needles or size needed to obtain gauge
- Tapestry needle
- Waste yarn for stitch holder

Gauge

21 sts and 32 rows = 4 inches/10 cm with larger needles in pat after washing.
To save time, take time to check gauge.

Pattern Stitch

(multiple of 14 sts)
Row 1 (RS): *K7, [p1, k1] 3 times, p1, rep from * across.
Row 2: *[K1, p1] 3 times, k1, p7, rep from * across.
Row 3: *P8, [k1, p1] 3 times, rep from * across.
Row 4: Rep Row 2.
Row 5: Rep Row 1.
Row 6: *K1, [p1, k1] 3 times, k7, rep from * across.
Rows 7–11: Rep Rows 1–5.
Row 12: *P7, [k1, p1] 3 times, k1, rep from * across.
Row 13: *[P1, k1] 3 times, p1, k7, rep from * across.
Row 14: *K7, [k1, p1] 3 times, rep from * across.
Row 15: Rep Row 13.

Row 16: Rep Row 12.

Row 17: *[P1, k1] 3 times, p8, rep from * across

Rows 18–22: Rep Rows 12–16.

Repeat Rows 1–22 for pat.

Pattern Notes

Cotton yarn in combination with this stitch pattern has a big "droop factor," so sleeves are slightly shorter than you might expect for this size—they will "grow" to fit.

To keep border in shape, elastic is applied to finished ribbing.

Back

With smaller needles, cast on 111 (125, 139, 153) sts and beg rib as follows:

Row 1 (RS): K1, *p1, rep from * across.

Row 2: P1, *k1, rep from * across.

Rep Rows 1 and 2 until piece measures 2½ inches, inc 1 in first st of last (WS) row so pat ribs will line up.

Change to larger needles and begin pat on Row 1. (112, 126, 140, 154 sts)

Work even until piece measures 15 (16, 16½, 17) inches from beg.

Shape underarms

Bind off 9 (11, 11, 14) sts at beg of next 2 rows. (94, 104, 118, 126 sts) Work even until piece measures 23 (24, 25, 26) inches from beg.

Back neck shaping

Maintaining established pat, work 38 (42, 49, 53) sts, join another ball of yarn and bind off next 18 (20, 20, 20) sts, work to end. Working both sides at once, bind off at each neck edge [5 sts] once, [3 sts] 1 (1, 2, 2) times, [2 sts] 1 (1, 1, 2) times and [1 st] 1 (2, 1, 0) times. (27, 30, 35, 38 sts rem each side)

Work even until piece measures 25 (26, 27, 28) inches from beg, place sts on holders.

Front

Work as for back until piece

measures 21½ (22½, 23, 23¾) inches from beg.

Maintaining established pat, work 41(46, 52, 56) sts, join another ball of yarn and bind off next 12 (12, 14, 14) sts, work to end.

Working both sides at once, bind off at each neck edge [3 sts] twice, [2 sts] 1 (2, 3, 3) times and [1 st] 6 times. (27, 30, 34, 38 sts)

Work even until piece measures same as back. Place sts on holders, leaving 36-inch tail on each side.

Sleeves

With smaller needles, cast on 55 (55, 69, 69) sts and rib as for back until piece measures 2½ inches, inc 1 in first st of last (WS) row.

Change to larger needles and beg pat with Row 1. Maintaining established pat, and working new sts in pat, inc 1 st each side [every 4th row] 11 (11, 0, 10) times, then [every 6th row] 14 (14, 20, 13) times. (106, 106, 110, 116 sts)

Work even in pat until sleeve measures 21 inches or desired length from beg. Bind off loosely in pat.

Finishing

Bind off front and back shoulder sts tog as follows:

Place 27 (30, 34, 38) sts from front left shoulder on one end of circular needle and back left shoulder sts on other end of circular needle. Hold needles containing shoulder sts parallel, right sides tog; with attached tail and larger needle, knit first st on front and back needles tog, *knit next st on both needles tog, bind off 1, rep from * until all sts are worked, fasten off. Rep for right shoulder.

Neck band

With circular needle, attach yarn at center back neck. Pick up and knit 100 (100, 104, 108) sts around neck. Work in rnds of k1, p1 rib for 1 inch. Bind off loosely in pat.

Set in sleeves. Sew sleeve and body underarms.

Cut a piece of elastic thread the desired measurement for ribbing, plus 5–6 inches. Thread a tapestry needle with one end of elastic. On row above cast on, run needle under one half of each knit st as it appears on WS of ribbing, and pull up gently until ribbing is slightly smaller than desired measurement. Secure both ends in seam. Rep this procedure twice, once on top row of ribbing, and once in middle. ◆

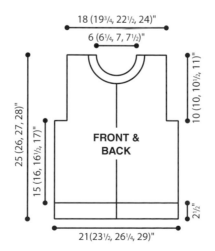

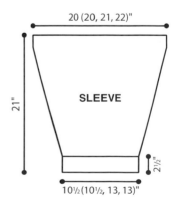

HIS WEEKEND PULLOVER

This sweater's casual styling and easy good looks will be appreciated by men of all ages.

DESIGN FROM BERNAT

Size

Men's medium (large, extra-large, 2X) Instructions are given for smallest size, with larger sizes in parentheses. When only 1 number is given, it applies to all sizes.

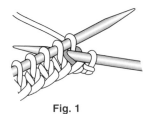

Finished Measurement

Chest: 42½ (48½, 53¾, 57) inches

Materials

- Bernat Denimstyle 70 percent acrylic/30 percent cotton worsted weight yarn (196 yds/100g per ball): 7 (8, 8, 9) balls sweatshirt #3044
- Size 7 (4.5mm) needles
- Size 8 (5mm) needles or size needed to obtain gauge
- Stitch holders

Gauge

18 sts and 25 rows=4 inches/10cm in pat with larger needles
To save time, take time to check gauge.

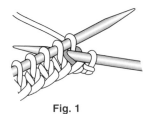

Fig. 1

Special Abbreviation

K1B (Knit 1 Below): K 1 in st 1 row below, sl both sts off needle. (Fig. 1)

Front
Rib Border

With smaller needles, cast on 97 (111, 123, 131) sts
Row 1 (RS): [K1, p1] 0 (0, 0, 2) times, k0 (0, 6, 6), [p1, k1] 0 (3, 3, 3) times, p0 (1, 1, 1), *k6, [p1, k1] 3 times, p1; rep from * 6 (7, 7, 7) times more, end k6 (0, 6, 6), [p1, k1] 0 (0, 0, 2) times.
Row 2: [P1, k1] 0 (0, 0, 2) times, k6 (0, 6, 6), *k1, [p1, k1] 3 times, k6; rep from * 6 (7, 7, 7) times more, end k0 (1, 1, 1), [p1, k1] 0 (3, 3, 3) times, k0 (0, 6, 6), [k1, p1] 0 (0, 0, 2) times.

Body

Change to larger needles and work in garter rib pat as follows:
Row 1 (RS): [K1B, p1] 0 (0, 0, 2) times, k0 (0, 6, 6), [p1, k1B] 0 (3, 3, 3) times, p0 (1, 1, 1), *k6, [p1, k1B] 3 times, p1; rep from * 6 (7, 7, 7) times more, end k6 (0, 6, 6), [p1, k1B] 0 (0, 0, 2) times.
Row 2: [P1, k1] 0 (0, 0, 2) times, k6 (0, 6, 6), *k1, [p1, k1] 3 times, k6; rep from * 6 (7, 7, 7) times more, end k0 (1, 1, 1), [p1, k1] 0 (3, 3, 3) times, k0 (0, 6, 6), [k1, p1] 0 (0, 0, 2) times.
Rep these 2 rows for garter rib pat.

Continue to work in established pat until front measures 17½ (17½, 18, 18½) inches from beg, ending with a WS row.

Shape left neck edge

Next row: Work in pat across 48 (55, 61, 65) sts; turn. Leave rem sts on a spare needle or holder.
Work 3 rows even.
Beg on next row, dec 1 st at neck edge by k2tog [every 4th row] 11 (12, 13, 14) times, then [every 6th row] 2 (1, 1, 1) times. (35, 42, 47, 50 sts)
Continue to work even in pat until front measures 24½ (25, 26, 27) inches from beg, ending with a WS row.

Shape shoulder

Maintaining pat, bind off 12 (14, 16, 17) sts at beg of next 2 RS rows. (11, 14, 15, 16 sts)
Work 1 row even in pat.
Bind off.

Shape right neck edge

With RS of work facing, sl next st from spare needle onto a safety pin. Join yarn to rem sts and work in pat to end of row.
Work 3 rows even.
Beg on next row, dec 1 st at neck edge by ssk [every 4th row] 11 (12, 13, 14) times, then [every 6th row] 2 (1, 1, 1) times. (35, 42, 47, 50 sts)

Continue to work even in pat until front measures 24½ (25, 26, 27) inches from beg, ending with a RS row.

Shape shoulder

Maintaining pat, bind off 12 (14, 16, 17) sts at beg of next 2 WS rows. Work 1 row even in pat.

Bind off rem 11 (14, 15, 16) sts.

Back

Work as for front, omitting neck shaping, until back measures 24½ (25, 26, 27) inches from beg, ending with a WS row.

Shape shoulders

Maintaining pat, bind off at beg of row [12 (14, 16, 17) sts] 4 times, then [11 (14, 15, 16) sts] twice. Place rem 27 (27, 29, 31) sts on a holder for back neck.

Sleeves

With smaller needles, cast on 46 (46, 52, 52) sts.

Row 1 (RS): K0 (0, 3, 3), *[p1, k1] 3 times, p1, k6; rep from * twice more, end [p1, k1] 3 times, p1, k0 (0, 3, 3).

Row 2: K0 (0, 3, 3), *k1, [p1, k1] 3 times, k6; rep from * twice more, end k1, [p1, k1] 3 times, k0 (0, 3, 3).

Beg garter st rib

Row 1: K0 (0, 3, 3), *[p1, k1B] 3 times, p1, k6; rep from * twice more, end [p1, k1B] 3 times, p1, k0 (0, 3, 3).

Row 2: K0 (0, 3, 3), *k1, [p1, k1] 3 times, k6; rep from * twice more, k1, [p1, k1] 3 times, k0 (0, 3, 3).

Rows 3–10: [Rep Rows 1 and 2] 4 times.

Change to larger needles and continue in established pat, at the same time, inc 1 st at each end [every 4th row] 19 (22, 18, 24) times, then [every 6th row] 3 (2, 5, 2) times. (90, 94, 98, 104 sts)

Continue to work even in pat until sleeve measures 17 (17½, 18½, 19) inches from beg. Bind off all sts.

Assembly

Block all pieces to measurements and allow to dry.

Sew right shoulder seam.

Neck band

With RS of work facing and smaller needles, pick up and k 38 (40, 42, 44) sts along left front neck edge; knit st from safety pin and mark as center st; pick up and k 38 (40, 42, 44) sts along right front neck edge; knit across 27 (27, 29, 31) back neck sts from holder, dec 2 sts evenly across. (102, 106, 112, 118 sts)

Row 1 (WS): *Knit to center 5 sts, k2tog-tbl, k1, k2tog, knit to end of row.

Bind off knitwise, dec at center as before.

Finishing

Sew left shoulder and neck band seam.

Place markers on front and back side edges 9½ (10, 10½, 11) inches down from shoulder seams. Sew in sleeves between markers. Sew side and sleeve seams. Do not press. ◆

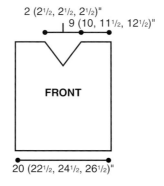

2 (2½, 2½, 2½)"
9 (10, 11½, 12½)"

FRONT

20 (22½, 24½, 26½)"

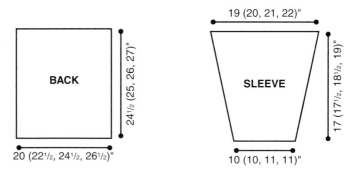

BACK

24½ (25, 26, 27)"

20 (22½, 24½, 26½)"

19 (20, 21, 22)"

SLEEVE

17 (17½, 18½, 19)"

10 (10, 11, 11)"

WEEKEND IN THE WOODS

This relaxed-fit sweater with its twiglike pattern is perfect for a walk in the woods.

DESIGN BY PAULINE SCHULTZ

Size

Man's small (medium, large, extra-large) Instructions are given for smallest size, with larger sizes in parentheses. When only 1 number is given, it applies to all sizes.

Finished Measurements

Chest: 40 (44, 48, 52) inches
Length: 25 (26, 27, 28) inches
Sleeve length: 21 inches

Materials

- Plymouth Encore Colorspun 75 percent acrylic/25 percent wool worsted weight yarn (200 yds/100g per skein): 6 (7, 7, 8) skeins earth #7301 (MC)
- Plymouth Encore D.K. 75 percent acrylic/25 percent wool DK weight yarn (150 yds/50g per ball): 5 (5, 5, 6) balls chocolate #1444 (CC)
- Size 5 (3.75mm) 16- and 32-inch circular needles
- Size 6 (4mm) 16- and 32-inch circular needles or size needed to obtain gauge
- Small amount smooth waste yarn
- Stitch markers
- Stitch holders
- Tapestry needle

Gauge

26 sts and 34 rnds = 4 inches/10cm in Crossed Ridges pat on larger needles
To save time, take time to check gauge.

Special Abbreviation

C4 (Cross 4): Drop first slipped st off needle to front of work, sl next 2 sts to RH needle, drop 2nd sl st off needle to front, pick up first

dropped st with LH needle, sl 2 sts from RH needle back to LH needle, then pick up 2nd dropped st with RH needle and replace it on LH needle. Knit these 4 sts.

Pattern Stitch

Crossed Ridges (multiple of 7 sts)

Rnd 1: With MC, *k3, p2, k2; rep from *around.

Rnd 2: Knit.

Rnds 3 and 4: Rep Rnds 1 and 2.

Rnd 5: Rep Rnd 1.

Rnd 6: With CC, *k2, sl 1, k2, sl 1, k1; rep from * around.

Rnd 7: *P2, sl 1, p2, sl 1, p1; rep from * around.

Rnd 8: Rep Rnd 6.

Rnd 9: With MC, *k2, C4, k1; rep from * around.

Rep Rnds 1–7 for pat.

Pattern Notes

To minimize the jog when changing colors, with the new color knit into the st of the row below the last st of the round.

When picking up sts around the armholes, pick up and knit the bar between the first and second pat st.

Sl all sts with yarn in back.

Steek sts are not included in st counts.

Body

With smaller needles and CC, cast on 228 (254, 280, 306) sts. Join without twisting, place marker between first and last st.

Work in k1, p1 rib for 4 rows.

[Change to MC and knit 1 row, rib 1 row. Change to CC, knit 1 row, rib 3 rows] twice. Change to larger needles.

With MC knit 1 row, inc 24 (26, 28, 30) sts evenly. (252, 280, 308, 336 sts)

Place marker after 126th (140th, 154th, 168th) st.

Work even in Crossed Ridges pat until body measures 15 (15½, 16, 16½) inches.

Begin armhole steeks

Sl marker, cast on 8 sts for steek, place marker, work to next marker, cast on 8 sts, place marker, work to end of rnd.

Keeping 8 sts between markers in chosen steek pat, work even in established pat on rem sts until armhole measures 7 (7½, 7½, 8) inches.

Shape front neck

Work across 52 (58, 64, 70) sts, bind off next 22 (24, 26, 28) sts for neck, work to end of rnd.

Neck steek and shaping

Work to bound-off neck sts, place marker, cast on 8 sts for steek, place marker, work to end of rnd.

[Dec 1 st each side of neck every rnd] 11 (13, 14, 15) times. (41, 45, 50, 55 sts on each side of neck)

Work even until armhole measures 10 (10½, 11, 11½) inches, ending at beg of neck steek.

Bind off neck steek sts, work to armhole steek and bind off 8 sts, work across 41 (45, 50, 55) sts, bind off 44 (50, 54, 58) back neck sts, work to armhole steek and bind off 8 sts, work to end of rnd.

Place shoulder sts on holders.

Sew and cut steeks.

Join shoulder seams using 3-needle bind off.

Sleeves

With smaller needles and MC, beg at underarm, pick up and knit 134 (141, 148, 155) sts around armhole, place marker between first and last st.

Change to larger needles and CC.

Beg with Rnd 6 of Crossed Ridges pat, work around ending last rep with k2.

Working in established pat, [dec 1 st each side of marker every 4th rnd] 35 times, changing to shorter needles when necessary. (64, 71, 78, 85 sts)

Work even until sleeve measures 19 inches.

Begin cuff

Change to smaller needles and CC.

Knit 1 row dec 16 (19, 20, 21) sts evenly. (48, 52, 58, 64 sts)

Work in k1, p1 rib for 3 rows.

[Change to MC, knit 1 row, rib 1 row. Change to CC, knit 1 row, rib 3 rows] twice.

Bind off in pat.

Neck Band

With smaller needles and CC, beg at right shoulder, pick up and knit 44 (50, 54, 58) sts across back neck, 20 (22, 24, 26) along left side of neck, 22 (24, 26, 28) across front neck, 20 (22, 24, 26) sts along RS of neck. Join, place marker between first and last st. (106, 118, 128, 138 sts)

Work in k1, p1 ribbing for 4 rnds on larger needles, 8 rnds on smaller needles, then 3 rnds on larger needles.

Do not bind off. Place sts on waste yarn.

Finishing

Turn armhole steeks to inside and sew in place.

Cut neck steek to 2 sts wide and overcast.

Turn neck band to inside and sew in place, enclosing neck steeks. ◆

FLIRTY IN LIME

Dainty seed stitch, bell sleeves and a lively lime color make a flirty combination in a cardigan any woman will love!

DESIGN BY SCARLET TAYLOR

Size
Woman's extra-small (small, medium, large) Instructions are given for smallest size, with larger sizes in parentheses. When only 1 number is given, it applies to all sizes.

EASY

5 BULKY

Finished Measurements
Chest: 35½ (39, 41, 45½) inches
Length: 21 (21, 22½, 23) inches

Materials
- Brown Sheep Lamb's Pride Bulky 85 percent wool/15 percent mohair bulky weight yarn (125 yds/4 oz per skein): 8 (9, 10, 11) skeins limeade #M120
- Size 8 (5mm) needles
- Size 10½ (6.5mm) needles or size needed to obtain gauge
- 1 (1-inch) button, La Mode #34575
- Tapestry needle

Gauge
14 sts and 24 rows = 4 inches/10cm in Seed st with larger needles
To save time, take time to check gauge.

Special Abbreviations
Ssp-b: Sl 2 sts knitwise 1 at a time, return these 2 sts to LH needle keeping them twisted, purl these 2 sts tog through the back lps.
M1 (Make 1): Insert LH needle under horizontal bar between st just worked and next st, knit through the back.

Pattern Stitch
Seed Stitch (even number of stitches)
Row 1 (RS): *K1, p1, rep from * across.
Row 2: *P1, k1, rep from * across.
Rep Rows 1 and 2 for pat.

Back
With smaller needles, cast on 62 (68, 72, 80) sts.
Work in garter st for 1 inch, ending with a WS row.
Change to larger needles.
Work even in Seed st until back measures 13 (13, 14, 14) inches, ending with a WS row.

Shape armholes
Next 2 rows: Bind off 4 (4, 4, 6) sts, work to end of row. (54, 60, 64, 68 sts)
Work even until armhole measures 8 (8, 8½, 9) inches, ending with a WS row.
Bind off in pat.

Left Front
With smaller needles, cast on 32 (34, 36, 40) sts.
Work even in garter st for 1 inch, ending with a WS row.
Change to larger needles.
Work even in Seed st until front measures same as for back to underarm, ending with a WS row.

Shape armhole
Next row (WS): Bind off 4 (4, 4, 6) sts, work to end of row. (28, 30, 32, 34 sts)
Work even until armhole measures 3 (3, 3½, 4) inches, ending with a RS row.

Shape neck

At neck edge, bind off 3 sts once, then 2 sts once. (23, 25, 27, 29 sts)

Dec row (RS): Work to last 3 sts, k2tog, k1.

Rep dec row [every other row] twice more, then [every 4th row] 4 times. (16, 18, 20, 22 sts)

Work even until armhole measures same as back to shoulders.

Bind off in pat.

Right Front

Work as for left front to neck shaping, working armhole shaping on a RS row and ending with a WS row.

Shape neck

At neck edge, bind off 3 sts once, then 2 sts once. (23, 25, 27, 29 sts)

Dec row (WS): Work to last 3 sts, ssp-b, p1.

Rep dec row [every other row] twice more, then [every 4th row] 4 times. (16, 18, 20, 22 sts)

Work even until armhole measures same as back.

Bind off in pat.

Sleeves

With larger needles, cast on 44 (44, 46, 46) sts.

Work in Seed st until sleeve measures 4 inches, ending with a WS row.

Shape cuff

Sizes extra-small and small only: K3, [k2tog, k2] 9 times, k2tog, k3. (34 sts)

Sizes medium and large only: [K4, k2tog, k3, k2tog] 2 times, [k3, k2tog] 4 times, k4. (38 sts)

All sizes: Work 1 row garter st. Change to Seed st.

Inc 1 st (M1) each end [every 6th row] 0 (0, 0, 7) times, [every 8th row] 11 (11, 10, 6) times, then [every 10th row] 0 (0, 1, 0) times. (56, 56, 60, 64 sts)

Work even until sleeve measures 20¼ (20½, 21, 20¾) inches ending with a WS row.

Bind off in pat.

Sew shoulder seams.

Neck Band

With smaller needles and RS facing, pick up and knit 59 sts evenly around neckline.

Work in garter st for 1 inch.

Bind off all sts loosely.

Button Band

With smaller needles and RS facing, pick up and knit 52 (52, 54, 56) sts evenly along left front edge.

Work in garter st for 1 inch.

Bind off all sts loosely.

Buttonhole Band

Work as for button band until band measures ½ inch, ending with a WS row.

Place marker for button ½ inch from top of neck band.

Buttonhole row: Work to marker, bind off 2 sts, work to end of row.

On following row, cast on 2 sts over bound-off sts of previous row. Continue in garter st until band measures 1 inch from beg.

Bind off all sts loosely.

Assembly

Sew sleeves into armhole.

Sew sleeve and side seams.

Sew on button. ◆

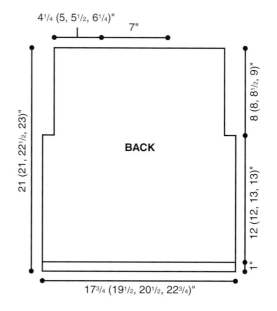

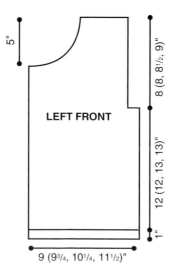

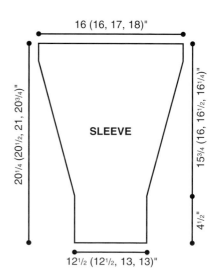

MULTICOLOR DREAM

Winter warmth meets colorful fashion yarn in this roomy coat with separate cozy neck cowl.

DESIGN BY ANN REGIS FOR NY YARNS

Size
Woman's medium/large
Body will fit almost any size. Shorten sleeves if desired for small/medium size.

Finished Measurements
Chest: Approx 63 inches
Length: 31½ inches

Materials
- N.Y. Yarns Action 70 percent acrylic, 30 percent wool super bulky weight yarn (49 yds/50g per ball): 4 balls neutrals (A) #1, 2 balls girly #2 (B), 5 balls pastel #3 (C), 9 balls cool #4 (D), 3 balls earthtones #6 (E), 3 balls denim #7 (F)
- Size 13 (9mm) needles or size needed to obtain gauge

- Size 17 (12mm) 24-inch circular needle
- Size K/10½/6.5mm crochet hook

Gauge
8 sts and 14 rows = 4 inches/10cm in St st with smaller needles
7 sts = 4 inches/10cm in St st with larger needles
To save time, take time to check gauge.

Special Abbreviations
Inc (Increase): Inc by knitting in front and back of st on knit side or by purling in front and back of st on purl side. Four sts total Inc every 2 out of 3 rows.
Dec (Decrease): K2tog on knit side, p2tog on purl side. Four sts total dec every 2 out of 3 rows.

Pattern Notes
Back and fronts are knit on the diagonal. Color stripe sequence varies for each piece. Sleeves are knit from cuff to upper edge.

Yarn amounts are sufficient to make both pieces.

COAT

Back
With size 13 needles and E, cast on 3 sts, p3.
Row 1 (RS): Inc 1, knit to last st, Inc 1. (5 sts)
Row 2: Inc 1, purl to last st, Inc 1. (7 sts)

Row 3: Knit across.
Row 4: Inc 1, purl to last st, Inc 1. (9 sts)
Row 5: Inc 1, knit to last st, Inc 1. (11 sts)
Row 6: Purl across all sts.
Rep Rows 1–6 with E, Inc 1 st on each side every 2 out of 3 rows, until piece measures 15 inches along each straight side.

Continue to Inc 1 st at each side as in Rows 1–6 until piece measures 31 inches along each straight side. Work 2 rows even, then dec 1 st on each side every 2 out of 3 rows until 3 sts rem. *At the same time,* work stripe pat as follows: [2 rows D, 4 rows A] 3 times, 22 rows D, 2 rows C, 2 rows D, 2 rows C, 4 rows D, 2 rows C, 8 rows D, 2 rows C, 2 rows D, [2 rows C, 2 rows D] twice, complete back with F.

When 3 sts rem, work first st, dec next 2 sts, pass first st over 2nd st. Fasten off.

Right Front
With A, cast on 3 sts, p3.
Working Rows 1–6 as for back, continue with A until front measures 13½ inches along straight edge.

Dec 1 st at front edge (right edge with RS facing) and Inc 1 st at side edge (left edge with RS facing) every 2 out of 3 rows until piece measures 31 inches along 1 long straight edge, then dec 1 st at beg and end of every 2 out of 3 rows until 3 sts rem. *At the same time,* work stripe pat as follows: 4 rows E, 4 rows A, 2 rows E, 2 rows A, 2 rows B, 2 rows E, 4 rows D, 4 rows E, 4 rows D, 2 rows B, 12 rows D, complete front with B.

Finish as for back.

Left Front

With F, cast on 3 sts, p3.

Working Rows 1–6 as for back, continue with F until piece measures 13½ inches along straight edge.

Dec 1 st at front edge (left edge with RS facing) and Inc 1 st at side edge (right edge with RS facing) every 2 out of 3 rows until piece measures 31 inches along 1 long straight edge, then dec 1 st at beg and end of every 2 out of 3 rows until 3 sts rem. *At the same time,* work stripe pat as follows: 2 rows E, 2 rows F, 4 rows E, 6 rows D, 2 rows C, 10 rows D, 6 rows C, 4 rows B, 12 C, 8 rows D, complete front with A. Finish as for back.

Right Sleeve

With D, cast on 28 sts. Work in St st for 3 inches. Change to C and

continue in St st, *at the same time,* Inc 1 st at each side [every 4th row] 6 times, [every 6th row] 4 times. Work even on 48 sts until sleeve measures 15 inches from beg. At beg of row, bind off [8 sts] twice, [6 sts] twice, [4 sts] twice. Bind off rem 12 sts.

Left Sleeve

With C, cast on 28 sts. Work in St st for 3 inches. Change to D and work as for right sleeve.

Assembly

Block pieces lightly and straighten grain if necessary. Sew shoulder seams. Set in sleeves. Sew sleeve seams. Sew side seams, leaving 7 inches open beg approx 9 inches above lower edge for pockets.

Left pocket lining

With RS facing and color of choice, pick up and knit 13 sts along side edge of left back pocket opening. Beg with a purl row, work in St st and Inc 1 st at each side [every knit row] twice. (17 sts)

Continue to Inc 1 st at end of knit rows twice more. (19 sts)

Work 14 rows even. Bind off all sts. Tack pocket into position and sew to left front.

Right pocket lining

With RS facing and color of choice, pick up and knit 13 sts along side edge of right back pocket opening. Beg with a purl row, work in St st and Inc 1 st at each side [every knit row] twice. (17 sts)

Continue to Inc 1 st at beg of knit rows twice more. (19 sts)

Work 14 rows even. Bind off all sts. Tack pocket into position and sew to right front.

Lower edge

With size K crochet hook, RS facing and color of choice, work 1 row of sl st crochet evenly across lower edge of right front, back, and left front.

If desired, work whipstitch around pocket and front edges.

COWL

With size 17 needles and D, cast on 50 sts. Place marker and join without twisting. Knit every rnd until piece measures 15 inches from beg. Bind off all sts. If desired, work whipstitch around top and bottom edges. ◆

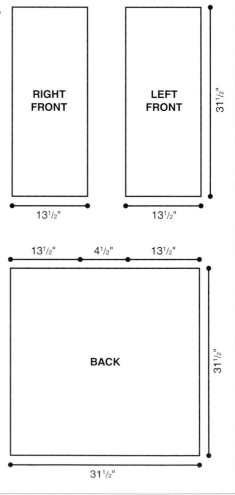

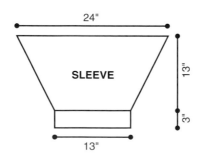

FALL COMFORT COAT

Add the perfect layer to your wardrobe with this quick-to-knit casual coat.

DESIGN BY JOHN LACHETT FOR CARON INTERNATIONAL

Size

Woman's extra-small (small, medium, large, extra-large) Instructions are given for smallest size, with larger sizes in parentheses. When only 1 number is given, it applies to all sizes.

Finished Measurements

Chest: 35 (38½, 41½, 45, 51¼) inches
Length: 30 (31, 32, 33, 34) inches

Materials

- Caron Simply Soft Quick 100 percent acrylic super bulky yarn (50 yds/86g per skein): 18 (21, 22, 23, 24) skeins autumn red QK1000-7
- Size 10½ (6.5mm) or size needed to obtain gauge
- Size J/10/6mm crochet hook
- Clasp for neck

Gauge

10 sts and 18 rows = 4 inches/10cm in Body and Border pats
10 sts and 17 rows = 4 inches/10cm in Yoke pat
To save time, take time to check gauge.

Special Abbreviation

T2R (2-st right-slanting twist): Knit 2nd st on LH needle, but do not drop st, knit first st on LH needle, sl both sts off needle.

Pattern Stitches

Border Cable (multiple of 4 sts + 2)
Row 1 (WS): Knit across.
Rows 2 and 3: Knit across.
Row 4 (RS): K2, *p2, k2; rep from * across.
Row 5: P2, *k2, p2; rep from * across.
Row 6: K2, *p2, k2; rep from * across.
Row 7: P2, *k2, p2; rep from * across.
Row 8: T2R, *p2, T2R; rep from * across.
Row 9: P2, *k2, p2; rep from * across.
Row 10: Rep Row 4.
Row 11: P2, *k2, p2; rep from * across.
Row 12: Rep Row 4.
Rows 13–15: Knit across.

Body Cable (multiple of 4 sts + 2)
Row 1 (RS): K2, *T2R, k2; rep from * across.
Rows 2, 4 and 6: Purl.
Row 3: Knit.
Row 5: T2R, *k2, T2R; rep from * across.
Row 7: Knit.
Row 8: Purl.
Rep Rows 1–8 for pat.

Yoke Cable (multiple of 5 sts + 3)
Row 1 (RS): P1, k1, p1, *T2R, p1, k1, p1; rep from * across.
Row 2: K1, p1, k1, *p2, k1, p1, k1; rep from * across.
Row 3: P1, k1, p1, *k2, p1, k1, p1; rep from * across.
Row 4: Rep Row 2.
Rep Rows 1–4 for pat.

Back

Cast on 46 (50, 54, 58, 66) sts.

Border

Work Rows 1–15 of Border Cable pat.

Body

Work Rows 1–8 of Body Cable pat until back measures approx 22 (22½, 23, 23½, 24) inches from beg, ending with a RS row.

Yoke

Beg with a WS row, knit 3 rows.
For size small only: Inc 1 st on last knit row. (51 sts)
For size medium only: Dec 1 st on last knit row. (53 sts)

For all sizes

Row 1 (RS): P0 (0, 1, 1, 0), k1, p1, T2R, *p1, k1, p1, T2R; rep from * to last 2 (2, 3, 3, 2) sts, end k1, p1, k0 (0, 1, 1, 0).
Row 2: K0 (0, 1, 1, 0), p1, k1, p2, *k1, p1, k1, p2; rep from * to last 2 (2, 3, 3, 2) sts, end k1, p1, k0 (0, 1, 1, 0).

Working in established Yoke Cable pat for rest of yoke, bind off 2 (3, 3, 4, 6) sts at beg of next 2 rows. (42, 45, 47, 50, 54 sts)

Maintaining pat, dec 1 st at each side by ssk at beg, work in pat to last 2 sts, k2tog, [every RS row] 3 (3, 4, 4, 5) times. (36, 39, 39, 42, 44 sts)
Note: For size large only, after armhole shaping is completed, to make setting in sleeves easier, discontinue cable on first and last 2 sts of row. Work these 2 sts in St st for rem of back.

Work even until armhole measures 7½ (8, 8½, 9, 9½) inches from underarm, ending with a WS row.

Shape shoulders and neck

Bind off 10 (11, 11, 12, 13) sts at beg of next 2 rows for shoulders. Bind off rem 16 (17, 17, 18, 18) sts for neck.

Left Front

Cast on 23 (25, 27, 29, 33) sts.

Border

Row 1 (WS): K3 (1, 3, 1, 1) for center front, place marker, knit across.
Rows 2 and 3: Knit across.
Row 4 (RS): [K2, p2] 5 (6, 6, 7, 8) times, end k3 (1, 3, 1, 1).

Work Rows 5–15 of established Border Cable pat, keeping 3 (1, 3, 1, 1) front edge sts in garter st.

Body

Row 1 (RS): *K2, T2R; rep from * to marker, end k3 (1, 3, 1, 1).

Work Rows 2–8 of Body Cable pat, then work Rows 1–8 of Body Cable pat until front measures approx 22 (22½, 23, 23½, 24) inches from beg, ending with a RS row and removing marker.

Yoke

Beg with a WS row, knit 3 rows.
Row 1 (RS): P0 (0, 1, 1, 0), k1, p1, T2R, [p1, k1, p1, T2R] 3 (4, 4, 4, 5) times, end p1, k1 (0, 1, 1, 1), p1 (0, 0, 1, 1), k1 (0, 0, 1, 1).

Work in established Yoke Cable Pat, binding off 2 (3, 3, 4, 6) sts at beg of next RS row. (21, 22, 24, 25, 27 sts)

Continue in pat, dec 1 st by ssk at beg of row (armhole edge) [every RS row] 3 (3, 4, 4, 5) times, and *at the same time*, beg on this row, dec 1 st at end of row (neck edge) [every 4th row] 8 (3, 5, 3, 1) times, then [every 5th row] 0 (5, 4, 6, 8) times. (10, 11, 11, 12, 13 sts rem)

Work even in pat until armhole measures 7½ (8, 8½, 9, 9½) inches from underarm, ending with a WS row.
Bind off all sts.

Right Front

Cast on 23 (25, 27, 29, 33) sts.

Border

Row 1 (WS): Knit to last 3 (1, 3, 1, 1) sts, place marker for center front, k3 (1, 3, 1, 1).
Rows 2 and 3: Knit across.
Row 4 (RS): K3 (1, 3, 1, 1), [p2, k2] 5 (6, 6, 7, 8) times.

Work Rows 5–15 of established Border Cable pat, keeping 3 (1, 3, 1, 1) front edge sts in garter st.

Body

Row 1 (RS): K3 (1, 3, 1, 1), *T2R, k2; rep from * across.

Work Rows 2–8 of Body Cable pat then work Rows 1–8 of Body Cable pat until front measures approx 22 (22½, 23, 23½, 24) inches from beg, ending with a RS row and removing marker.

Yoke

Beg with a WS row, knit 3 rows.
Row 1 (RS): K1 (0, 0, 1, 1), p1 (0, 0, 1, 1), k1 (0, 1, 1, 1), p1, [T2R, p1, k1, p1] 3 (4, 4, 4, 5) times, T2R, p1, k1, p0 (0, 1, 1, 0).

Work in established Yoke Cable pat, binding off 2 (3, 3, 4, 6) sts at beg of next WS row. (21, 22, 24, 25, 27 sts)

Continue in pat, dec 1 st by k2tog at end of row (armhole edge) [every RS row] 3 (3, 4, 4, 5) times, and at the same time, beg on this row, dec 1 st at beg of row (neck edge) [every 4th row] 8 (3, 5, 3, 1) times, then [every 5th row] 0 (5, 4, 6, 8) times. (10, 11, 11, 12, 13 sts rem)

Work even in pat until armhole measures 7½ (8, 8½, 9, 9½) inches from underarm, ending with a RS row.
Bind off all sts.

Sleeves

Cast on 30 (34, 34, 38, 38) sts.

Border

Work Rows 1–5 of Border Cable pat.

Body

Row 1 (RS): K2, *T2R, k2; rep from * across.

Work Rows 1–8 of Body Cable pat, *at the same time*, inc 1 st at each side [every 40th (0, 44th, 44th, 15th) row] 1 (0, 1, 1, 4) times. (32, 34, 36, 40, 46 sts)

Work even until sleeve measures 17 (17½, 18, 18, 18) inches from beg, ending with a WS row.

Shape cap

Maintaining pat, bind off 2 (3, 3, 4, 6) sts at beg of next 2 rows. (28, 28, 30, 32, 34 sts)

Dec 1 st at each side [every RS row] 10 times. (8, 8, 10, 12, 14 sts)
Bind off rem sts.

Assembly

Block pieces to measurements. Join shoulder seams.

Front bands and neck edging

Row 1: With RS facing, with crochet hook and beg at lower right front, sc evenly along front edge to beg of neck shaping, work 2 sc in corner st, continue along neck shaping to left front, work 2 sc in corner st, work along left front to lower edge of front, turn.
Row 2: Ch 3, sc in first sc, *ch 1, sc in next sc; rep from * around. Fasten off.

Finishing

Set in sleeves; sew side and sleeve seams. Sew clasp to fronts at beg of neck shaping. ◆

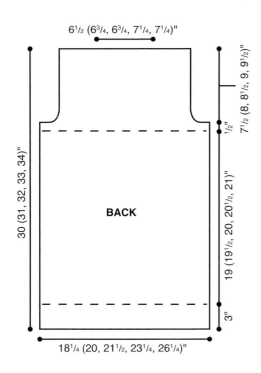

6¹/₂ (6³/₄, 6³/₄, 7¹/₄, 7¹/₄)"

7¹/₂ (8, 8¹/₂, 9, 9¹/₂)"

¹/₂"

30 (31, 32, 33, 34)"

BACK

19 (19¹/₂, 20, 20¹/₂, 21)"

3"

18¹/₄ (20, 21¹/₂, 23¹/₄, 26¹/₄)"

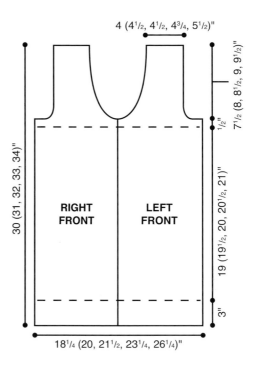

4 (4¹/₂, 4¹/₂, 4³/₄, 5¹/₂)"

7¹/₂ (8, 8¹/₂, 9, 9¹/₂)"

¹/₂"

30 (31, 32, 33, 34)"

RIGHT FRONT   **LEFT FRONT**

19 (19¹/₂, 20, 20¹/₂, 21)"

3"

18¹/₄ (20, 21¹/₂, 23¹/₄, 26¹/₄)"

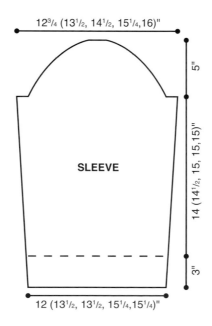

12³/₄ (13¹/₂, 14¹/₂, 15¹/₄,16)"

5"

14 (14¹/₂, 15, 15,15)"

SLEEVE

3"

12 (13¹/₂, 13¹/₂, 15¹/₄,15¹/₄)"

FINE LINES PULLOVER

This flattering hip-length tunic is cleverly detailed with vertical line detailing.

DESIGN BY LORNA MISER FOR SOUTH WEST TRADING CO.

Size

Woman's small (medium, large, extra-large) Instructions are given for smallest size, with larger sizes in parentheses. When only 1 number is given, it applies to all sizes.

Finished Measurements

Chest: 40 (44, 48, 52) inches

Materials

- South West Trading Co. Diva 72 percent acrylic/28 percent nylon bulky weight yarn (56 yds/50g per skein): 14 (16, 18, 20) skeins Arizona sunset (MC)
- South West Trading Co. Beyond Bold 100 percent cotton worsted weight yarn (146 yds/100g per skein): 1 skein purple (CC)
- Size 10 (6mm) straight and 24-inch circular needles or size needed to obtain gauge
- Stitch holders
- Size J/10/6mm crochet hook

Gauge

12 sts and 20 rows = 4 inches/10cm in St st with MC
To save time, take time to check gauge.

Pattern Stitch

Dipped Edging (multiple of 6 sts + 1)

Rows 1–4: With CC, knit.
Row 5: With MC, knit.
Row 6: With MC, purl.
Rows 7 and 8: Rep Rows 5 and 6.
Row 9: With CC, *k3, knit into st 4 rows below next st by inserting tip of needle through st from front to back, wrap yarn around needle and pull it back through front of work, drop next st off needle (it is locked in place on CC row), k2; rep from * to last st, k1.
Row 10: With CC, knit.

Back

With CC, cast on 61 (67, 73, 79) sts. Work Dipped Edging pat, then continue with MC and St st until body measures 24 (25, 26, 27) inches. Place all sts on holder for shoulders and back neck.

Front

With CC, cast on 61 (67, 73, 79) sts. Work Rows 1–10 of Dipped Edging pat. Continue with MC and St st until piece measures 21 (22, 23, 24) inches.

Divide for neck

Work across 25 (27, 30, 32) sts, join 2nd ball of yarn and work next 11 (13, 15, 15) sts, place these sts on holder for front neck, work across rem sts. Working both sides separately, dec for neck. On next RS row, knit to last 3 sts, ssk, k1; k1, k2tog, knit to end. Rep this dec row [every RS row] 3 (5, 5, 4) times more. (21, 21, 24, 27 sts rem for each shoulder)

Place all sts on holder for shoulders.

Sleeves

With CC, cast on 31 (31, 33, 33) sts. Work Dipped Edging pat, then continue with MC and St st, inc 1 st at each edge [every 6th (4th, 4th, 4th) row] 15 (15, 17, 17) times, working inc 1 st in from edge. (61, 61, 67, 67 sts)

Work even in St st until sleeve measures 20 (19, 18, 17) inches from beg.

Bind off all sts.

Assembly

Bind off front and back shoulders tog using 3-Needle Bind Off, see Knit Techniques on page 70.

Mark 10 (10, 11, 11) inches down from shoulder seams on front and back for sleeve placement.

Sew sleeve to body, centering at shoulder seam, and beg and ending at markers on body edge. Sew side and sleeve seams.

Neck Edging

With circular needle and CC, pick up and knit approx 50 (54, 58, 60) sts from around neck edge and neck holders. Purl 1 rnd, knit 1 rnd, purl 1 rnd. Bind off knitwise.

Fine Lines

Holding yarn behind work insert hook from front to back through "dipped" st at top of front hem and pull up a lp. Insert hook into knit stitch in 2nd MC row above dipped stitch and pull a lp to right side and through loop on hook forming a slip stitch. Continue working a slip stitch through every other knit row, following the line of knit stitches up the front (Photo below).

Work as many fine lines as desired. Sample sweater shows 6 lines centered on front only.

Fasten off each line at shoulder, hem and neck. ◆

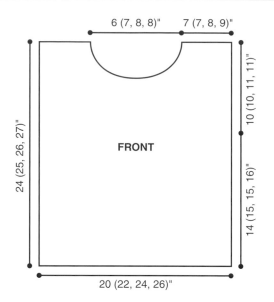

FRONT

6 (7, 8, 8)"   7 (7, 8, 9)"

10 (10, 11, 11)"

24 (25, 26, 27)"

14 (15, 15, 16)"

20 (22, 24, 26)"

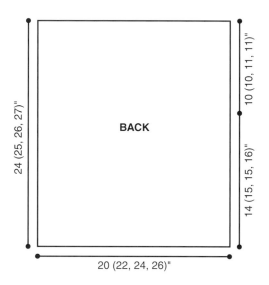

BACK

10 (10, 11, 11)"

24 (25, 26, 27)"

14 (15, 15, 16)"

20 (22, 24, 26)"

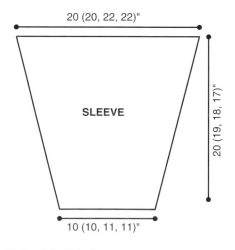

SLEEVE

20 (20, 22, 22)"

20 (19, 18, 17)"

10 (10, 11, 11)"

SNAZZY STRIPES

This comfortable turtleneck works up easily in eye-catching stripes.

DESIGN BY MELISSA LEAPMAN FOR COATS & CLARK

Size

Woman's small (medium, large, extra-large, 2x-large, 3x-large) Instructions are given for smallest size, with larger sizes in parentheses. When only 1 number is given, it applies to all sizes.

Finished Measurements

Chest: 34 (37, 40, 43, 46, 49) inches
Length: 21 (22, 22½, 23, 24, 24) inches

Materials

- Coats & Clark TLC Amoré 80 percent acrylic/20 percent nylon worsted weight yarn (290 yds/ 170g per skein): 2 (2, 2, 2, 3, 3) skeins each celery #3625 (A) and plum #3534 (B)
- Size 6 (4mm) needles
- Size 8 (5mm) needles or size needed to obtain gauge

Gauge

16 sts and 24 rows = 4 inches/10cm in St st with larger needles
To save time, take time to check gauge.

Special Abbreviation

M1 (Make 1): Insert LH needle under the horizontal thread between st just worked and the next st, and knit into the back loop.

Stripe Sequences

Body Stripe Pat
Work *10 rows A, 10 rows B; rep from * for pat.

Sleeve Stripe Pat
Work *4 rows A, 4 rows B; rep from * for pat.

Special Technique

Fully fashioned dec
On RS rows: K2, ssk, work across in established pat to last 4 sts, end k2tog, k2.
On WS rows: P2, p2tog, work across in established pat to last 4 sts, end p2tog-tbl, p2.

Fully fashioned inc
Work 1 st, M1, work across to last st, end M1, work last st.

Back

With smaller needles and A, cast on 62 (68, 74, 80, 86, 92) sts. Change to B and work k1, p1 rib until piece measures approx 1½ inches from beg.

Change to larger needles, beg St st in Body Stripe pat, work fully fashioned inc at each side [every 20th row] 3 times. (68, 74, 80, 86, 92, 98 sts)

Maintaining established Body Stripe pat throughout, continue to work even until back measures approx 12½ (13¼, 13½, 13½, 14, 14) inches from beg, ending with a WS row.

Shape armholes

Bind off 2 (3, 3, 4, 5, 5) sts at beg of next 2 rows. Work fully fashioned

dec each side [every row] 0 (1, 2, 3, 4, 10) times, then [every other row] 6 (6, 6, 7, 7, 4) times. (52, 54, 58, 58, 60, 60 sts rem)

Continue to work even until piece measures approx 20 (21, 21½, 22, 23, 23) inches from beg, ending with a WS row.

Shape shoulders

Bind off 4 (4, 5, 5, 6, 6) sts at beg of next 4 rows, then 4 (5, 5, 5, 4, 4) sts at beg of next 2 rows. Bind off rem 28 sts for back of neck.

Front

Work as for back until piece measures approx 18½ (19½, 20, 20½, 21½, 21½) inches from beg, ending with a WS row.

Shape neck

Next row (RS): Work across first 18 (19, 21, 21, 22, 22) sts; join 2nd skein of yarn and bind off center 16 sts; complete row in established stripe.

Working both sides at once with separate skeins of yarn, bind off at each neck edge [4 sts] once, then [2 sts] once. (12, 13, 15, 15, 16, 16 sts on each side)

Work even as needed, until piece measures same as back to shoulders, ending with a WS row.

Shape shoulders

Bind off at each shoulder edge [4 (4, 5, 5, 6, 6) sts] twice, then [4 (5, 5, 5, 4, 4) sts] once.

Sleeves

With smaller needles and A, cast on 36 (36, 40, 40, 44, 44) sts. Change to B and work k1, p1 rib until cuff measures approx 1½ inches from beg, ending with a WS row.

Change to larger needles, beg St st in Sleeve Stripe pat, work fully fashioned inc at each side on next row and [every 6th row] 0 (3, 0, 2, 2, 2) times, then [every 8th row] 10 (8, 10, 9, 9, 9) times. (58, 60, 62, 64, 68, 68 sts)

Continue to work even in established pat until sleeve measures approx 17½ (17½, 18, 18, 18, 18) inches from beg, ending with a WS row.

Shape cap

Bind off 2 (3, 3, 4, 5, 5) sts at beg of next 2 rows. Work fully fashioned dec each side [every other row] 4 (7, 9, 12, 13, 13) times, then [every row] 15 (12, 11, 8, 8, 8) times. (16 sts)

Bind off 2 sts at beg of next 4 rows. (8 sts)

Bind off all sts.

Assembly

Sew left shoulder seam.

Neckband

With smaller needles and B, RS facing, pick up and knit 60 sts around neckline. Work k1, p1 rib until band measures approx 4 inches from beg. Change to larger needles and continue even

in pat until neckband measures approx 8¼ inches from beg. Change to A and work 1 more row of rib.

Bind off loosely in rib.

Finishing

Sew right shoulder seam, including side of neckband. Set in sleeves. Sew sleeve and side seams. ◆

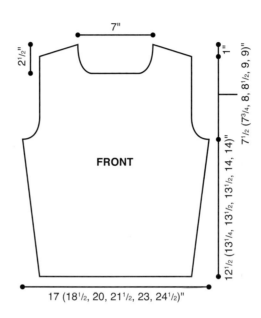

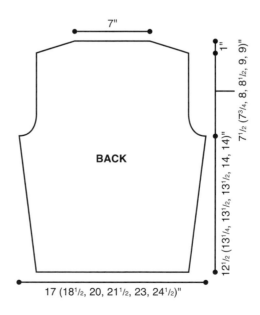

BABY CABLE SWEATER

This saucy sweater features broad bands of mock baby cables at the hemline and neckline to keep things interesting, but they won't slow you down.

DESIGN BY KATHLEEN POWER JOHNSON

Size

Woman's extra-small (small, medium, large, 1X-large, 2X-large, 3X-large) Instructions are given for smallest size, with larger sizes in parentheses. When only 1 number is given, it applies to all sizes.

Finished Measurements

Chest: 34 (36, 38½, 42½, 47, 51¼, 56½) inches

Length: 22½ (23, 23½, 24, 25, 26½, 28) inches

Materials

- Reynolds Cabana 65 percent polyester/35 percent acrylic bulky weight yarn* (135 yds/100g per ball): 8 (8, 10, 11, 12, 14, 16) balls coral #935
- Size 8 (5mm) 16-inch circular needle
- Size 10 (6mm) knitting needles or size needed to obtain gauge
- Stitch holders

Gauge

15 sts and 20 rows = 4 inches/10cm in St st with larger needles

To save time, take time to check gauge.

Special Abbreviations

C2F (Cross 2 Sts to Front): Knit next 2 sts tog, leave on left needle, knit into first st, sl both sts off needle.

M1 (Make 1): Insert left needle from front to back under horizontal loop between sts and knit into back of this loop with right needle.

Back

Ribbing

Cast on 66 (70, 74, 82, 90, 98, 106) sts.

Row 1 (WS): K2, *p2, k2; rep from * across.

Row 2: P2, *C2F, p2; rep from * across.

Rep Rows 1 and 2 until back measures 5 (5, 5, 5, 5½, 5½, 5½) inches from beg.

Body

Continue to work in St st until back measures 15¼ (15¾, 16, 16, 17, 17¾, 18) inches or desired length to underarm, ending with a WS row.

Shape armhole

Row 1 (RS): Bind off 3 (4, 4, 5, 5, 6, 6) sts, knit across.

Row 2: Bind off 3 (4, 4, 5, 5, 6, 6) sts, purl across.

Row 3 (extra-small–large): Ssk, knit across to last 2 sts, k2tog.

Row 3 (1X-large–3X-large): Bind off 2 (2, 3) sts, knit across.

Row 4: Bind off 0 (0, 0, 0, 2, 2, 3) sts, purl across.

Row 5 (all sizes): Ssk, knit across to last 2 sts, k2tog.

Row 6: Purl across.

Dec 1 st at each end [every other row] 1 (1, 1, 3, 4, 6, 8) times. (54, 56, 60, 62, 66, 68, 70 sts)

Work even in St st until back measures 22½ (23, 23½, 24, 25, 26¼, 28) inches from beg, ending with a RS row.

Next row: P12 (13, 15, 16, 18, 19, 20) and place sts on holder; p30 and place on holder, p12 (13, 15, 16, 18, 19, 20) and place on holder.

Front

Cast on and work as for back until front measures 19½ (20, 20½, 21, 22, 23½, 25) inches from beg, ending with a WS row.

Beg neck

Row 1: K26 (27, 29, 30, 32, 33, 34), C2F, k26 (27, 29, 30, 32, 33, 34).

Row 2: Purl.

Row 3: K24 (25, 27, 28, 30, 31, 32), p2, C2F, p2, k24 (25, 27, 28, 30, 31, 32).

Row 4: P24 (25, 27, 28, 30, 31, 32), k2, p2, k2, p24 (25, 27, 28, 30, 31, 32).
Row 5: K22 (23, 25, 26, 28, 29, 30), [C2F, p2] twice, C2F, k22 (23, 25, 26, 28, 29, 30).
Row 6: P24 (25, 27, 28, 30, 31, 32), k2, p2, k2, p24 (25, 27, 28, 30, 31, 32).
Row 7: K20 (21, 23, 24, 26, 27, 28), [p2, C2F] 3 times, p2, k20 (21, 23, 24, 26, 27, 28).
Row 8: P20 (21, 23, 24, 26, 27, 28), [k2, p2] 3 times, k2, p20 (21, 23, 24, 26, 27, 28).
Row 9: K18 (19, 21, 22, 24, 25, 26) [C2F, p2] 4 times, C2F, k18 (19, 21, 22, 24, 25, 26).
Row 10: P20 (21, 23, 24, 26, 27, 28), [k2, p2] 3 times, k2, p20 (21, 23, 24, 26, 27, 28).
Row 11: K16 (17, 19, 20, 22, 23, 24), [p2, C2F] 5 times, p2, k16 (17, 19, 20, 22, 23, 24).
Row 12: P16 (17, 19, 20, 22, 23, 24), [k2, p2] 5 times, k2, k16 (17, 19, 20, 22, 23, 24).
Row 13: K14 (15, 17, 18, 20, 21, 22), [C2F, p2] 6 times, C2F, k14 (15, 17, 18, 20, 21, 22).
Row 14: P16 (17, 19, 20, 22, 23, 24), [k2, p2] 5 times, k2, p16 (17, 19, 20, 22, 23, 24).
Row 15: K12 (13, 15, 16, 18, 19, 20), [p2, C2F] 7 times, p2, k12 (13, 15, 16, 18, 19, 20).

Row 16: P12 (13, 15, 16, 18, 19, 20), [k2, p2] 7 times, k2, p12 (13, 15, 16, 18, 19, 20).
Row 17: K12 (13, 15, 16, 18, 19, 20), [p2, C2F] 7 times, p2, k12 (13, 15, 16, 18, 19, 20).
Row 18: P12 (13, 15, 16, 18, 19, 20) and place sts on holder; [k2, p2] 7 times, k2 and place sts on holder for neck, p12 (13, 15, 16, 18, 19, 20) and place sts on holder.

Sleeves

Note: *Work inc sts in rev St st until there are 4 inc, enabling you to add 1 full rep.*

Cast on 38 (38, 38, 38, 42, 42, 42) sts. Work as for Rows 1 & 2 of back ribbing, at the same time, work M1 at each end [every 4th row] 0 (0, 0, 0, 0, 0, 1) times, [every 6th row] 0 (0, 3, 9, 9, 10, 13) times, [every 8th row] 1 (8, 7, 3, 3, 3, 0) times, then [every 10th row] 6 (1, 0, 0, 0, 0, 0) times. (52, 56, 58, 62, 66, 68, 70 sts)

Continue to work even until sleeve measures 14½ (15¾, 15¾, 16¾, 16¾, 16¾, 17½) inches or desired length to underarm, ending with a WS row.

Shape sleeve cap

Bind off 3 (4, 4, 5, 5, 6, 6) sts at beg of next 2 rows. Bind off 0 (0, 0, 0, 2, 2, 3) sts at beg of next 2 rows, dec by ssk at beg and k2tog at end [every other row] 9 (10, 9, 11, 11, 10, 9) times, then [every 4th row] 1 (1, 2, 1, 1, 2, 2) times. Beg with a RS row, bind off 3 sts at beg of next 4 rows. Bind off rem 14 (14, 16, 16, 16, 16, 18) sts.

Assembly

Knit each set of shoulder sts tog using a 3-needle bind off. Leave final st from each shoulder seam on needle rather than fastening off.

Neck

Sl shoulder seam sts along with 30 back neck sts and 30 front neck sts to circular needle. (62 sts)

Beg at right shoulder seam, place marker after right shoulder seam st for beg of rnd.

Rnd 1: *[C2F, p2] 7 times, C2F, p2tog; rep from * once more. (60 sts)
Rnd 2: *K2, p2; rep from * around.
Rnd 3: *C2F, p2; rep from * around.

Rep Rnds 2 and 3 until back of collar measures 2½ inches from Rnd 1, ending with Rnd 3. Bind off loosely in k2, p2 rib.

Sew in sleeves, then sew side and sleeve seams. ◆

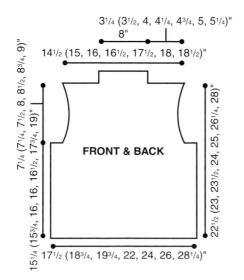

3¼ (3½, 4, 4¼, 4¾, 5, 5¼)"
8"
14½ (15, 16, 16½, 17½, 18, 18½)"
7¼ (7¼, 7½, 8, 8½, 8¾, 9)"
FRONT & BACK
22½ (23, 23½, 24, 25, 26¼, 28)"
15¼ (15¾, 16, 16, 16½, 17¾, 19)"
17½ (18¾, 19¾, 22, 24, 26, 28¼)"

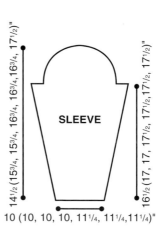

14½ (15¾, 15¾, 16¾, 16¾, 16¾, 17½)"
SLEEVE
16½ (17, 17, 17½, 17½, 17½, 17½)"
10 (10, 10, 10, 11¼, 11¼, 11¼)"

AFGHANS
SLEEK & COZY

Tantalizing textures for cuddly afghans and
a latest-fashion throw to toss across a chair
will give you lots of knitting fun!

SUMMER GARDEN COVERLET

Quick-to-knit panels combine to turn a solid color into a multi-textured coverlet.

DESIGN BY KATHLEEN POWER JOHNSON

Finished Size
Approx 48 x 60 inches

Materials
- Plymouth Wildflower DK weight 51 percent mercerized cotton/49 percent acrylic yarn (137 yds/50g per ball): 32 balls green #11
- Size 9 (5.5mm) needles or size needed to obtain gauge
- Size 10½ (6.5mm) needles
- Tapestry needle

Gauge
17 sts and 23 rows = 4 inches/10cm in pat with smaller needles and 2 strands of yarn
To save time, take time to check gauge.

Pattern Note
Afghan is worked with 2 strands of yarn held tog throughout.

Special Abbreviation
Twist 3: K3tog but do not sl off needle. Knit first st on LH needle and

sl off needle, knit 2nd st in same way, sl last st off needle without knitting it.

Pattern Stitches
Cable & Leaf Panel (33 sts)
Row 1 (RS): P2, *k7, p3, k3, p3, rep from *, end last rep p2.
Row 2 and all even rows: Purl.
Row 3: P2, *k7, p3, twist 3, p3, rep from *, end last rep p2.
Row 5: P2, *ssk, k3, k2tog, p3, [k1, yo] twice, k1, p3, rep from *, end last rep p2.
Row 7: P2, *ssk, k1, k2tog, p3, k2, yo, k1, yo, k2, p3, rep from *, end p2.
Row 9: P2, *twist 3, p3, k7, p3, rep from *, end p2.
Row 11: P2, *k3, p3, k7, p3, rep from *, end p2.
Row 13: Rep Row 9.
Row 15: P2, *[k1, yo] twice, k1, p3, ssk, k3, k2tog, p3, rep from *, end p2.
Row 17: P2, *k2, yo, k1, yo, k2, p3, ssk, k1, k2tog, p3, rep from *, end p2.
Row 19: Rep Row 3.
Row 20: Purl.
  Rep Rows 1–20 for pat.
Fencepost Lace Panel (49 sts)
Rows 1 and 3 (WS): K1, p1, *k3, p1, rep from *, end k3.
Rows 2 and 6: Knit.
Row 4: K1, k2tog, *yo, k1, yo, k3tog, rep from *, end yo, k2.
Rows 5 and 7: K3, *p1, k3, rep from *, end p1, k1.
Row 8: K2, yo, *k3tog, yo, k1, yo,

rep from *, end k2tog, k1.
  Rep Rows 1–8 for pat.

Cable & Leaf Panel
Make 3
With smaller needles and 2 strands of yarn, cast on 33 sts and work in pat for 330 rows, ending with Row 10 (approx 58 inches), maintaining purl garter selvage throughout. Bind off all sts.

Fencepost Panel
Make 2
With smaller needles and 2 strands of yarn, cast on 49 sts and work in pat for 330 rows, ending with Row 2 (approx 58 inches), maintaining knit garter selvage throughout. Bind off all sts.

Finishing
Assemble panels in this sequence: leaf—lace—leaf—lace—leaf. Sew with a single strand of yarn, working from a garter st bump on 1 edge to a corresponding bump on opposite edge for a nearly invisible seam.

Border
On lower edge with RS facing and smaller needles, pick up and knit 212 sts, knit 6 rows. Bind off with larger needles.
  Rep for top edge. Damp block if necessary. ◆

WISHBONE

Chunky cables on a seed stitch background highlight a brawny afghan.

DESIGN BY BARBARA VENISHNICK

Finished Size
Approx 46 x 58 inches, excluding fringe

Materials
- Brown Sheep Burly Spun, 100 percent wool super-bulky weight yarn (132 yds/8 oz per hank): 8 hanks fuchsia #BS23
- Size 17 (12mm) 29-inch circular needle or size needed to obtain gauge
- Cable needle
- Size G/6 crochet hook for placing fringe

Gauge
8 sts and 12 rows = 4 inches/10cm in Seed Stitch Rib pat
To save time, take time to check gauge.

Special Abbreviations
C4b (cable 4 back): Sl 2 sts to cn and hold in back, k2, k2 from cn.

C4f (cable 4 front): Sl 2 sts to cn and hold in front, k2, k2 from cn.

Pattern Stitch
Seed Stitch Rib

Rows 1, 5 and 7 (RS): [K1, p1] 3 times, [k8, {p1, k1} 8 times, p1] 3 times, k8, [p1, k1] 3 times.

Row 2 and all WS rows: P5, [k1, p8, k1, p15] 3 times, k1, p8, k1, p5.

Row 3: [K1, p1] 3 times, [c4b, c4f, {p1, k1} 8 times, p1] 3 times, c4b, c4f, [p1, k1] 3 times.

Row 8: Rep Row 2.
Rep Rows 1–8 for pat.

Pattern Note
Circular needle is used to accommodate large number of sts. Do not join; work in rows.

Afghan
Cast on 95 stitches.

Work even in Seed Stitch Rib pat until afghan measures approx 58 inches, ending with Row 4 of pat.

Bind off.

Fringe
Cut 190 strands of yarn, each 12 inches long.

Fold 1 strand in half and knot in each Row 1 st at beg of afghan just above cast-on edge.

Pull tails through folded loop and pull tightly.

Rep fringe in each Row 4 st just below bound-off edge. ◆

RASPBERRY AFGHAN

Twisted rib stripes work up into a unique and elegant afghan. Knit in dark raspberry yarn, it would also make a great Christmas afghan.

DESIGN BY SHARI HAUX

BEGINNER

4
MEDIUM

Finished Size
Approx 58 x 63 inches

Materials
- Plymouth Encore worsted weight 75 percent acrylic/25 percent wool yarn (200 yds/100g per ball): 12 balls dark raspberry #1607
- Size 8 (5mm) needles or size needed to obtain gauge
- Stitch markers
- Tapestry needle

Gauge
18 sts and 24 rows = 4 inches/10cm in pat
To save time, take time to check gauge.

Afghan
Cast on 258 sts. Knit 10 rows.

Beg pat
Row 1 (RS): K6, pm, p4, *k1tbl, [p1, k1tbl] 3 times, p4, rep from * to last 6 sts, end k6.

Row 2: K6, k4, *p1, [k1tbl, p1] 3 times, k4, rep from * to last 6 sts, end k6.

Rep Rows 1 and 2 until piece measures approximately 61½ inches from beg.

Knit 10 rows. Bind off all sts. ◆

CELTIC TRADITION

Small cables and easy stitches form a block pattern in this traditional throw.

DESIGN BY JOYCE ENGLUND

Finished Size
Approx 48 x 63 inches

Materials
• Brown Sheep Lamb's Pride Superwash Worsted, 100 percent washable wool worsted weight yarn (200 yds/100g per skein): 17 skeins stonewashed denim #SW150
• Size 11 (8mm) 29-inch circular needle or size needed to obtain gauge
• Cable needle
• Stitch markers

Gauge
15 sts and 20 rows = 4 inches/10cm in Cable pat
To save time, take time to check gauge.

Special Abbreviation
C4 (cross 4): Slip next st to cn and hold in front, k 3rd st on LH needle, k first and 2nd sts, k1 from cn.

Pattern Stitch
Cables
Rows 1, 3 and 5 (RS): Knit.
Rows 2 and 4: P3, k2, *p5, k2; rep from * across, end last rep p3.
Rows 6 and 8: [K2, sl 1] twice, *k3, sl 1, k2, sl 1; rep from * across, end last rep k2.
Row 7: P2, sl 1, k2, sl 1, *p3, sl 1, k2, sl 1; rep from * across, end last rep p2.
Row 9: K2, C4, *k3, c4; rep from * across, end last rep k2.
Row 10: Rep Row 2.
  Rep Rows 1–10 for pat.

Pattern Notes
Two strands of yarn are held tog for entire afghan.
  Circular needle is used to accommodate large number of sts. Do not join; work in rows.

Afghan
With 2 strands of yarn held tog, cast on 162 sts.

Border
Knit 7 rows.
Set up pat: K7, place marker, work in pat to last 7 sts, place marker, k7.
  Keeping first and last 7 sts in garter st and remaining sts in Cable pat, work even until afghan measures approximately 61 inches, ending with Row 2 of pat.
  Knit 7 rows.
  Bind off knitwise. ◆

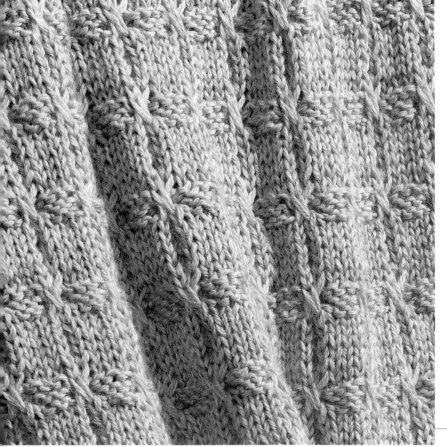

FLYING CABLES

Increases and decreases in the areas between cables form a natural scallop along the edges of this afghan.

DESIGN BY BARBARA VENISHNICK

Finished Size
Approx 44 x 59 inches

Materials
• Brown Sheep Lamb's Pride Worsted, 85 percent wool/15 percent mohair worsted weight yarn (190 yds/4 oz per hank): 6 hanks blue heirloom #M75
• Brown Sheep Handpaint Originals 70 percent mohair/30 percent wool worsted weight yarn (88 yds/50g per hank): 12 hanks tropical water #HP60
• Size 15 (10mm) 29-inch circular needle or size needed to obtain gauge
• Cable needle

Gauge
9 sts and 13 rows = 4 inches/10cm in St st with 2 strands of yarn held tog
To save time, take time to check gauge.

Special Abbreviation
C6f (cable 6 front): Sl 3 sts to cn and hold in front, k3, k3 from cn.

Pattern Stitch
Flying Cables
Rows 1, 3, 7, 9 and 13 (RS): K1-tbl, [k1, p1, k6, p1, k1, ssk, k4, yo, k1, yo, k4, k2tog] 5 times, k1, p1, k6, p1, k1, sl 1 wyif.
Rows 2, 4, 6, 8, 10 and 12: K1-tbl, [p1, k1, p6, k1, p14] 5 times, p1, k1, p6, k1, p1, sl 1 wyif.
Row 5: K1-tbl, [k1, p1, c6f, p1, k1, ssk, k4, yo, k1, yo, k4, k2tog] 5 times, k1, p1, c6f, p1, k1, sl 1 wyif.
Row 11: Rep Row 5.
Row 14: K1-tbl, [p1, k1, p6, k1, {p1, k6} twice] 5 times, p1, k1, p6, k1, p1, sl 1 wyif.
Rep Rows 1–14 for pat.

Pattern Notes
One strand of each color are held tog for entire afghan.
Circular needle is used to accommodate large number of sts. Do not join; work in rows.

Afghan
With 2 strands of yarn held tog, cast on 127 sts.
[Work Rows 1–14 of Flying Cables pat] 14 times, rep Rows 1–13.
Bind off knitwise on WS.
Block. ◆

GUY'S GUERNSEY AFGHAN

The stitch pattern on this afghan was inspired by patterns on English Guernsey sweaters worn by fishermen.

DESIGN BY LOIS S. YOUNG

Finished Size
Approx 48 x 64 inches

Materials
- Plymouth Fantasy Naturale worsted weight 100 percent cotton yarn (140 yds/100g per ball): 15 balls taupe #7360
- Size 9 (5.5mm) 29-inch circular needle or size needed to obtain gauge
- Cable needle
- Tapestry needle

Gauge
16 sts and 24 rows = 4 inches/10cm in St st
To save time, take time to check gauge.

Pattern Note
Sl first st of each row knitwise.

Special Abbreviation
M1 (Make 1): Inc by making a backward loop over right needle.

Pattern Stitch
(multiple of 24 sts + 22)
Rows 1, 3, 7 and 9 (RS): Sl 1, k6, *p1, k6, p1, k16, rep from *, end last rep k7 instead of k16.
Rows 2, 4, 6 and 8: Sl 1, k4, p2, *k1, p6, k1, p16, rep from *, end last rep p2, k5 instead of p16.
Row 5: Sl 1, k6, p1, *sl next 3 sts to cn, hold in front, k3, return sts from cn to left needle and k3, p18, rep

from *end last rep p1, k7 instead of p18.
Row 10: Rep Row 2.
Rep Rows 1–10 for pat.

Afghan
Loosely cast on 182 sts.

Border
Rows 1–7: Sl 1, knit across.
Set up pat: Sl 1, k6, *p1, k3, M1, k2, p1, k16, rep from *, end last rep k7 instead of k16. (190 sts)
Work Rows 2–10 of pat, then work [Rows 1–10] 35 times. Rep [Rows 1–8] once more.
Dec row: Sl 1, k6, *p1, k3, k2tog, k1, p1, k16, rep from *, end last rep k7 instead of k16. (182 sts)

Border
Rows 1–6: Sl 1, knit across. Bind off knitwise on WS.
Block lightly. ◆

CHOCOLATE MOUSSE

A soft cotton and wool-blend yarn is used in a delicious, casual throw.

DESIGN BY KATHY CHEIFETZ

Finished Size
Approx 45 x 60 inches

Materials
- Brown Sheep Cotton Fleece, 80 percent cotton/20 percent Merino wool light worsted weight yarn (215 yds/100g per skein): 18 skeins teddy bear #CW820
- Size 15 (10mm) 32-inch circular needle or size needed to obtain gauge
- Cable needle
- Size K/10 crochet hook

Gauge
11 sts and 14 rows = 4 inches/10cm in pat st
To save time, take time to check gauge.

Special Abbreviation
Mc (mini cable): Sl next stitch to cn and hold in front, k1, k1 from cn.

Pattern Stitch
Mini Cables
Rows 1, 3, 5, 7, 9 and 11 (RS): P4, *Mc, p4, rep from * across row.
Rows 2, 4, 6, 8, 10 and 12: K or p the sts as they present themselves.
Row 13: K4, *Mc, k4; rep from * across row.
Row 14: Purl.
Rows 15, 17, 19 and 21: Rep Row 1.
Rows 16, 18, 20 and 22: Rep Row 2.
Rows 23 and 24: Rep Rows 13 and 14.
   Rep Rows 1–24 for pat.

Pattern Notes
Three strands of yarn are held tog for entire afghan.
   Circular needle is used to accommodate large number of sts. Do not join; work in rows.

Afghan
With 3 strands of yarn held tog, cast on 124 sts.
   [Work Rows 1–24 of Mini Cables pat] 8 times, rep Rows 1–12.
   Bind off in pat, do not cut yarn.

Edging
Place last st on crochet hook. *Sl st loosely in every other st or row to corner st, ch 1, sc in corner st, ch 1, rep from * around entire afghan. ◆

FIVE EASY CABLES

Garter stitch and cable panels give a lot of bang for your buck in this easy afghan.

DESIGN BY DIXIE BUTLER

Finished Size
Approx 44 x 52 inches

Materials
- Brown Sheep Prairie Silks, 72 percent wool/18 percent mohair/10 percent silk worsted weight yarn (88 yds/50g per skein): 32 skeins buck #PS450
- Size 13 (9mm) 29-inch circular needle or size needed to obtain gauge
- Cable needle

Gauge
11 sts and 16 rows = 4 inches/10cm in Garter & Cable pat.
To save time, take time to check gauge.

Special Abbreviations
Cf (cable front): Sl 3 sts to cn and hold in front, k3, k3 from cn.
Cb (cable back): Sl 3 sts to cn and hold in back, k3, k3 from cn.

Pattern Stitch
Garter & Cable
Rows 1 and 5 (RS): K10, [p2, k9] 9 times, p2, k10.
Row 2 and all WS rows: K9, p 1, [k2, p9, k2, p1, k7, p1] 4 times, k2, p9, k2, p1, k9.
Row 3: K10, [p2, cf, k3, p2, k9] 4 times, p2, cf, k3, p2, k10.
Row 7: K10, [p2, k3, cb, p2, k9] 4 times, p2, k3, cb, p2, k10.

Row 8: Rep row 2.
Rep rows 1-8 for pat.

Pattern Notes
Two strands of yarn are held tog for entire afghan.

Circular needle is used to accommodate large number of sts. Do not join; work in rows.

Afghan
With 2 strands of yarn held tog, cast on 121 sts.

Work even in Garter & Cable pat until afghan measures approximately 52 inches, ending with Row 4 or 8 of pat.
Bind off in pat.
Block. ◆

AUTUMN BLAZE

A colorful blaze of leaves and berries is featured on this lovely afghan. Worked in panels, it is a handy carry-along project.

DESIGN BY NAZANIN S. FARD

Finished Size
Approx 50 x 50 inches

Materials
- Brown Sheep Lamb's Pride Superwash Worsted, 100 percent washable wool worsted weight yarn (200 yds/100g per skein): 18 skeins blaze #SW145
- Size 10 (6mm) needles or size needed to obtain gauge
- Tapestry needle

Gauge
14 sts and 22 rows = 4 inches/10cm in St st
To save time, take time to check gauge.

Special Abbreviations
M1 (Make 1): Lift the running thread between st just worked and next st, k into the back of this thread.
P inc: P into front and back of next st.
K inc: K into front and back of next st.
Cdd (centered double decrease): Sl 2 tog knitwise, k1, p2sso.

Pattern Notes
Two strands of yarn are held tog for entire afghan.

Pay special attention to increases and decreases, as st count varies in both panels.

Afghan

Leaves Panel
Make 4
With 2 strands of yarn held tog, cast on 26 sts.
Rows 1 (WS)–4: Knit.
Row 5: K5, p5, k4, p3, k9.
Row 6: P7, p2tog, k inc, k2, p4, k2, yo, k1, yo, k2, p5.
Row 7: K5, p7, k4, p2, k1, p1, k8.
Row 8: P6, p2tog, k1, p inc, k2, p4, k3, yo, k1, yo, k3, p5.
Row 9: K5, p9, k4, p2, k2, p1, k7.
Row 10: P5, p2tog, k1, p inc, p1, k2, p4, ssk, k5, k2tog, p5.
Row 11: K5, p7, k4, p2, k3, p1, k6.
Row 12: P4, p2tog, k1, p inc, p2, k2, p4, ssk, k3, k2tog, p5.
Row 13: K5, p5, k4, p2, k4, p1, k5.
Row 14: P5, yo, k1, yo, p4, k2, p4, ssk, k1, k2tog, p5.
Row 15: K5, p3, k4, p2, k4, p3, k5.
Row 16: P5, [k1, yo] twice, k1, p4, k1, M1, k1, p2tog, p2, cdd, p5.
Row 17: K9, p3, k4, p5, k5.
Row 18: P5, k2, yo, k1, yo, k2, p4, k1, k inc, k1, p2tog, p7.
Row 19: K8, p1, k1, p2, k4, p7, k5.
Row 20: P5, k3, yo, k1, yo, k3, p4, k2, p inc, k1, p2tog, p6.
Row 21: K7, p1, k2, p2, k4, p9, k5.
Row 22: P5, ssk, k5, k2tog, p4, k2, p1, p inc, k1, p2tog, p5.
Row 23: K6, p1, k3, p2, k4, p7, k5.
Row 24: P5, ssk, k3, k2tog, p4, k2, p2, p inc, k1, p2tog, p4.
Row 25: K5, p1, k4, p2, k4, p5, k5.
Row 26: P5, ssk, k1, k2tog, p4, k2, p4, yo, k1, yo, p5.
Row 27: K5, p3, k4, p2, k4, p3, k5.
Row 28: P5, cdd, p2, p2tog, k1, M1, k1, p4, [k1, yo] twice, k1, p5.
[Rep Rows 5–28] 10 times.
Knit 4 rows.
Bind off all sts loosely.

Berries Panel
Make 3
With 2 strands of yarn held tog, cast on 26 sts.
Rows 1 (WS)–4: Knit.
Row 5: *K2, p1; rep from * across, end last rep k2.
Row 6: *P2, [k1, p1] twice in next st, p2, k1; rep from * across, end last rep p2.
Rows 7 and 9: K2, *p1, k8; rep from * across.
Row 8: *P2, k4, p2, k1; rep from * across, end last rep p2.
Row 10: * P2, [k2tog] twice, pass first k2tog over 2nd, p2, k1; rep from * across, end last rep p2.
Row 11: Rep Row 5.
Row 12: *P2, k1, p2, [k1, p1] twice in the next st; rep from * across, end last rep p2.
Rows 13 and 15: *K8, p1; rep from * across, end last rep k2.
Row 14: *P2, k1, p2, k4; rep from * across, end last rep p2.
Row 16: *P2, k1, p2, [k2tog] twice, pass first k2tog over 2nd; rep from * across, end last rep p2.

[Rep rows 5–16] 20 times.
Knit 4 rows.
Bind off all sts loosely.

Finishing

Alternating Leaves and Berries
panels, sew panels tog using
single strand of yarn.

Side Border

With RS facing, pick up and
k 130 sts evenly along one
side edge.
Knit 3 rows.
Bind off loosely.
Rep for remaining side. ◆

FLORA DORA

This afghan is worked in one piece in bands of repeating blossoms. Each band is separated by picot-accented edging that is applied after the afghan is complete.

DESIGN BY KATHLEEN POWER JOHNSON

Finished Size
Approx 48 x 60 inches, without edging

Materials
- Brown Sheep Lamb's Pride Worsted, 85 percent wool/15 percent mohair worsted weight yarn (190 yds/4 oz per skein): 13 skeins lotus pink #M38 (MC), 2 skeins white frost #M11 (A)
- Brown Sheep Lamb's Pride Bulky, 85 percent wool/15 percent mohair bulky weight yarn (125 yds/4 oz per skein): 1 skein white frost #M11 (B)
- Size 10 (6mm) 24-inch circular needle
- Size 11 (8mm) 36-inch circular needle or size needed to obtain gauge

Gauge
12 sts and 16 rows = 4 inches/10cm in St st with 2 strands of yarn on larger needles
To save time, take time to check gauge.

Special Abbreviation
Picot: Cast on 2 sts, bind off these two sts.

Pattern Stitch
Eyelet Blossoms

Row 1 (RS): K8, *[k2tog] twice, yo, (k1, p1, k1) into next st, yo, [ssk] twice, k10, rep from * across, end last rep k8.

Row 2 (and all even-numbered rows): Purl.

Row 3: K8, *[k2tog, yo] twice, k1, [yo, ssk] twice, k10, rep from * across, end last rep k8.

Row 5: K7, *k2tog, yo, k2tog, [k1, yo] twice, k1, ssk, yo, ssk, k8, rep from * across, end last rep k7.

Row 7: K6, *k2tog, yo, k2tog, k2, yo, k1, yo, k2, ssk, yo, ssk, k6, rep from * across.

Row 9: K6, *k2tog, yo, k1, k2tog, yo, k3, yo, ssk, k1, yo, ssk, k6, rep from * across.

Row 11: K6, *[k2tog, yo] twice, k5, [yo, ssk] twice, k6, rep from * across.

Row 13: K10, *yo, ssk, k1, k2tog, yo, k14, rep from * across, end last rep k10.

Row 15: K11, *yo, sl 1 knitwise, k2tog, psso, yo, k16, rep from * across, end last rep k11.

Row 16: Purl.

Pattern Notes

Two strands of yarn are held tog for entire afghan.

Circular needles are used to accommodate large number of sts. Do not join; work in rows.

Afghan

With larger needles and MC, loosely cast on 139 sts.

*Work in St st for 6 rows, ending with a WS row.

Work 16 rows of Eyelet Blossoms pat, then 6 rows of St st.

With A, knit 2 rows.

Rep from * 6 times, ending last rep with 2nd 6 rows of St st.

Bind off loosely.

Picot Bands

Work in each garter-st stripe that separates bands.

Row 1: With smaller needles and 1 strand of B, beg with 2nd st pick up and knit 1 st in each down-curving garter st "bump" across row. Do not work last st. (137 sts)

Row 2: Bind off 4 sts, *slip last st back to LH needle, picot, bind off 3 sts, rep from * across, binding off last st.

Side Edging

With RS facing using larger needles and MC, pick up and k 179 sts along one long edge.

Knit 1 row.

Change to A and knit 1 more row.

Bind off.

Rep along remaining side edge.

Edging

With RS facing using larger needles and MC, pick up and knit 144 sts across bound-off edge, including edge of trim.

Knit 1 row.

Change to A.

Next row: K1, *yo, k2tog, rep from * across, end last rep k1.

Purl 1 row.

Bind off purlwise.

Rep along cast-on edge. ◆

HYACINTH BEAUTY

Puffy bud stitches combine with multiple yarn-overs to create a light and airy summer afghan.

DESIGN BY FRANCES HUGHES

INTERMEDIATE

3
LIGHT

Finished Size
Approx 52 x 62 inches excluding fringe

Materials
• Brown Sheep Wildfoote Luxury Sock Yarn,
75 percent washable wool/25 percent nylon fingering weight yarn (215 yds/50g per skein): 20 skeins little lilac #SY32
• Size 11 (8mm) 32-inch circular needle or size needed to obtain gauge

Gauge
14 sts and 10 rows = 4 inches/10cm in pat st
To save time, take time to check gauge.

Pattern Stitch
Hyacinths
Row 1 (WS): K1, *p5tog, (k1, p1, k1, p1, k1) all in next st, rep from * across, end last rep k1.
Row 2: K1, purl to last st, k1.
Row 3: K1, *(k1, p1, k1, p1, k1) all in next st, p5tog, rep from * across, end last rep k1.

Row 4: K1, purl to last st, k1.
Row 5: Knit, wrapping yarn twice around needle for each st.
Row 6: K1, purl to last st dropping extra wrap for each st, k1.
Rep Rows 1–6 for pat.

Pattern Notes
Three strands of yarn are held tog for entire afghan.

Circular needle is used to accommodate large number of sts. Do not join; work in rows.

Afghan
With 3 strands of yarn held tog, cast on 176 sts.

Knit 2 rows.

Work even in Hyacinth pat until afghan measures 62 inches, ending with Row 3 of pat.
Next 2 rows: K1, purl to last st, k1.
Bind off loosely.

Double Knot Fringe
Cut strands of yarn, each 18 inches long.

Hold 5 strands tog and fold in half. Knot 1 group of strands in every 3rd cast-on st.

Divide strands, using 5 from left and 5 from right groups, and tie again about ¾ inch below first row of knots using an overhand knot.

Rep for another row of knots.

Rep fringe along bound-off edge. ◆

GRAY ROSE

A combination of two colors gives a heathery look to a first-project afghan.

DESIGN BY DIXIE BUTLER

Finished Size
Approx 46 x 60 inches, without fringe

Materials
- Brown Sheep Nature Spun, 100 percent wool worsted weight yarn (245 yds/100g per skein): 10 skeins grey heather #N03 (MC), 5 skeins cranberry fog #N81 (CC)
- Size 17 (12mm) needles or size needed to obtain gauge

Gauge
9 sts and 13 rows = 4 inches/10cm in pat st
To save time, take time to check gauge.

Pattern Notes
Afghan is worked with 2 strands of MC and 1 strand of CC held tog throughout.
SI all sts purlwise.

Afghan
Cast on 100 sts.
Rows 1 (RS) and 2: SI 1, k1, *p1, k1; rep from * across row.
Rows 3 and 7: SI 1, k to end of row.
Row 4: SI 1, p to last st, k1.
Rows 5 and 6: SI 1, *p1, k1; rep from * across row.
Row 8: Rep Row 4.
Rep Rows 1–8 until afghan measures approximately 60 inches, ending with Row 2 or 6 of pat.
Bind off.

Fringe
Cut strands of yarn, each 12 inches long.
For each fringe, use 2 strands CC and 4 strands MC held tog.
Fold group in half and knot into each st of bound-off edge.
Rep along cast-on edge. ◆

DOTTED STRIPES

This colorway is mindful of spring flowers and would make a charming accent in a girl's room.

DESIGN BY LOIS S. YOUNG

Finished Size
Approx 44 x 66 inches

Materials
- Brown Sheep Cotton Fleece, 80 percent cotton/20 percent Merino wool light worsted weight yarn (215 yds/100g per skein): 14 skeins cotton ball #CW100 (MC), 2 skeins each lime light CW840 (A) and tea rose CW210 (B)
- Size 13 (9mm) 36-inch circular needle or size needed to obtain gauge

Gauge
10 sts and 14 rows = 4 inches/10cm in Picot Stripes pat
To save time, take time to check gauge.

Special Abbreviations
Ssp: Sl 2 sts separately knitwise, return sts to LH needle in this reversed position, p2tog through back of sts.
Picot: (K1, [yo, k1] 3 times) in next st, making 7 sts out of 1.

Pattern Stitches
A. Seed Stitch
All rows: *K1, p1; rep from * across, end last rep k1.
B. Picot Stripes
Row 1 (WS): With MC, k1, purl to last st, k1.
Row 2: With A k3, *picot, k9; rep from * across, end last rep picot, k3.
Row 3: With A knit.
Row 4: With MC, k2 *k2tog, k5, ssk, k7; rep from * across, end last rep

k2tog, k5, ssk, k2.
Row 5: K1, p1, *ssp, p1, sl 1 wyif, p1, p2tog, p7; rep from * across, end last rep p1, k1.
Row 6: K2, *k2tog, sl 1 wyib, ssk, k7; rep from * across, end last rep k2.
Row 7: K1, purl to last st, k1.
Row 8: With B, k8, *picot, k9; rep from * across, end last rep picot, k8.
Row 9: With B, knit.
Row 10: With MC, k7, *k2tog, k5, ssk, k7; rep from * across row.
Row 11: K1, p6, *ssp, p1, sl 1 wyif, p1, p2tog, p7; rep from * across, end last rep p6, k1.
Row 12: K7, *k2tog, sl 1 wyib, ssk, k7; rep from * across row.
Rows 13–18: Rep Rows 1–6.
Rows 19–38: Work in St st, keeping first and last st in knit.
Rows 39–76: Rep Rows 1–38, working color stripe sequence as B, A, B.

Pattern Notes
Afghan is worked with 3 strands of yarn held tog throughout.

Circular needle is used to accommodate large number of sts. Do not join, work in rows.

Afghan
With MC, cast on 87 sts loosely.
Work in Seed St for 6 rows.
Knit 1 row.
Next row: P1, knit to last st, p1.
[Work Picot Stripe pat] 3 times.
Rep Rows 1–18.
Work in Seed St for 6 rows.
Bind off in pat.

Side Borders
With MC and RS facing, pick up and knit 148 sts along one side edge.
Work in Seed St for 6 rows.
Bind off in pat. ◆

MONET MITERS THROW

Soft mohair combines with glitz in an interesting twist on shape and color. The mitered squares are knit in garter stitch and joined as they are worked. Garter bands separate the rows of blocks.

DESIGN BY DIANE ZANGL

Finished Size
Approx 44 x 56 inches

Materials
• Plymouth Le Fibre Nobili Imperiale 80 percent mohair/20 percent nylon worsted weight yarn (110 yds/ 25g per ball): 10 balls each olive #4122 (A) and taupe #4121 (B); 7 balls off-white #4102 (C)
• Plymouth Odyssey Glitz 60 percent nylon/37 percent wool/3 percent lamé bulky weight novelty yarn (65 yds/50g per ball): 21 balls spring #900 (CC)
• Size 11 (8mm) 36-inch circular and 2 (10-inch) double pointed needles

Gauge
10 sts and 20 rows = 4 inches/10cm in garter st
To save time, take time to check gauge.

Special Techniques & Abbreviations
Cable Cast On: *Insert RH needle between last 2 sts on LH needle, wrap yarn around needle as if to knit and pull through to make a

new st, place new st on LH needle; rep from * as directed.
CDD (Centered Double Decrease): Sl 2 sts as if to k2tog, k1, pass 2 sl sts over knit st. Center st will lie on top.

Pattern Stitch
Basic Square
Row 1 (WS): Knit to marked st, p1, knit to end of row.
Row 2: Knit to 1 st before marked st, CDD, knit to end of row.
Rep Rows 1 and 2 until 1 st rem.

Leave last st on needle, cut mohair only. Join next color.

Pattern Notes
Two dpns are used for squares; circular needle is used for dividing bands and outer borders.

One strand of glitz and 2 strands of mohair (either A, B or C) are held tog throughout throw. Colors are referred to by the mohair letter only.

When changing colors, cut mohair only. Glitz is carried through entire throw.

Throw

With dpn, using 2 strands of A and 1 strand of CC held tog, Cable Cast On 33 sts. Mark center st.

Work Basic Square, change to B.

Pick up and knit 16 sts (1 st in each ridge) along left edge of square just worked, mark last st, Cable Cast On 16 sts. (33 sts)

Work Basic Square, change to A.

Continue alternating squares of A and B until there are 6 squares in the row. Fasten off last st.

Dividing Band

With circular needle and RS facing, using 2 strands of C and 1 strand of CC held tog, pick up and knit 16 sts along top edge of each square. (96 sts)

Knit 5 rows.

Cut C; leave sts on needle.

Second Row of Squares

With B and dpn, cable cast on 17 sts, mark last st, knit across 16 sts of dividing band, turn. (33 sts on dpn, remainder left on circular needle)

Work Basic Square, leaving last st on needle. Change to A.

Continue adding squares in alternating colors by picking up and knitting 16 sts along square just completed and knitting another 16 sts along top of dividing band. (33 sts when beg each square)

Rep from Dividing Band until there are 7 rows of squares with a dividing band between each row.

Rep dividing band.

Bind off loosely.

End Border

With 2 strands of C and 1 strand of CC held tog, pick up and knit 96 sts along beg end of throw.

Knit 5 rows.

Bind off loosely.

Side Border

Work as for end border, picking up and knitting 16 sts in each square and 3 sts in each dividing band. (136 sts)

Knit 5 rows.

Bind off loosely.

Rep for 2nd side. ◆

HEART OF MINE

Here is a perfect afghan for that special little person who has captured your heart!

DESIGN BY KATHY SASSER

Finished Size
Approx 32 x 40 inches

Materials
• Brown Sheep Cotton Fleece, 80 percent cotton/20 percent Merino wool light worsted weight yarn (215 yds/100g per skein): 9 skeins coral sunset #CW225
• Size 13 (9mm) 32-inch circular needle or size needed to obtain gauge
• Cable needle

Gauge
9 sts and 17 rows = 4 inches/10cm in Irish Moss pat
To save time, take time to check gauge.

Pattern Stitches
A. Irish Moss
(multiple of 2)
Row 1 (WS) and 2: *K1, p1, rep from * across.
Rows 3 and 4: *P1, k1, rep from * across.
   Rep Rows 1–4 for pat.
B. Front Cable
(worked over 8 sts)
Rows 1 and 3 (WS): K1, p6, k1.
Row 2: P1, k6, p1.
Row 4: P1, sl 3 sts to cn and hold in front, k3, k3 from cn, ends with p1.
   Rep Rows 1–4 for pat.
C. Back Cable
(worked over 8 sts)
Rows 1 and 3 (WS): K1, p6, k1.

Row 2: P1, k6, p1.
Row 4: P1, sl 3 sts to cn and hold in back, k3, k3 from cn, ends with p1. Rep Rows 1–4 for pat.

Pattern Notes

Circular needle is used to accommodate sts.

Work in rows, do not join.

Three strands of yarn are held tog throughout afghan.

Work Rows 1–19 of Cabled Heart chart once, [rep Rows 4–19] 7 times.

Afghan

Holding 3 strands tog, cast on 96 sts.

Knit 4 rows.

Set up pat (WS): Garter st over 3 sts, place marker, work Row 1 of [Irish Moss pat over 10 sts, Back Cable pat over 8 sts] twice, place marker, Cabled Heart pat from chart over 18 sts, place marker, [Front Cable pat over 8 sts, Irish Moss pat over 10 sts] twice, place marker, garter st over 3 sts.

Work even in established pats until 8 heart pats have been completed.

Knit 4 rows.

Bind off. ◆

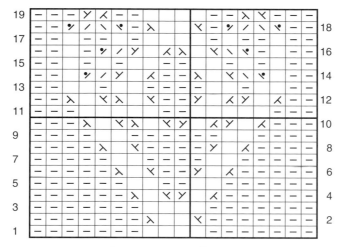

CABLED HEART CHART

STITCH KEY

☐	K on RS, p on WS
−	P on RS, k on WS
⅄⅄	Sl 1 to cn and hold in front, k1, k1 from cn
⅄⅄	Sl 1 to cn and hold in back, k1, k1 from cn
↘↘	Sl 1 to cn and hold in front, p1, k1 from cn
↗↗	Sl 1 to cn and hold in back, k1, p1 from cn
⅄⅄	Sl 2 to cn and hold in front, p1, k2 from cn
⅄⅄	Sl 1 to cn and hold in back, k2, p1 from cn
⅄ ⅄	Sl 2 to cn and hold in front, k2, k2 from cn

QUICK LACY THROW

Worked with three strands held together throughout, this cozy afghan is the perfect project for a snowbound weekend.

DESIGN BY CAROL MAY

BEGINNER

4 MEDIUM

Finished Size
Approx 42 x 56 inches

Materials
- Plymouth Encore worsted weight 75 percent acrylic/25 percent wool yarn (200 yds/100g per ball): 4 balls each light green #801, medium green #9401, dark green #1604
- Size 15 (10mm) 29-inch circular needle or size needed to obtain gauge
- Tapestry needle
- 9-inch-wide piece of stiff cardboard

Gauge
6 sts = 4 inches/10cm in garter st
To save time, take time to check gauge.

Pattern Notes
Throw is worked with 1 strand of each color held tog throughout.

Circular needle is used to accommodate large number of sts. Do not join at end of row.

Afghan
Using 3 strands of yarn, loosely cast on 69 sts. Knit every row until there are 3 ridges of garter st, ending with a WS row.

Row 1 (RS): K3, *k2tog, yo, rep from * to last 4 sts, end k4.

Row 2: Knit across.

Row 3: K4, *yo, k2tog, rep from * to last 3 sts, end k3.

Row 4: Knit across.

Rep Rows 1–4 until piece measures 54 inches or 2 inches less than desired length.

Work in garter st until there are 3 ridges on front of work. Bind off all sts loosely and knitwise.

Tassels
Make 4
Using 3 strands tog, wrap 24 times around stiff cardboard. Cut yarn, leaving a 12-inch end. Thread strands into tapestry needle, run strands around all strands at 1 end of cardboard several times, pulling tight. Fasten off securely. Cut all strands at opposite end. With separate length of yarn, wrap tassel tightly about 2 inches below top, fasten off and run ends into tassel. Trim bottom, then fasten to corner of throw with ends at top. ◆

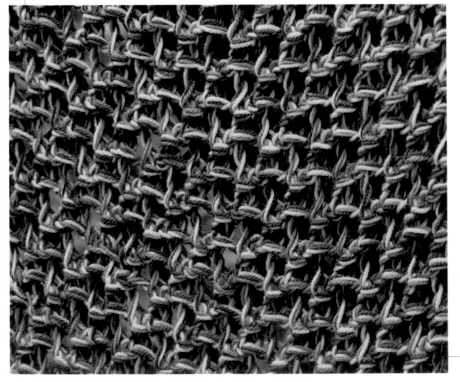

JEWEL TONES

Jewel-like colors and a luxurious triple fringe highlight an afghan fit for a queen.

DESIGN BY JANET REHFELDT

Finished Size
Approx 50 x 64 inches, without fringe

Materials
- Brown Sheep Lamb's Pride Worsted, 85 percent wool/15 percent mohair worsted weight yarn (190 yds/4 oz per skein): 6 skeins each periwinkle #M59, RPM pink #M105, sunburst gold #M14, Aztec turquoise #M78
- Brown Sheep Handpaint Originals 70 percent mohair/30 percent wool worsted weight yarn (88 yds/50g per skein): 11 skeins tropical waters #HP60
- Size 35 (20mm) 47-inch circular needle or size needed to obtain gauge

Gauge
6 sts and 8 rows = 4 inches/10cm in garter st
To save time, take time to check gauge.

Pattern Stitch
Rows 1 (RS)–6: K2, *yo, k2tog; rep from * across, end last rep k2.
Rows 7–14: Knit.
Rep Rows 1–14 for pat.

Pattern Notes
Afghan is worked with 5 strands of yarn (one of each color) held tog throughout.
Circular needle is used to accommodate large number of stitches. Do not join; work in rows.

Afghan
Cast on 94 sts.
Beg with a RS row, knit 4 rows.
Work even in pat until afghan measures approximately 47 inches, ending with Row 6 of pat.
Knit 3 rows.
Bind off knitwise on WS.

Triple Knot Fringe
Cut strands into 35-inch lengths.
Using 5 strands held tog (1 of each color), fold strands in half.
Knot 1 group of strands in each row along edge of afghan.
Take half of strands from first group, and knot them tog with half of strands of adjoining group about 1½ inches below first knots. Rep across row.
Beg with free half of first group, make a 3rd row of knots about 1½ inches below previous ones.
Trim ends even.
Rep for opposite edge of afghan. ◆

ACORN AFGHAN

This warm and cozy afghan is worked with two strands throughout. It's a fast and interesting project, even for a beginner.

DESIGN BY FATEMA HABIBUR-RAHMAN

Finished Size
Approx 50 x 55 inches

Materials
- Plymouth Encore worsted weight 75 percent acrylic/25 percent wool yarn (200 yds/100g per ball): 12 balls cranberry #560
- Size 15 (10mm) 29- or 36-inch circular needle or size needed to obtain gauge
- Tapestry needle

Gauge
6 sts = 4 inches/10cm in St st with 2 strands of yarn
To save time, take time to check gauge.

Pattern Notes
Circular needle is used to accommodate large number of sts. Do not join at end of row.

Afghan is worked with 2 strands of yarn held tog throughout.

Pattern Stitch
Acorn Stitch (multiple of 6 sts + 2)
Row 1 (WS): K1, *p5tog, [k1, p1, k1, p1, k1] into next st, rep from * to last st, k1.
Row 2: Purl across.
Row 3: K1, *[k1, p1, k1, p1, k1] into next st, p5tog, rep from * to last st, k1.
Row 4: Purl across.
Row 5: Knit, wrapping yarn around needle 3 times for each st.
Row 6: Purl, dropping extra loops.
Rep Rows 1–6 for pat.

Afghan
With 2 strands of yarn held tog, cast on 182 sts.

Work Rows 1–6 of pat until piece measures approximately 49 inches from beg, ending with Row 4. Bind off all sts loosely.

Finishing
Wet-block afghan. ◆

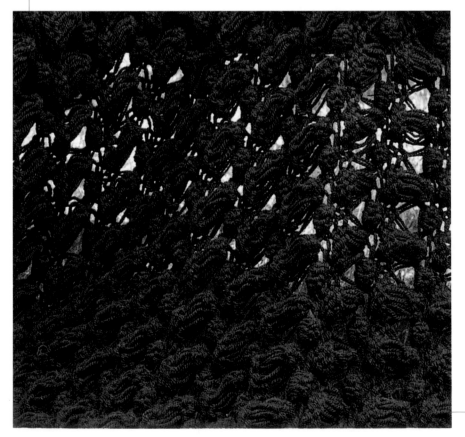

BY THE SEA

Combine a lacy shell and wave pattern with seaside colors to create a truly unique summer afghan.

DESIGN BY KATHLEEN POWER JOHNSON

INTERMEDIATE

4 MEDIUM

Finished Size
Approx 48 x 60 inches

Materials
• Plymouth Fantasy Naturale worsted weight 100 percent cotton yarn (140 yds/100g per ball): 11 balls variegated #9936
• Size 10 (6mm) needles or size needed to obtain gauge
• Crochet hook (for fringe)

Gauge
14 sts and 24 rows = 4 inches/10cm in garter st
To save time, take time to check gauge.

Pattern Note
Double-Wrapped Sts: When knitting or slipping these sts on following row, drop 2nd wrap.

Pattern Stitch
Shell and Wave Pat
(multiple of 12 sts + 1)
Row 1: Knit across, wrapping yarn twice around needle for each st.
Row 2: Sl 4 sts purlwise, insert LH needle into front of these 4 sts from left to right and k4tog, *yo, [k1, yo] 5 times, sl 7 sts purlwise, insert LH needle into front of these 7 sts from left to right and k7tog, rep from *, ending last rep sl 4, insert LH needle into front of these 4 sts from left to right and k4tog.
Row 3: Knit across (there should be one yo after each st except last st).

Rows 4, 5 and 6: Knit.
Rep Rows 1–6 for pat.

Afghan
Cast on 169 sts. Knit 6 rows, then beg pat. Work even in pat until afghan measures approximately 59½ inches, ending with Row 6. Knit 3 rows. Bind off all sts.

Fringe
For each end, cut 96 (15-inch) strands. Beg at corner, *fold 3 strands in half, pull through st and knot close to afghan edge. Rep from * every 1½ inches across. ◆

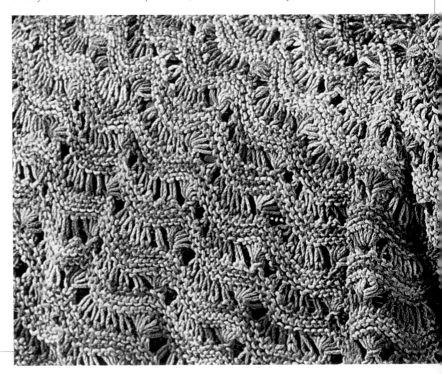

MORNING SUNLIGHT

Cables and long slip stitches resemble rays of sunshine on this cheery sun porch throw.

DESIGN BY JANET REHFELDT

Finished Size
Approx 34 x 46 inches

Materials
- Brown Sheep Lamb's Pride Superwash Worsted, 100 percent washable wool worsted weight yarn (200 yds/100g per skein): 10 skeins corn silk #SW13
- Size 17 (13mm) 29-inch circular needle
- Cable needle

Gauge
9½ sts and 10 rows = 4 inches/10cm in pat st
To save time, take time to check gauge.

Special Abbreviation
C3F (cable 3 front): Sl 1 st to cn and hold in front, k2, k1 from cn.

Pattern Notes
Afghan is worked with 3 strands of yarn held tog throughout.

Circular needle is used to accommodate large number of sts. Do not join, work in rows.

Afghan
With 3 strands held tog, cast on 81 sts.

Knit 4 rows.

Beg pat

Row 1 (RS): K3, p2, sl 1 wyib, p2, k1, *p2, k3, p2, k1, p2, sl 1 wyib, p2, k1, rep from * to last 2 sts, k2.

Row 2: K2, p1, k2, sl 1 wyif, k2, p1, *k2, p3, k2, p1, k2, sl 1 wyif, k2, p1, rep from * to last 2 sts, k2.

Row 3: K3, p2, k1, p2, k1, *p2, k3, [p2, k1] 3 times, rep from * to last 2 sts, k2.

Row 4: Rep Row 2.

Row 5: K3, p2, sl 1 wyib, p2, k1, *p2, C3F, p2, k1, p2, sl 1 wyib, p2, k1, rep from * to last 2 sts, k2.

Row 6: [K2, p1] 3 times, *k2, p3, [k2, p1] 3 times, rep from * to last 2 sts, k2.

Row 7: K3, p2, sl 1 wyib, p2, k1, *p2, k3, p2, k1, p2, sl 1 wyib, p2, k1, rep from * to last 2 sts, k2.

Row 8: Rep Row 2.

Row 9: K3, p2, k1, p2, k1, *p2, k3, [p2, k1] 3 times, rep from * to last 2 sts, k2.

Row 10: Rep Row 2.

Rep Rows 5–10 until afghan measures approximately 48 inches, ending with Row 8.

Knit 3 rows.

Bind off knitwise on WS. ◆

TIBETAN CHECK AFGHAN

A checkerboard is overlaid with bands of horizontal garter stitch, giving a three-dimensional effect. The afghan is constructed in one piece using intarsia technique.

DESIGN BY BARBARA VENISHNICK

Finished Size
Approx 49 x 63 inches

Materials
- Plymouth Encore worsted weight 75 percent acrylic/25 percent wool yarn (200 yds/100g per ball): 5 balls rose heather #433 (A), 4 balls each beige heather #1415 (B), grey heather #389 (C)
- Size 10 (6mm) 40-inch circular needle or size needed to obtain gauge
- Size H/8 (5mm) crochet hook (for cast on)
- Tapestry needle

Gauge
15 sts and 26 rows = 4 inches/10cm in pat
To save time, take time to check gauge.

Pattern Notes
Afghan is worked using intarsia technique. Attach separate ball of yarn for each square of checkerboard. Keep them all in a basket to avoid tangling. When changing colors, pick up new color under old to avoid holes.

Carry colors B and C up behind color A stripes. Cut yarn and reposition colors only when color B and C blocks change position. Color A may be carried up side when not in use.

Circular needle is used to accommodate large number of sts. Do not join at end of row.

Special Abbreviations
M1 (Make 1): Inc by lifting running thread between st just knit and next st onto LH needle. K1 in back loop.

Provisional cast on: With crochet hook and scrap yarn, loosely ch number of sts needed for afghan plus a few more. With working needle and afghan yarn, pick up 1 st in each purl bump on back side of ch. Ch can be undone leaving live sts to work trim. This makes a more flexible edge than a regular cast on.

With crochet hook, ch 176 sts plus a few extra. With circular needle, provisionally cast on as follows: [22 B, 22 C] 4 times.
Note: *Cast-on row counts as Row 1 of first rep of pat.*

Pattern
Row 1: Knit [22 B, 22 C] 4 times.

Row 2: Purl [22 C, 22 B] 4 times.
Rows 3 and 4: Rep Rows 1 and 2.
Rows 5–8: With A, k176.
Rows 9–40: [Rep Rows 1–8] 4 more times to complete row of checks.
Row 41: Knit [22 C, 22 B] 4 times.
Row 42: Purl [22 B, 22 C] 4 times.
Rows 43 and 44: Rep Rows 41 and 42.
Rows 45–48: With A, k176.
Rows 49–80: [Rep Rows 41–80] 4 more times to complete row of checks.

Rep [Rows 1–80] 4 times more, ending last rep with Row 76. Do not work last 4 rows of A. Finished grid will be 8 blocks wide and 10 blocks high. Do not bind off.

Top Border
Rows 1 and 2: With A, knit.
Row 3: With C, k1, M1, k to last st, M1, k1.
Row 4: With C, knit.
Rows 5 and 6: With A, knit.
Rows 7 and 8: With B, rep Rows 3 and 4.
Row 9: With A, knit.
With A, bind off all sts knitwise.

Bottom Border
Undo crochet ch and place all sts

on needle. **Note:** *Undo 1 st at a time and sl resulting st onto needle as you go.* Work as for top border.

Side Borders

With A and circular needle, pick up and k 1 st in every other row along side of afghan, with first st in first color A row of top border, and last st in first color A row of bottom border.

Row 1: With A, knit.

Row 2: With C, pick up and k 1 st in color C row of top border, knit across, pick up and k 1 st in color C row of bottom border.

Row 3: With C, knit.

Row 4: With A, pick up and k 1 st in 2nd color A row of top border, knit across, pick up and k 1 st in 2nd color A row of bottom border.

Row 5: With A, knit.

Row 6: With B, pick up and k 1 st in color B row of top border, knit across, pick up and k 1 st in color B row of bottom border.

Row 7: With B, knit.

Row 8: With A, pick up and k 1 st in last color A row of top border, knit across, pick up and k 1 st in last color A row of bottom border.

With A, bind off all sts knitwise. Rep on other side.

Block lightly. ◆

THIS WAY & THAT WAY

Garter stitch squares face in opposite directions to give an interesting look to this jewel of an afghan. It makes a great carry-along project.

DESIGN BY BARBARA VENISHNICK

Finished Size
Approx 38 x 50 inches

Materials
• Brown Sheep Nature's Spectrum, 100 percent wool bulky weight yarn (81 yds/2 oz per hank): 14 hanks ocean treasures #W8300 (MC)
• Brown Sheep Handpaint Originals 70 percent mohair/30 percent wool worsted weight yarn (88 yds/50g hanks): 6 hanks peacock #HP65 (CC)
• Size 11 (8mm) straight, 2 double-pointed and (2) 29-inch circular needles or size needed to obtain gauge
• Size J/10 crochet hook

Gauge
10 sts and 20 rows (10 ridges) = 4 inches/10cm in garter st with MC
To save time, take time to check gauge.

Pattern Note
Afghan is made in garter st squares; squares are joined with three-needle bind off.

Squares
Make 48
With MC, cast on 18 stitches.

Every row: K1-tbl, k16, sl 1 wyif. [Rep this row] 31 times. (16 ridges) Bind off.

Joining Squares

Afghan is organized into 6 rows of 8 squares each.

With 2 strands of CC held tog and dpn, pick up and knit 16 sts along bound-off edge of first square. Do not cut yarn.

Continuing with same double strand of yarn and 2nd dpn, pick up and knit 16 sts along side edge of 2nd square.

Fold 2nd square behind first, having WS tog and needles parallel.

Working end of yarn will be at the right of work; "folded" end of picked-up sts will be at the left.

Keeping working yarn between needles at all times, work three-needle bind off as follows:

*Insert RH needle into first st of front square knitwise, then into first st of back square purlwise, wrap yarn around needle and pull through both sts, sl both sts off needles. Rep from * once (2 sts on RH needle). Pass first st over 2nd st as in regular bind off. Continue to work in this manner until all sts are bound off. Cut yarn and fasten off final st.

A flat knit chain has been created between first and 2nd squares.

Continue to join squares in same manner, alternating directions of ridges by joining selvage edges to cast-on or bound-off edges until you have a long strip of 8 squares. Make 5 more strips, making sure that 3 strips have beginning squares facing in opposite directions as others.

Joining Strips

Hold first strip with RS facing, using double strand of CC and circular needle, pick up and knit 16 sts in each square along right edge of strip. Cut yarn.

With 2nd circular needle pick up and knit 16 sts in each square along left edge of 2nd strip. Hold strips with WS tog, making sure squares form a checkerboard pat. Join strips with three-needle bind off as for individual squares.

Join remaining strips to those previously finished.

Edging

With double strand of CC, work 16 single crochet in each square along outside edge of afghan, working 2 single crochet in each corner st and making sure to keep work flat. Join with sl st.

Block. ◆

SAND DUNES AFGHAN

The thick, warm fabric of this afghan makes it great for the den or cabin. The easy overall cable pattern gives the impression of complexity.

DESIGN BY LAURA POLLEY

Finished Size
Approx 54 x 67½ inches

Materials
- Plymouth Encore Chunky bulky weight 75 percent acrylic/25 percent wool yarn (143 yds/100g per ball): 34 balls off-white #256
- Size 15 (10mm) 32-inch circular needle or size needed to obtain gauge
- Cable needle
- Tapestry needle

Gauge
15 sts and 15 rows = 4 inches/10cm in pat with 2 strands held tog
To save time, take time to check gauge.

Pattern Notes
Afghan is worked with 2 strands of yarn held tog throughout.
Circular needle is used to accommodate large number of sts. Do not join at end of row.

Special Abbreviations
BC (Back Cross): Sl next 3 sts to cn and hold in back, k3, k3 from cn.
FC (Front Cross): Sl next 3 sts to cn and hold in front, k3, k3 from cn.

Pattern Stitch
Sand Dunes Pat (multiple of 12 sts + 2)

Rows 1 and 5 (RS): Knit across.
Rows 2, 4 and 6: Purl across.
Row 3: K1, *FC, k6, rep from * to last st, end k1.
Row 7: K1, *k6, BC, rep from * to last st, end k1.
Row 8: Purl across.
Rep Rows 1–8 for pat.

Afghan
With 2 strands of yarn, cast on 194 sts.
Rows 1–240: [Work Rows 1–8 of pat] 30 times. Piece should measure approximately 64 inches from beg.
Bind off all sts, leaving last st on RH needle.

Finishing
Note: Pick up and knit sts along edge at a rate of 2 sts for every 3 sts or rows on all 4 edges. This will give the number of sts given for each border section.

Left Border
Turn afghan ¼-turn clockwise so left edge is at top. Counting loop on RH needle as first st, pick up and knit 160 more sts along afghan edge. (161 sts)
Turn and work border in rows.
Row 1 (WS): P1, *k1, p1 rep from * across.
Row 2: K2, *p1, k1, rep from * to last st, k1.

Row 3: P2, *k1, p1, rep from * to last st, p1.
Row 4: K1, *p1, k1, rep from * across.
Rows 5–7: Rep Rows 1–3.
Bind off in pat as Row 4, leaving last st on needle.

Bottom Border
Turn afghan clockwise again, so bottom (cast-on) edge is at top. Counting loop on RH needle as first st, pick up and knit 5 sts along edge of left border and 129 more sts along afghan edge. (135 sts)
Work as for left border, leaving last st on needle.

Right Border
Turn afghan clockwise again, so right edge is at top. Counting loop on RH needle as first st, pick up and knit 5 sts along edge of bottom border and 161 more sts along afghan edge. (167 sts)
Work as for left border, leaving last st on needle.

Top Border
Turn afghan clockwise again, so bound off edge is at top. Counting loop on RH needle as first st, pick up and knit 5 sts along edge of right border, 129 sts across bound off edge, then 6 more sts along side edge of left border. (141 sts) ◆

FUNKY FOURSOME

Four yarns in varying textures combine in a chevron-stripe pattern in this sumptuous afghan. Tassels decorate the points of each chevron.

DESIGN BY NAZANIN FARD

Finished Size
Approx 40 x 53 inches (excluding tassels)

Materials
- Plymouth Rimini Rainbow 60 percent acrylic/40 percent wool super bulky yarn (38 yds/50g per ball): 6 balls orange sunset #19 (A)
- Plymouth 24K 82 percent nylon/18 percent lamé worsted weight yarn (187 yds/50g per ball): 3 balls rust sparkle #1356 (B)
- Plymouth Alpaca Bouclé 90 percent alpaca/10 percent nylon super bulky yarn (70 yds/50g per ball): 8 balls burnt orange #17 (C)
- Plymouth Spazzini 75 percent wool/25 percent nylon bulky weight yarn (72 yds/50g per ball): 9 balls autumn leaves #936 (D)

- Size 15 (10mm) 30-inch circular needle or size needed to obtain gauge
- Size J/10 (6mm) crochet hook
- 6-inch piece of cardboard

Gauge
8 sts and 18 rows (9 ridges) = 4 inches/10cm in pat st
To save time, take time to check gauge.

Special Abbreviation
M1 (Make 1): Make a backward lp and place on RH needle.

Pattern Stitches
A. Ridges
Row 1 (WS): Knit.
Row 2: *K1, M1, k8, ssk, k1, k2tog, k8, M1; rep from * to last st, k1.
   Rep Rows 1–2 for pat.

B. Color Stripe Sequence
Work 2 rows each of A, 3 strands B held tog, 2 strands C held tog, 3 strands D held tog.

Pattern Note
Circular needle is used to accommodate large number of sts. Do not join; work in rows.

Afghan
With A, cast on 112 sts.
   Work even in Color Stripe sequence until 17 reps (68 ridges) have been completed.
   Knit 2 rows A.
   Bind off loosely.

Side Edging
With C, work 1 row of sc along side edge of afghan.
   Rep for other side.

Tassel
Make 11
Cut 2 strands of B, each about 8 inches long and set aside.
   Holding 1 strand of each yarn tog, wrap yarn around cardboard 4 times.
   Using 1 reserved strand, tie one end; cut opposite end.
   Wrap 2nd strand around tassel, about 1 inch below fold.
   Tie tightly and hide ends in tassel.
   Trim ends even.
   Attach 1 tassel to each point of afghan. ◆

HOMESPUN STRIPES

Knit this comfy afghan in your favorite colors, using chunky yarn. It's sure to please any member of the family.

DESIGN BY EDIE ECKMAN

BEGINNER

5
BULKY

Finished Size
Approx 46 x 59 inches

Materials
- Plymouth Encore Chunky bulky weight 75 percent acrylic/25 percent wool yarn (143 yds/100g per ball): 7 balls blue #515 (A), 6 balls natural #256 (B)
- Size 10 (6mm) 29- or 36-inch circular needle
- Tapestry needle

Gauge
13 sts and 19 rows = 4 inches/10cm in pat
To save time, take time to check gauge.

Pattern Notes
Circular needle is used to accommodate large number of sts. Do not join at end of row.

Measure length by holding piece vertically; weight of afghan will make it stretch.

Afghan
With A, cast on 139 sts. Knit 5 rows, ending with a WS row. (3 ridges garter st)

Rows 1 and 3 (RS): With B, knit.
Rows 2 and 4: With B, purl.
Row 5: With A, k3, *put tip of RH needle into next st in first row of B, pull up loop, k1, pass loop over st just knitted, k3, rep from * across.
Rows 6 and 8: With A, purl.
Row 7: With A, knit.
Row 9: With B, k1, * put tip of RH needle into next st in first row of A, pull up loop, k1, pass loop over st just knitted, k3, rep from *, ending last rep k1 instead of k3.
Rows 10 and 12: With B, purl.
Row 11: With B, knit.
Rep Rows 5–12 for pat until afghan measures approximately 57 inches from beg, ending with Row 5 of pat. With A, knit 5 rows. Bind off all sts.

Side Border
*With A, pick up and k 215 sts along long edge of afghan. Knit 5 rows. Bind off all sts. Rep from * for other side. ◆

CROSS-STITCH SQUARES

This traditional design features the checkerboard effect of cross-stitch squares and stockinette stitch. Each square is surrounded by knit stitches.

DESIGN BY JOYCE ENGLUND

Finished Size
Approx 48 x 56 inches

Materials
- Plymouth Encore Chunky bulky weight 75 percent acrylic/25 percent wool yarn (143 yds/100g per ball): 11 balls butter yellow #215
- Size 11 (8mm) 29-inch circular needle or size needed to obtain gauge
- Stitch markers
- Tapestry needle

Gauge
12 sts and 16 rows = 4 inches/10cm in St st
To save time, take time to check gauge.

Special Abbreviation
Right Twist (RT): K1 in front of 2nd st on LH needle, k1 in back of first st on LH needle, sl both sts off needle at once.

Afghan
Cast on 142 sts. Work 4 ridges of garter st, ending with a RS row, and placing a marker 6 sts from each end for side borders.

Row 1 (WS): K6, purl to 2nd marker, k6.

Row 2: K6, [RT] 5 times (10 sts), *p2, k10, p2, [RT] 5 times, rep from * to marker, end k6.

Rows 3–12: [Rep Rows 1 and 2] 5 times.

Row 13: Rep Row 1.

Rows 14–18: Knit.

Row 19: K6, purl to 2nd marker, k6.

Row 20: K16, *p2, [RT] 5 times, p2, k10, rep from * to marker, end k6.

Rows 21–30: [Rep Rows 19 and 20] 5 times.

Row 31: Rep Row 19.

Rows 32–36: Knit.

Rows 37–216: [Rep Rows 1–36] 5 times.

Rows 217–229: [Rep Rows 1–13] once. Remove markers.

Knit 8 rows. Bind off all sts knitwise on RS. ◆

COMPLEMENTARY GEOMETRICS

Stripes and squares are balanced in an asymmetrical repeat on a modern-looking throw.

DESIGN BY KENNITA TULLY

Finished Size
Approx 36 x 45 inches

Materials
• Plymouth Alpaca Bouclé 90 percent alpaca/10 percent nylon bulky weight yarn (70 yds/50g per ball): 9 balls each burnt orange #17 (A) and turquoise #20 (B)

• Size 11 (8mm) 30-inch circular needle or size needed to obtain gauge

Gauge
11 sts and 9 rows = 4 inches/10cm in garter st
To save time, take time to check gauge.

Pattern Stitches
Intarsia Blocks A
All RS rows: *K10 B, k10 A; rep from * across.
All WS rows: *K10 A, k10 B; rep from * across.
Intarsia Blocks B
All RS rows: *K10 A, k10 B; rep from * across.
All WS rows: *K10 B, k10 A; rep from * across.

Pattern Notes
Circular needle is used to accommodate large number of sts. Do not join; work in rows.

Throw is worked in garter st throughout.

Wind separate balls or bobbins for each color area of intarsia blocks.

To avoid holes when changing colors, always bring new color up over old.

Throw
With A, cast on 100 sts.

Work even in following sequence:
[8 rows A, 8 rows B] 3 times.
16 rows Intarsia Blocks A, 16 rows Intarsia Blocks B.
8 rows each of A, B, A.
16 rows Intarsia blocks A.
8 rows each of B, A, B.
16 rows Intarsia Blocks A, 16 rows Intarsia Blocks B.
[8 rows A, 8 rows B] 3 times.
Bind off knitwise. ◆

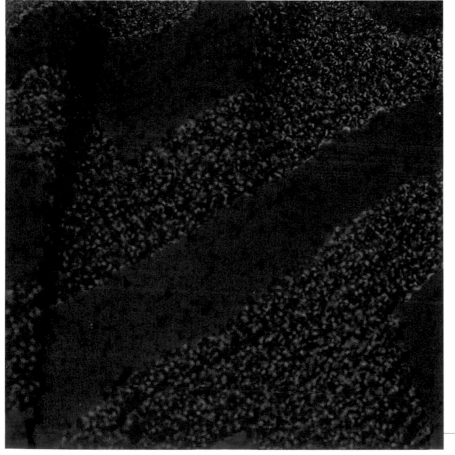

LUXURY LAP AFGHAN

Wrap yourself in luxury with this combination of soft and silky yarns.

DESIGN BY LYNDA ROPER

Finished Size
Approx 36 x 36 inches

Materials
- Plymouth Firenze 40 percent nylon/30 percent wool/30 percent acrylic bulky weight eyelash yarn (55 yds/50g per ball): 7 balls purple/blue #445 (MC)
- Plymouth Flash 100 percent nylon worsted weight eyelash yarn (190 yds/50g per ball): 4 balls soft white #900 (CC)
- Size 11 (8mm) 24-inch circular needle or size needed to obtain gauge

Gauge
11½ sts and 20 rows = 4 inches/10cm in St st
To save time, take time to check gauge.

Pattern Notes
Circular needle is used to accommodate large number of sts.
Do not join; work in rows.

Afghan is worked in 1 piece with single strand MC; 2 strands of CC are held tog throughout for border.

Side borders may be worked by using both ends of same ball of CC.

To avoid holes when changing colors, always bring new color up over old.

Afghan
With 2 strands of CC held tog, cast on 102 sts.

Knit 6 rows.

Set up pat:
Row 1: K6 CC, join MC and knit to last 6 sts, join double strand of CC, k6.

Row 2: K6 CC, with MC purl to last 6 sts, k6 CC.

Keeping first and last 6 sts in CC garter st, and center in MC and St st, work even until afghan measures 35 inches, ending with a WS row.

Cut MC and 2nd ball of CC.

With CC, knit 6 rows.

Bind off. ◆

JIFFY RIB AFGHAN

The surprise element of this design is the I-cord fringe. It is knitted on to look like a continuation of the knitted ribs.

DESIGN BY BARBARA VENISHNICK

Finished Size
Approx 40 x 48 inches (excluding fringe)

Materials
- Cleckheaton Mohair 12-ply bulky weight 92 percent mohair/4 percent wool/4 percent nylon yarn (110 yds/50g per ball) from Plymouth Yarn: 10 balls light blue #252
- Plymouth Wildflower DK weight 51 percent cotton/49 percent acrylic yarn (137 yds/50g per ball): 9 balls light blue #33
- Size 10 (6mm) double-pointed and 40-inch circular needles or size needed to obtain gauge
- Tapestry needle

Gauge
13 sts and 18 rows = 4 inches/10cm in pat with 1 strand of each yarn held tog
To save time, take time to check gauge.

Pattern Notes
Afghan is worked with 1 strand of each color held tog throughout.

Circular needle is used to accommodate large number of sts. Do not join at end of row.

Reserve 1 ball of mohair and an equal amount of cotton for fringe.

Afghan
With 1 strand of each yarn, cast on 129 sts.

Row 1 (RS): K1 tbl, *k2, p3, rep from * to last 3 sts, end k2, wyif, sl last st purlwise.

Row 2: K1 tbl, purl to last st, sl 1 purlwise.

Rep Rows 1 and 2 for pat until piece measures 48 inches, ending with Row 2.

Bind off all sts in pat.

I-Cord Fringe
With dpn and 1 strand of each yarn, pick up and knit 1 st in each of 2 knit sts of first rib. Cast on 2 more sts (a total of 4 sts). Do not turn.

*Sl all sts to other end of needle, bring yarn across back of work, k4. Do not turn. Rep from * until a total of 13 rows of I-Cord have been worked.

Cut yarn and draw through all sts using a tapestry needle. Weave ends into cord.

Work an I-Cord fringe at top and bottom of each knit rib. ◆

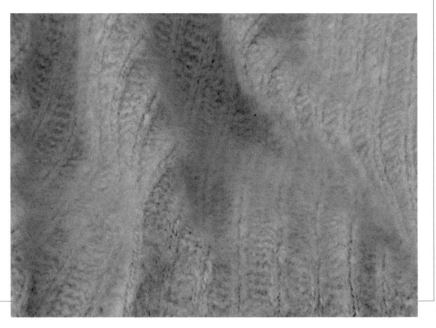

BOLD MACAW THROW

As bright as the parrot it is named for, this throw will add a wild touch of color and excitement wherever it is located.

DESIGN BY ANITA CLOSIC

Finished Size
Approx 42 x 48 inches

Materials
• Plymouth Eros 100 percent nylon worsted weight novelty yarn (165 yds/50g per ball): 4 balls black #3017 (A)
• Plymouth Parrot 100 percent nylon super bulky ribbon yarn (28 yds/50g per ball): 10 balls rainbow #24 (B)
• Plymouth Colorlash 100 percent polyester carry-along eyelash yarn (220 yds/50g per ball): 2 balls gold #23 (C)
• Plymouth Fantasy Naturale 100 percent mercerized cotton worsted weight yarn (140 yds/100 g per skein): 4 skeins red #3611 (D)
• Size 11 (8mm) 30-inch circular needles or size needed to obtain gauge

Gauge
14 sts and 18 rows = 4 inches/10cm in pat st
To save time, take time to check gauge.

Pattern Stitches
Feathers (multiple of 17 sts + 4)
Row 1 (RS): K2, *[k2tog] 3 times, [yo, k1] 5 times, yo, [k2tog] 3 times; rep from * to last 2 sts, k2.
Rows 2 and 3: Knit.

Row 4: K2, purl to last 2 sts, k2.
Rep Rows 1–4 for pat.
Color Sequence (28 rows)
Knit 4 rows with 2 strands A held tog, knit 4 rows with 1 strand each B and C held tog, work 12 rows in Feathers pat with 1 strand D, knit 4 rows with 1 strand each B and C held tog, knit 4 rows with 2 strands A held tog.

Pattern Note
Circular needle is used to accommodate large number of sts. Do not join; work in rows.

Throw
With 2 strands of A held tog, loosely cast on 123 sts.
Work even in color sequence until 8 reps have been completed. (224 rows)
Bind off loosely.

Fringe
Cut strands of A and B, each 20 inches long.
Holding 2 strands of each tog, fold each group of 4 in half.
Working along cast-on edge, insert crochet hook from WS to RS between scallops.
Pull fold of fringe through fabric. Draw ends through lp and fasten tightly.
Trim fringe evenly. ◆

SAWTOOTH STRIPES

No need to carry extra colors in this afghan. Slip stitches create the sawtooth design.

DESIGN BY JOANNE TURCOTTE

Finished Size

Approx 40 x 50 (50 x 60) inches. Instructions are given for smaller size, with larger size in parentheses. When only 1 number is given, it applies to both sizes.

Materials

- Plymouth Alpaca Bouclé 90 percent alpaca/10 percent nylon super bulky weight yarn (70 yds/50g per ball): 7 (8) balls plum #2028 (A), 9 (11) balls plum tweed #3676 (B), 5 (6) balls pumpkin #2037 (C)
- Size 10½ (6.5mm) 29-inch circular needle
- Size 11 (8mm) 29-inch circular needle or size needed to obtain gauge

Gauge

10 sts and 16 rows = 4 inches/10cm in St st with larger needles
To save time, take time to check gauge.

Pattern Stitch

Sawtooth (multiple 3 sts + 1)
Row 1: With B, k3, sl 1, *k2, sl 1; rep from * to last 3 sts, k3.
Row 2: P3, sl 1, *p2, sl 1; rep from * to last 3 sts, p3.
Rows 3–10: Work in St st for 8 rows.
Row 11: With C, k3, sl 1, *k2, sl 1; rep from * to last 3 sts, k3.
Row 12: P3, sl 1, *p2, sl 1; rep from * to last 3 sts, p3.
Rows 13–20: Work in St st for 8 rows.
Row 21: Rep Row 1.

Row 22: Rep Row 2.
Rows 23–30: Work in St st for 8 rows.
Row 31: With A, k3, sl 1,*k2, sl 1; rep from * to last 3 sts, k3.
Row 32: P3, sl 1, *p2, sl 1; rep from * to last 3 sts, p3.
Rows 33–40: Work in St st for 8 rows.
Rep Rows 1–40 for pat.

Pattern Note

Circular needle is used to accommodate large number of sts. Do not join; work in rows.

Afghan

With smaller needle and A, loosely cast on 97 (121) sts.
Work even in garter st for 6 rows. Change to larger needle.
Work even in St st for 10 rows.
Work even in Sawtooth pat until afghan measures approx 49 (59) inches, ending with Row 40.
Change to A and knit 6 rows.
Bind off loosely.

Side Border

With RS facing, using A and smaller needle, pick up and knit 125 (150) sts along one side edge of afghan.
Knit 5 rows.
Bind off loosely.
Rep on opposite side. ◆

RETRO 1930'S BOUDOIR THROW

Recapture the past with a softly romantic throw in serene colors.

DESIGN BY ANITA CLOSIC

Finished Size
Approx 42 x 48 inches

Materials
- Plymouth Sinsation 80 percent rayon/20 percent wool bulky weight yarn (38 yds/50g per ball): 6 balls cream #3301 (A)
- Plymouth Parrot 100 percent nylon super bulky novelty yarn

(28 yds/50g per ball): 5 balls ivory #43 (B)
- Plymouth Yukon 35 percent mohair/35 percent wool/30 percent acrylic super bulky weight yarn (59 yds/100g per ball): 5 balls pink #959 (C)
- Size 15 (10mm) 32-inch circular needle or size needed to obtain gauge
- Stitch markers

Gauge
8 sts and 11 rows = 4 inches/10cm in 1930s Fan pat
To save time, take time to check gauge.

Pattern Notes
Circular needle is used to accommodate large number of sts. Do not join; work in rows.

Place markers between each pat rep.

Pattern Stitch
1930s Fan (Multiple of 17sts + 4)
Rows 1 (RS)–4: With A, knit.
Row 5: With C, k2, *[k2tog] 3 times, [yo, k1] 5 times, yo, [k2tog] 3 times; rep from * to last 2 sts, k2.
Row 6: With C, k2, purl to last 2 sts, k2.
Rows 7–12: [Rep Rows 5 and 6] 3 times.
Rows 13–16: With A, knit.
Rows 17–20: With B, knit.
Rows 21–24: With A, knit.
Rep Rows 1–24 for pat.

Throw
With B, loosely cast on 89 sts. Knit 4 rows.
Work even in 1930s Fan pat until 6 full reps have been completed.
Rep Rows 1–20.
Bind off loosely with B. ◆

FIRESIDE WARMER AFGHAN

Create the tweed look of this striking afghan by using a slip-stitch pattern with alternating variegated and solid colors within a black framework.

DESIGN BY CAROLYN PFEIFER

Finished Size
Approx 50 x 62 inches

Materials
- Red Heart Super Saver 100 percent acrylic worsted weight yarn from Coats & Clark (452 yds/8 oz per skein): 3 skeins black #312 (MC), 50 yds each of 14 variegated colors (A), 40 yds each of 16 solid colors (CC)
- Size 9 (5.5mm) 29-inch circular needle or size needed to obtain gauge
- Size H/8 (5mm) crochet hook (optional)
- Tapestry needle

Gauge
17 sts and 26 rows = 4 inches/10cm
To save time, take time to check gauge.

Pattern Notes
Sample was made with a different color for each stripe, alternating variegated and solid colors. Stripes are separated by 4 rows of MC.

Sl all sts purlwise unless otherwise instructed.

Afghan
With MC, cast on 211 sts.

Row 1 (RS): Sl 1 knitwise, *sl 1 wyif, k1, rep from * across.

Row 2: Sl 1, purl across.

Row 3: Sl 1 knitwise, *k1, sl 1 wyif, rep from * across, end k2.

Row 4: Sl 1, purl across.
Rows 1–4 form pat.

Rows 5 and 6: Drop MC but do not break off, attach first solid color (CC), rep Rows 1 and 2.

Rows 7 and 8: With MC, rep Rows 3 and 4.

Rows 9–14: Rep Rows 5–8, then rep Rows 5 and 6. Cut CC.

Rows 15–18: With MC only, work Rows 3 and 4, then Rows 1 and 2. Cut MC.

Rows 19–26: With first variegated color (A), work pat, beg with Row 3 and ending with Row 2. Cut A, attach MC.

Rows 27–30: With MC, rep Rows 15–18.
Drop MC but do not cut, attach next solid color (CC).

Rows 31–40: Beg with pat Row 3, work 2 rows CC, [2 rows MC, 2 rows CC] twice, ending with pat Row 4. Cut CC.

Rows 41–44: With MC, rep Rows 1–4. Cut MC.

Rows 45–52: Attach next variegated color (A), work [Rows 1–4] twice.

Rep [Rows 1–52] 6 times, then rep [Rows 1–44] once. This should give you 16 tweed stripes and 14 variegated stripes or approximately 62 inches.

Bind off all sts knitwise.

Finishing
Edge (optional)
With MC and crochet hook, work one rnd of single crochet around entire afghan.

Fringe
Cut a 3-inch-wide cardboard piece. Wrap MC yarn around it as many times as needed to have 1 strand in each st across top and bottom edges of afghan. Cut yarn on 1 edge of cardboard so that each piece is 6 inches. Fold each piece and loop through sts on top and bottom edges of afghan. Trim fringe evenly.

Steam block lightly with pressing cloth, being careful not to touch iron to fabric. ◆

PATCHWORK TRIO AFGHAN

Large needles, basic stitches—stockinette, seed and cable—and a checkerboard arrangement best show the texture of this fast-knitting project.

DESIGN BY DIANE ZANGL

Finished Size
Approx 40 x 50 inches (blocked)

Materials
- Plymouth Encore worsted weight 75 percent acrylic/25 percent wool yarn (200 yds/100g per ball): 4 balls each plum #959 (A), dark mauve #958 (B), dusty rose #2340 (C)
- Size 11 (7mm) needle or size needed to obtain gauge
- Cable needle
- Tapestry needle

Gauge
13 sts and 16 rows = 4 inches/10cm in St st with 2 strands of yarn held tog
To save time, take time to check gauge.

Pattern Notes
Afghan is worked with 2 strands of yarn held tog throughout. Use 2 strands for sewing squares tog.

If desired, afghan may be knit in 4 panels of 5 squares each. Refer to Fig. 1 for sequence, do not bind off after each square is completed. Cut old color, join new color at beg of next row. Work as directed for next square.

Special Abbreviation
C6 (Cable 6): Sl 3 sts to cn and hold in front, k3, k3 from cn.

Square 1
Make 7
With 2 strands of A, cast on 32 sts. Knit 3 rows.
Row 1 (RS): Knit.
Row 2: K3, p to last 3 sts, k3.
   [Rep Rows 1 and 2] 19 times more. Knit 4 rows. Bind off all sts.

Square 2
Make 6
With 2 strands of B, cast on 32 sts. Knit 3 rows.
Row 1 (RS): K3, p2, [k2, p2] 6 times, k3.
Rows 2 and 3: K5, [p2, k2] 6 times, k3.
Row 4: Rep Row 1.
   [Rep Rows 1–4] 9 times more. Knit 4 rows. Bind off all sts.

Square 3
Make 7
With 2 strands of C, cast on 32 sts. Knit 3 rows.
Rows 1 and 5 (RS): [K6, p1] twice, k4, [p1, k6] twice.
Rows 2, 4 and 6: K3, p3, k1, p6, k1, p4, k1, p6, k1, p3, k3.
Row 3: K6, p1, C6, p1, k4, p1, C6, p1, k6.
   [Rep Rows 1–6] 5 times more. Work Rows 1–4.
   Knit 4 rows. Bind off.

Finishing
Referring to Fig. 1, sew squares tog as shown. Block. ◆

2	3	1	2
1	2	3	1
3	1	2	3
2	3	1	2
1	2	3	1

FIG. 1

VELVET STRIPES LAP ROBE

Sensuous velvet stripes alternate with delicate openwork rows in a richly colored lap robe.

DESIGN BY LOIS S. YOUNG

Finished Size
Approx 36 x 46 inches (excluding fringe)

Materials
- Plymouth Sinsation 80 percent rayon/20 percent wool chenille bulky weight yarn (38 yds/50g per ball): 17 balls ruby #4475 (A)
- Plymouth Encore Worsted 75 percent acrylic/25 percent wool worsted weight yarn (200 yds/100g per ball): 5 balls dark red #9601 (B)
- Size 10 (6mm) 29-inch circular needle or size needed to obtain gauge
- Size Q (16mm) crochet hook

Gauge
12 sts and 20 rows = 4 inches/10cm in pat
To save time, take time to check gauge.

Pattern Stitch
Velvet Stripes
Rows 1(RS)–8: With A, sl 1p, knit to end of row.
Row 9: With B, sl 1p, knit to end of row.
Rows 10 and 12: Sl 1p, k2, purl to last 3 sts, k3.

Row 11: Sl 1p, k2, *yo, k2tog; rep from * to last 2 sts, k2.
Rep Rows 1–12 for pat.

Pattern Notes
Chenille part of afghan should be knitted as tightly as possible to prevent chenille from "worming."

Two strands of B are held tog for entire lap robe, except for fringe.

Lap Robe
With A, loosely cast on 113 sts.
Slipping first st of every row purlwise, work in garter st for 7 rows.
[Work Rows 1–12 of Velvet Stripes pat] 20 times.

Rep Rows 1–7.
Bind off knitwise on WS.

Fringe
Cut strands of B, each 14 inches long.

Holding 3 strands tog, fold each group in half.

Working along cast-on edge, insert crochet hook from WS to RS (adding two fringe for every three stitches).

Pull fold of fringe through fabric. Draw ends through lp and fasten tightly.

Rep along bound-off edge.
Trim fringe even. ◆

CLIMBING ROSES

A soft color and petite cables embellish a timeless afghan. Picot-hemmed borders add a romantic touch.

DESIGN BY SHARI HAUX

Finished Size
Approx 52 x 59 inches

Materials
- Plymouth Encore Worsted 75 percent acrylic/25 percent wool worsted weight yarn (200 yds/100g per ball): 11 balls medium rose #180
- Size 10 (6mm) 30-inch circular needle or size needed to obtain gauge
- Stitch markers

Gauge
24 sts and 20 rows = 4 inches/10cm in pat st
To save time, take time to check gauge.

Pattern Stitch
Mock Cable
Row 1 (RS): P3, *sl 1k, k2, psso, p2; rep from *, end last rep p3.
Row 2: K3, *p1, yo, p1, k2; rep from *, end last rep k3.
Row 3: P3, *k3, p2; rep from *, end last rep p3.
Row 4: K3, *p3, k2; rep from *, end last rep k3.
Rep Rows 1–4 for pat.

Pattern Note
Circular needle is used to accommodate large number of sts. Do not join; work in rows.

Afghan
Cast on 286 sts.
Beg with a WS row, work even in St st for 9 rows.
Turning row (RS): K17, *yo, k2tog; rep from * to last 17 sts, k17.
Work even in St st for 9 rows.

Set up pat
Next row (RS): K16, place marker, work Mock Cable pat to last 16 sts, place marker, k16.
Keeping sts between markers in Mock Cable pat and rem sts in St st, work even until afghan measures approx 52 inches above turning row, ending with Row 4 of pat.

Top Border
Work even in St st for 8 rows.
Turning row (RS): K17, *yo, k2tog; rep from * to last 17 sts, k17.
Work even in St st for 9 rows.
Bind off.

Finishing
Fold side border to WS, forming hem. Sew in place.
Rep for other side.
Fold lower border to WS on turning row. Sew in place.
Rep for top border. ◆

LAZY MAN'S PLAID

Brightly colored rows with a slip stitch background combine with a mitered border and tassels to create this handsome afghan.

DESIGN BY BARBARA VENISHNICK

Finished Size
Approx 44 x 56 inches

Materials
- Plymouth Wildflower DK weight 51 percent mercerized cotton/49 percent acrylic yarn (137 yds/50g per ball): 12 balls purple #45 (A), 4 balls each orange #56 (B), green #58 (C), yellow #48 (D)
- Size 11 (8mm) 29-inch circular needle or size needed to obtain gauge
- Size H/8 (5mm) crochet hook for cast on
- Tapestry needle

Gauge
12½ sts and 22 rows = 4 inches/ 10cm in pat with 2 strands held tog To save time, take time to check gauge.

Pattern Notes
Afghan is worked with 2 strands of yarn held tog throughout.

When working pat, sl sts purlwise with yarn on WS of fabric.

Work first and last sts of every row in selvage st: k first st tbl, sl last st wyib. Selvage sts are not included in pat instructions.

Special Abbreviation
M1 (Make 1): Inc by making a backward loop over right needle.

Special Technique
Provisional cast on: With crochet hook and scrap yarn, ch number of sts needed for cast on plus a few extra. With working yarn and needle, pick up 1 st in back purl bump of each ch st until desired number of sts is cast on.

Afghan
With A, provisionally cast on 129 sts (127 for pat + 1 selvage st on each side).
Note: Cast on row is counted as Row 1 of pat for first rep.
Row 1 (RS): With A, knit.
Row 2: With A, purl.
Rows 3–6: With B, [k3, sl 1] 31 times, end k3.
Row 7: With A, knit.
Row 8: With A, purl.
Rows 9 and 10: With C, k1, [sl 1, k3] 31 times, end sl 1, k1.
Row 11: With A, knit.
Row 12: With A, purl.
Rows 13–16: With D, [k3, sl 1] 31 times, end k3.
Row 17: With A, knit.
Row 18: With A, purl.
Rows 19 and 20: With C, k1, [sl 1, k3] 31 times, end sl 1, k1.
[Rep Rows 1–20] 12 more times. [Rep Rows 1–8] once more.

Top Border
Row 1: With A, knit all sts across (including selvage sts).

Row 2: With A, knit across.
Row 3: With C, k1, M1, k127, M1, k1.
Row 4: With C, k131.
Row 5: With A, k1, M1, k129, M1, k1.
Row 6: With A, k133.
Row 7: With D, k1, M1, k131, M1, k1.
Row 8: With D, k135.
Row 9: With A, k1, M1, k133, M1, k1.
Row 10: With A, k137.
Row 11: With B, k1, M1, k135, M1, k1.
Row 12: With B, k139.
Row 13: With A, k1, M1, k137, M1, k1.
Bind off all sts knitwise on WS.

Bottom Border
Undo crochet ch and place sts on needle. Work as for top border.

Side Border
Row 1: With A and circular needle, RS facing, pick up and knit 1 st in first row of bottom border, 1 st in every selvage st along side, and 1 st in first row of top border, turn.
Row 2: With A, knit back, turn.
Row 3: With C, pick up and knit 1 st in color C row of bottom border, knit across all sts of previous row, pick up and knit 1 st in color C row of top border, turn.
Row 4: With C, knit back, turn.
Continue in this fashion, picking up 1 more st at beg and end of each RS row, using same color sequence as for top and bottom borders.

Bind off on last WS row with A as for top and bottom borders.

Tassels
Make 4

Wrap a double strand of A around a 6-inch ruler or cardboard 35 times. Tie at top and cut bottom loops. With A, wrap tightly 1 inch below top tie. Using 1 strand each of B, C and D, wrap once around 1 inch below top tie, covering color A wrap. Tie strands tightly and using a tapestry needle, run ends into center of tassel. Trim bottom of tassel ends evenly. Attach 1 tassel to each corner of afghan. ◆

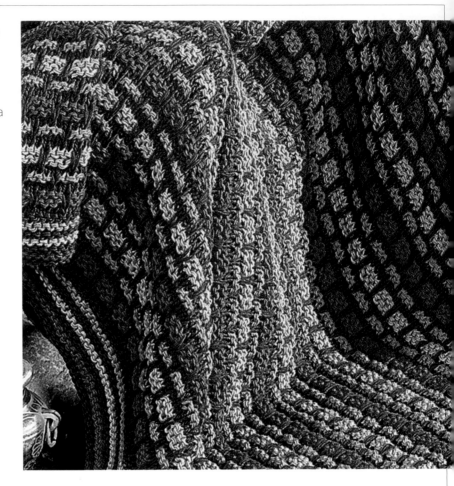

RIO GRANDE STRIPES

Beginning with the sheep that came into New Mexico with Coronado in 1540, wool and weaving have played an important part in the culture of the American Southwest. This afghan is based on woven blankets from the mid-1800s, worked in an easy pattern of garter, stockinette and simple slip-stitch stripes.

DESIGN BY E.J. SLAYTON

Finished Size
Approx 38 x 54 (43 x 66) inches. Instructions are given for smaller size, with larger size in parentheses. When only 1 number is given, it applies to both sizes.

Materials
- Brown Sheep Burly Spun, 100 percent wool super-bulky weight yarn (132 yds/8 oz per hank): 4 (5) hanks black #BS05 (MC), 2 (3) hanks limeade #BS120 (A), 1 (2) hanks orange you glad #BS110 (B), 1 hank periwinkle #BS59 (C)
- Size 13 (9mm) needles or size needed to obtain gauge
- Tapestry needle

Gauge
9 sts and 12 rows = 4 inches/10cm in St st
To save time, take time to check gauge.

Pattern Stitches
A. Wide Stripe (uneven number of sts)

Row 1 (RS): With A, k5, *sl 1, k1, rep from * to last 4 sts, end k4.

Row 2: With A, sl 1, k3, p1, *sl 1, p1, rep from * to last 4 sts, end k3, sl 1.

Row 3: With A, knit.

Row 4: With A, sl 1, k3, p to last 4 sts, end k3, sl 1.

Row 5: With B, k5, *sl 1, k1, rep from * to last 4 sts, end k4.

Row 6: With B, sl 1, k4, *sl 1, k1, rep from * to last 4 sts, end k3, sl 1.

Row 7: With B, knit.

Row 8: With B, sl 1, k to last st, end sl 1.

Rows 9–12: Rep Rows 1–4.

Row 13: With MC, k4, *sl 1, k1, rep from * to last 5 sts, end sl 1, k4.

Row 14: With MC, sl 1, k3, *sl 1, p1, rep from * to last 5 sts, end sl 1, k3, sl 1.

B. Narrow Stripe (multiple of 4 sts + 1)

Row 1 (RS): With C, knit.

Row 2: With C, sl 1, k to last st, sl 1.

Row 3: With A, k4, *sl 1, k3, rep from * to last 5 sts, end sl 1, k4.

Row 4: With A, *sl 1, k3, rep from * to last st, sl 1.

Rows 5 and 6: With C, rep Rows 1 and 2.

Pattern Notes

Sl all sts purlwise with yarn on WS of fabric.

Sl first and last st of all WS rows.

When working sl st stripes, be careful not to pull yarn too tightly behind sl sts.

Except in Narrow Stripe, break color not in use and re-attach next time it is needed.

Afghan

With A, cast on 77 (87) sts.

Row 1 (WS): Sl 1, knit to last st, sl 1.

Row 2: Knit.

Rows 3 and 4: Rep Rows 1 and 2.

Row 5: Rep Row 1.

Knit, inc 8 (10) sts evenly. (85, 97 sts)

Next row: Sl 1, k3, p to last 4 sts, k3, sl 1.

Work Rows 5–14 of Wide Stripe, then work 10 rows MC.

Work Narrow Stripe, then work 12 rows MC.

Work Rows 1–14 of Wide Stripe, then work 32 rows MC. Rep Narrow Stripe.

For larger size only: Work 12 rows MC, Rows 1–14 of Wide Stripe, 12 rows MC, rep Narrow Stripe.

Both sizes: Work 32 rows MC, Rows 1–14 of Wide Stripe, 12 rows MC, Narrow Stripe, 12 rows MC, rep Rows 1–12 of Wide Stripe.

Next row: With A knit, dec 8 (10) sts evenly. (77, 87 sts)

Knit 4 rows, sl first and last sts of WS rows.

Bind off knitwise on WS.

Block. ◆

BLUE CHRISTMAS AFGHAN

This lovely reversible afghan is perfect for the beginning knitter and looks great in any color.

DESIGN BY LYNNETTE HARTER

Finished Size
Approx 40 x 60 inches (excluding fringe)

Materials
- Plymouth Encore Chunky bulky weight 75 percent acrylic/25 percent wool yarn (143 yds/100g per ball): 10 balls blue #515
- Size 13 (9mm) 32-inch circular needle or size needed to obtain gauge
- Tapestry needle
- Crochet hook (for fringe)

Gauge
12 sts = 4 inches/10cm in pat
To save time, take time to check gauge.

Pattern Note
Circular needle is used to accommodate large number of sts. Do not join at end of row.

Afghan
Cast on 120 sts.
Rows 1–4: *K4, p4, rep from * across.
Rows 5 and 7: P2, *k4, p4, rep from * across, end p2.
Rows 6 and 8: K2, *p4, k4, rep from * across, end k2.
Rows 9–12: *P4, k4, rep from * across.
Rows 13 and 15: Rep Row 6.
Rows 14 and 16: Rep Row 5.

Rep Rows 1–16 for pat until afghan measures approximately 60 inches from beg, ending with Row 4, 8, 12 or 16. Bind off all sts.

Fringe
For each fringe, *cut 2 (12-inch) strands of yarn, fold in half. Insert crochet hook through st from back to front, pull folded ends through, pull ends through loop and pull snug. Rep from * in every other st across shorter edges of afghan. Trim fringe evenly. ◆

FINGERPAINT FUN

Chunky yarn and variegated colors create a snug afghan that may remind you of a child's fingerpaint drawing.

DESIGN BY EDIE ECKMAN

Finished Size
Approx 48 x 52 inches

Materials
• Plymouth Handpaint Wool 100 percent wool super bulky weight yarn (60 yds/100g skein): 14 skeins Santa Fe #160
• Size 17 (12.75mm) 29-inch circular needle
• Size 15 (10mm) double-pointed needles (2 only)

Gauge
8 sts and 11 rows = 4 inches/10cm in Double Moss pat
To save time, take time to check gauge.

Pattern Stitch
Double Moss (multiple of 4 sts)
Rows 1 and 2: *K2, p2; rep from * across row.
Rows 3 and 4: *P2, k2; rep from * across row.
Rep Rows 1–4 for pat.

Afghan
Cast on 86 sts.
Work even in Double Moss pat until afghan measures 50 inches.
Bind off loosely.

I-Cord Edging
With dpn, cast on 3 sts.
Insert needle into edge of afghan and pull up a st. (4 sts on RH needle)

Do not turn; slide sts to opposite end of needle.
*K2, k2tog-tbl, pick up and knit another st from edge of afghan. Rep from * picking up sts evenly along edge to first corner.

Unattached row: [K3, slide sts to opposite end of needle] twice. Continue working attached I-cord along edges and unattached I-cord in corner sts around entire afghan. Sew last 3 sts to cast-on sts. ◆

SEASIDE SUNSET THROW

Shades of royal purple capture the feeling of the last sunset rays at the beach. An added bonus: the throw is reversible.

DESIGN BY ANITA CLOSIC

Finished Size
Approx 42 x 48 inches

Materials
- Plymouth Yukon Print 35 percent mohair/35 percent wool/30 percent acrylic super bulky weight yarn (59 yds/100g per hank): 5 hanks purple print #8001 (A)
- Plymouth Odyssey Glitz 60 percent nylon/37 percent wool/3 percent lamé bulky weight novelty yarn (66 yds/50g per ball): 5 balls purple variegated #923 (B)
- Plymouth Yukon 35 percent mohair/35 percent wool/30 percent acrylic super bulky weight yarn (59 yds/100g per ball): 4 balls purple #578 (C)
- Plymouth Dazzlelash 78 percent polyester/22 percent rayon bulky weight novelty yarn (220 yds/50g per ball): 2 balls purple metallic #104 (D)
- Size 15 (10mm) 32-inch circular needles or size needed to obtain gauge

Gauge
8 sts and 10 rows = 4 inches/10cm in Fancy pat
To save time, take time to check gauge.

Pattern Stitch
Fancy
Rows 1–4: With A, knit.
Row 5: With B, knit.
Rows 6–8: With B, k2, *yo, k2tog; rep from * to last 2 sts, k2.
Rows 9–12: With 1 strand each of C and D held tog, knit.
Row 13: With B, knit.
Rows 14–16: Rep Row 6.
  Rep Rows 1–16 for pat.

Pattern Notes
Circular needle is used to accommodate large number of sts. Do not join; work in rows.
  Slightly scalloped edge forms automatically along sides of throw.

Throw
With A, loosely cast on 84 sts.
  Work even in Fancy pat until 8 reps have been completed.
  With C, knit 4 rows.
  Bind off loosely. ◆

SPORTY SQUARES

Cables and color mix together for a sporty afghan.
Make one in your favorite team colors.

DESIGN BY KATHARINE HUNT

Finished Size
Approx 42 x 59 inches, lightly blocked

Materials
- Brown Sheep Burly Spun, 100 percent wool super-bulky weight yarn (132 yds/8 oz per hank): 7 hanks prairie fire #BS181 (MC), 4 hanks oatmeal #BS115 (CC)
- Size 15 (10mm) needles or size needed to obtain gauge

Gauge
10 sts and 17 rows = 4 inches/10cm in Bicolor pat
To save time, take time to check gauge.

Pattern Notes
Afghan is worked in 5 panels of 7 squares each.

Slip all sts purlwise.

Solid Squares are worked in either MC or CC.

MC squares are used alternately with all others in each panel.

When working Bicolor Square: On Rows 1 and 5, wrap color not in use loosely over working strand before purling last st, to position it for color change on next row.

Solid Square
Setup pat: With color indicated,
For first square in a panel only:
Beg with a RS row, knit 3 rows.

For 2nd–7th squares in a panel:
Purl 2 rows, beg with a WS row.

Begin pat

Row 1 (WS): Purl.

Row 2: P1, k1, p1, *sl 1 wyib, k1, sl 1 wyib, p1; rep from * across, end last rep k1, p1.

Row 3: P5, *sl 1 wyif, p3; rep from * across row.

Row 4: P1, k1, *p1, drop sl st off needle to front of work, k2, pick up dropped st and knit it; rep from * across, end last rep p1, k1, p1.

  [Rep Rows 1–4] 6 times.

  Knit 2 rows.

Final square only: Bind off knitwise on WS.

Bicolor Square

Setup pat: With CC,

For first square in panel only:
With CC, beg with a RS row, knit 3 rows, purl 1 row, knit 1 row.

For 2nd–7th squares in a panel:
With CC, beg with a WS row, purl 3 rows, knit 1 row.

Begin pat

Row 1 (WS): With CC, purl.

Row 2: With MC, p1, k2, *sl 1 wyib, k1; rep from * across, end last rep sl 1 wyib, k2, p1.

Row 3: With MC, p5, *sl 1 wyif, p3; rep from * across row.

Row 4: With MC, p1, k2, *drop sl st off needle to front of work, k2, pick up dropped st and knit it, k1; rep from * across, end last rep k1, p1.

Row 5: With MC, purl.

Rows 6–8: With CC, rep Rows 2–4.

  [Rep Rows 1–8] twice.

  With CC, purl 1 row, knit 3 rows.

Final square only: Bind off knitwise on WS.

Afghan

Outside Panel
Make 2

With MC, cast on 21 sts.

[Work 1 Solid Square with MC, work 1 Bicolor Square] 3 times, work 1 Solid Square with MC.

Panels 2 and 4
Make both alike

With CC, cast on 21 sts.

  Work 1 Bicolor Square, [work 1 Solid Square with MC, work 1 Solid Square with CC] twice, work 1 Solid Square with MC, work 1 Bicolor Square.

Center Panel
Make 1

With MC, cast on 21 sts.

  [Work 1 Solid Square with MC, work 2 Solid Squares with CC] 3 times, work 1 Solid Square in MC.

Finishing

Block each panel.

  Sew panels tog in order indicated. Reblock lightly if necessary. ◆

GLITTERING CASHMERE

Sumptuous cashmere and alpaca yarns combine with a glittery carry-along yarn in a variation on a classic pattern stitch.

DESIGN BY SANDI PROSSER

Finished Size
Approx 44 x 55 inches (excluding fringe)

Materials
- Plymouth Royal Cashmere 100 percent fine Italian cashmere worsted weight yarn (154 yds/50g per hank): 6 hanks chocolate #344K (A)
- Plymouth Alpaca Boucle 90 percent alpaca/10 percent nylon super bulky weight yarn (70 yds/50g per ball): 6 balls brown #12 (B)
- Plymouth Baby Alpaca Brush 80 percent baby alpaca/20 percent acrylic bulky weight yarn (110 yds/ 50g per ball): 3 balls beige #1000 (C)
- Plymouth Glitterlash 50 percent polyester/50 percent metallic carry-along yarn (185 yds/25g per ball): 2 balls copper #6 (D)
- Plymouth Flash 100 percent nylon worsted weight yarn (190 yds/50g per ball): 2 balls dark chocolate #993 (E)
- Size 10 (6mm) 30-inch circular needle or size needed to obtain gauge

Gauge
14 sts and 18 rows = 4 inches/10cm in Wave pat
To save time, take time to check gauge.

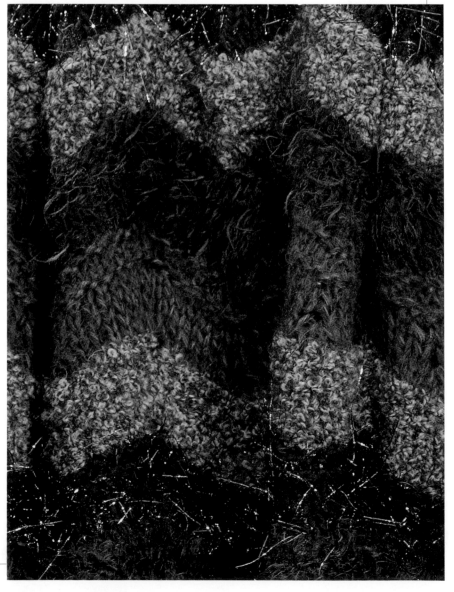

Special Abbreviation
CDD (Centered Double Decrease): Slip 2 sts as if to k2tog, k1, pass 2 slipped sts over knit st.

Pattern Stitches
Wave
Rows 1 and 3 (RS): K2, *yo, k6, CDD, k6, yo, k1; rep from * to last st, k1.
Rows 2 and 4: Purl.
Rows 5–8: Knit.
　Rep Rows 1–8 for pat.

Pattern Notes
Circular needle is used to accommodate large number of sts. Do not join; work in rows.

Color Stripe Sequence
Work 8 rows each of the following colors: 1 strand B, 1 strand C, 1 strand each of A and E held tog, 1 strand B, 1 strand each A and D held tog, 1 strand C, 1 strand each A and E held tog, 1 strand each A and D held tog.

Afghan
With 1 strand each of A and D held tog, cast on 163 sts.
　Knit 3 rows.
　Working even in Wave pat, [rep color stripe sequence] 4 times, ending with Row 7 of Wave pat on final stripe.
　Bind off knitwise on WS.

Fringe
Cut strands of yarn, each 18 inches long.
　Holding 1 strand of each color tog, fold each group of 6 yarns in half.
　Working in each point of pat, insert crochet hook from WS to RS.
　Pull fold of fringe through fabric. Draw ends through lp and fasten tightly.
　Rep along bound-off edge.
　Trim fringe evenly. ◆

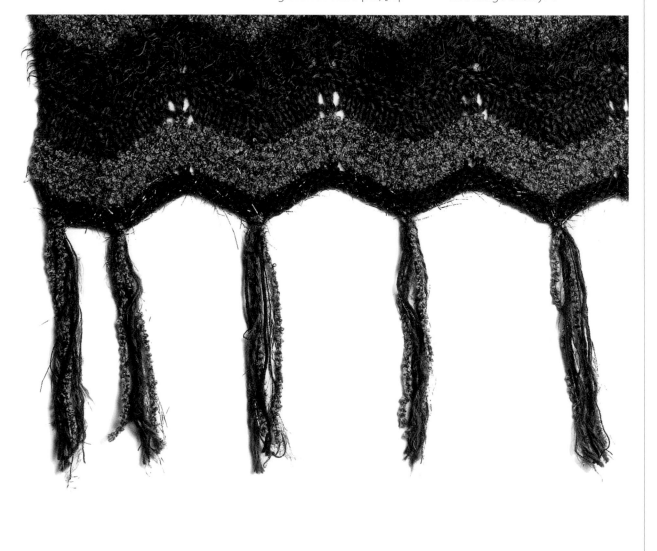

STAINED GLASS SQUARES

Combine small amounts of many different yarns for a beautiful afghan that glows!

DESIGN BY LAURA POLLEY

INTERMEDIATE

4 MEDIUM

Finished Size
Approx 48½ x 61 inches

Materials
- Lion Brand Imagine 80 percent acrylic/20 percent mohair worsted weight mohair-look yarn, (22 yds/2.5 oz per skein): 6 skeins black #153 (MC)
- 10–40 different yarns (DK to heavy worsted weight) in various shades of deep rose and violet (CC1's) (see Pattern Notes)
- 10–40 different yarns (DK to heavy worsted weight) in various shades of blues and greenish blues (CC2's) (see Pattern Notes)
- Size 9 (5.5mm) straight and 36-inch circular needles or size needed to obtain gauge
- Tapestry needle

Gauge
17 sts and 30 rows = 4 inches/10cm in chart pat
To save time, take time to check gauge.

Pattern Notes
Each block of color uses approximately 11 yds of CC. Use this number to determine if you have enough of a particular yarn to complete a block. If you run out of yarn in middle of a block, you may simply finish that block in a closely matched color and type of yarn.

There are 165 blocks of color in the afghan. Use this number to determine how many different colors/yarns you would like to use. Sample afghan uses 32 yarns plus MC. Total amount of CC's is approximately 1,815 yds.

St gauge is more important than row gauge, as length may be adjusted by adding more blocks to each strip. To check gauge, cast on 18 sts with desired CC1 and work Rows 1–30 of chart. Piece should measure approximately 4¼ inches wide and 4 inches long, measuring above cast-on row.

Circular needle is used to pick up sts along side edges of panels for joining, and to pick up sts for borders. When using circular needle, do not join, but turn and work in rows or in 3-needle bind-off as indicated in pat.

First and last sts of each row of chart are selvage sts, and if you work them as directed in chart, you will have a neat edge on both sides of each strip. These edge sts make it much easier to pick up sts for joining strips, and keep horizontal MC garter ridges aligned throughout afghan.

Carry MC loosely up side of work throughout strip.

Each strip may be joined upon completion to strips already worked, or you may prefer to work all strips and then begin joining. There are a total of 11 strips.

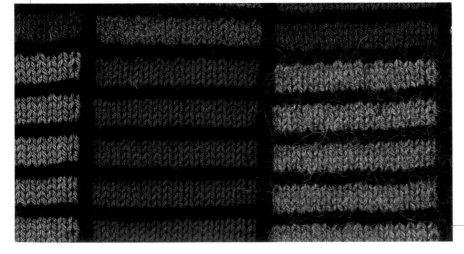

Afghan

Strip 1

With straight needles and desired CC1 (deep rose), cast on 18 sts. Work [Rows 1–30 of chart] 14 times, changing CC after each rep and alternating deep rose and blue blocks throughout, then work [Rows 1–28] once more. (448 total rows worked)

Last block worked should be deep rose (a CC1). Bind off all sts. Strip should measure approximately 59 inches.

Strips 2, 4, 6, 8 and 10

Work as for Strip 1, beg and ending with a CC2 block.

Strips 3, 5, 7, 9 and 11

Work as for Strip 1.

Join Strip 1 and Strip 2

With MC and circular needle, RS of Strip 1 facing, beg at lower right corner of strip (at cast on edge), pick up and knit 1 st in edge of cast-on row, then 1 st in each edge st to upper right corner of strip, then 1 st in edge of bind off row. Do not break yarn. (226 sts)

(There is 1 edge st for every 2 rows of knitting, so if you pick up 1 st in each edge st plus 1 st at upper and lower edges, you will not need to count sts.)

Hold Strip 2 directly to left of last picked-up st of Strip 1. With RS facing, using same strand of MC and same needle, beg at bound off edge of Strip 2, pick up 1 st in edge of bound off row, 1 st in each edge st to lower end of Strip 2, then 1 st in edge of cast on row. (226 more sts)

You will now have both strips hanging from needle, and a total of 552 sts. Fold needle so both tips are tog, with RS of each strip facing outward. Using straight needle and MC, knit first st on front and back needles tog, *knit next st on both needles tog, bind off 1, rep from * until all sts are worked, fasten off.

Join remaining strips in same way, alternating colors, treating joined strips as Strip 1 and next strip to be joined as Strip 2, until all 11 strips have been joined.

Right Side Border

With MC and circular needle, RS facing, beg at lower right edge of Strip 11, pick up and knit 1 st in edge of cast on row, 1 st in each edge st to upper right corner of strip, then 1 st in edge of bound off row. (226 sts)

Row 1 (WS): Knit into front and back of first st, knit to last st, knit into front and back of last st (228 sts)

Row 2 (RS): Knit.

Rep [Rows 1 and 2] twice more, then work Row 1 once more. (234 sts)

Bind off loosely purlwise on RS, leaving 10-inch tail for sewing corner.

Left Side Border

Pick up sts as for right border, beg at upper left (bound off) edge of Strip 1 and ending at lower left (cast on) edge of Strip 1.

Complete as for right border. (234 sts)

Upper Border

With MC and circular needle, RS facing, beg at upper right corner of Strip 11, pick up and knit 17 sts in each color block across upper edge to left corner of Strip 1. (Do not pick up sts in MC joining/bound off rows) (187 sts)

Complete as for right border. (195 sts)

Lower Border

Pick up sts as for upper border, beg at lower left corner of Strip 1 and ending at lower right corner of Strip 11. (187 sts)

Complete as above.

Finishing

With tails of MC, sew corner seams. Block piece by pinning flat without stretching, and steaming lightly above work. Do not rest iron on afghan. ◆

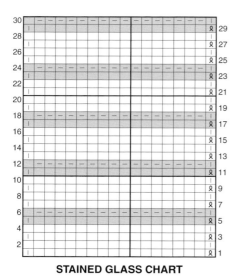

STAINED GLASS CHART

STITCH KEY
☐ K on RS, p on WS with CC
▨ K (RS) with MC
⊟ K (WS) with MC
Ꝑ K through back loop with CC
Ꝑ K through back loop with MC
Ɪ☐ Sl st with yarn held on WS

Tips for Working With Bits & Pieces

Afghan may be worked in any color scheme you desire. Choose odds and ends of many colors plus black or white for a vibrant afghan, or use odd balls of colors to match your home decor.

Squares are suggested, but if you have very small lengths of yarn, you can use them to make a crazy-strip design, keeping MC ridges in place.

Feel free to combine yarns of different weights, textures, and fibers. Any yarn between DK and heavy worsted weight can be used with this pattern, but try to balance weights by working a lighter weight square next to a heavier one and vice versa.

You can use fingering weight or sock weight yarns doubled to equal a strand of DK or worsted yarn. This is a great way to expand your possibilities.

Variegated yarns look great in this stained-glass pattern. Choose a yarn whose dominant color fits desired color scheme, even if there are several other colors present.

For a larger or smaller afghan, simply adjust number of blocks in each strip, as well as number of strips. A smaller version in primary colors plus black would make a great kid's afghan.

For blocking and laundering, determine care requirements for most delicate yarn used, and treat entire afghan in this manner. If one square is dry-clean only, it's best to dry-clean the entire afghan! In most cases, a gentle-cycle or hand washing will be suitable. Lay flat to dry.

GLITZY GLAMOUR THROW

This throw begins at one corner and increases to the center. Once there, decreasing begins to give it a unique diagonal shape.

DESIGN BY LANIE HERING

Finished Size

Approx 50 inches square, with fringe

Materials

- Plymouth Baby Alpaca Grande 100 percent baby alpaca bulky weight yarn (110 yds/100g per skein): 9 skeins plum #2213 (MC)
- Plymouth Eros Glitz 86 percent nylon/10 percent rayon/4 percent Lurex medium weight novelty yarn (158 yds/50g per ball): 2 balls grapevine #104 (A)
- Plymouth Dazzlelash 78 percent polyester/22 percent rayon bulky weight eyelash yarn (220 yds/50g per ball): 1 ball grape #104 (B)
- Size 11 (8mm) 29-inch circular needle or size needed to obtain gauge

Gauge

12 sts and 22 rows = 4 inches/10cm in garter st
To save time, take time to check gauge.

Pattern Stitch

Stripes
Working in garter st, work [2 rows CC, 4 rows MC] twice, 2 rows CC.

Pattern Notes

Circular needle is used to accommodate large number of sts. Do not join; work in rows.

One strand each of A and B are held tog throughout throw. This is referred to as CC in pattern instructions.

Throw

With MC, cast on 2 sts. Knit 1 row.
Rows 1 (RS)–13: Knit in front and back of first st, knit to end of row.
Row 14: Knit in front and back of first st, knit to last 2 sts, knit in front and back of next st, k1.

Rep Rows 1–14, working in color pat of 16 rows MC, 14 rows stripe pat, [24 rows MC, 14 rows stripe pat] 3 times, 24 rows MC, 7 rows stripe pat.

This is widest part of throw.

Beg dec shaping

Rows 1–13: K2tog, knit to end of row.
Row 14: K2tog, knit to last 2 sts, k2tog.

Rep Rows 1–14, working in color pat of rem 7 rows of stripe pat, [24 rows MC, 14 rows stripe pat] 4 times, 16 rows MC.

Bind off rem 2 sts.

Fringe

Cut 12-inch lengths of all yarns.

Holding 1 strand of each yarn tog, fold group in half and attach at 2-inch intervals on all 4 sides of throw. ◆

SIMPLE SENSATION

Bold black and white squares create a dramatic look in a very modern afghan.

DESIGN BY LYNDA ROPER

Finished Size
Approx 40 x 58 inches

Materials
- Plymouth Furlauro 100 percent nylon bulky weight eyelash yarn (82 yds/50g per ball): 3 balls white #1145 (A)
- Plymouth Sinsation 80 percent rayon/20 percnt wool bulky weight yarn (38 yds/50g per ball):

12 balls each black #3314 (B) and white #3300 (C)
- Size 10½ (6.5mm) 30-inch circular needle or size needed to obtain gauge

Gauge
10 sts and 16 rows = 4 inches/10cm in St st
To save time, take time to check gauge.

Pattern Notes
Circular needle is used to accommodate large number of sts. Do not join; work in rows. Use separate balls for each color section.

To avoid holes when changing colors, always bring new color up over old.

Afghan
With A, cast on 112 sts loosely.

Beg with knit row, work in St st for 8 rows.

Set up pat
Next row (RS): K8 A, [join B, k24, join C, k24] twice, join A, k8.

Work even in St st and established color pat for 35 more rows.

Keeping 8 sts at each end in A and reversing color block placement, work even for 36 more rows. (72 rows)

Work in established block pat until there is a total of 6 rows of blocks.

Change to A and work even in St st for 8 rows.

Bind off loosely. ◆

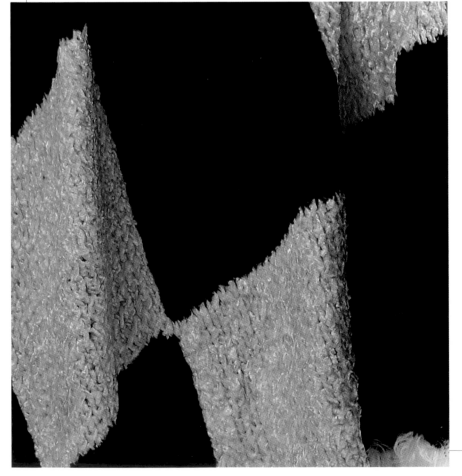

LACE BLOCKS

The unique combination of large needles and worsted weight yarn join to produce a light and lacy baby blanket, finished with a dainty crochet edging. The decreases and yarn overs produce squares that are at an angle.

DESIGN BY DIANE ZANGL

INTERMEDIATE

4 MEDIUM

Finished Size
Approx 42 x 42 inches after blocking

Materials
- Brown Sheep Cotton Fleece, 80 percent cotton/20 percent Merino wool light worsted weight yarn (215 yds/100g per skein): 5 skeins nymph #CW610
- Size 10½ (6.5mm) 24-inch circular needles or size needed to obtain gauge
- Size H/8 (5mm) crochet hook
- Tapestry needle

Gauge
14 sts and 22 rows = 4 inches/10cm in pat
To save time, take time to check gauge.

Pattern Note
Circular needles are used to accommodate large amount of sts. Do not join; work back and forth in rows.

Blanket
Cast on 140 sts. Purl 1 row.
Set up pat: K2, referring to chart [work from A–B] 8 times, [work from B–C] once, k2.

Work even, keeping first and last 2 sts in St st and rem sts in established pat.

[Rep Rows 1–24] 9 times, [rep Rows 1–12] once.
Knit 1 row.
Bind off. Do not cut yarn. Sl last st to crochet hook.

Edging
Work 1 rnd single crochet around blanket, making sure to keep work flat. Join with sl st.
Rnd 2: *Ch 2, sl st in next single crochet, rep from * around.
Join with sl st, fasten off.
Block. ◆

STITCH KEY
- ☐ K on RS, p on WS
- ⊟ P on RS, k on WS
- ⊡ Yo
- ☑ K2tog
- ◹ Ssk

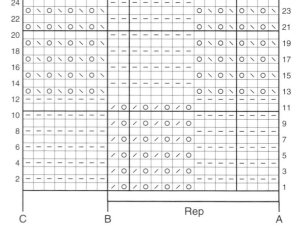

LACE BLOCKS CHART

DIAMOND LACE THROW

A diamond lace pattern worked on a garter stitch background makes a cozy afghan that is completely reversible.

DESIGN BY NAZANIN S. FARD

Finished Size
Approx 50 x 60 inches

Materials
• Brown Sheep Lamb's Pride Superwash Bulky, 100 percent washable wool bulky weight yarn (110 yds/100g per skein): 15 skeins plum crazy #SW55
• Size 10½ (6.5mm) needles or size needed to obtain gauge
• Size J/10 crochet hook

Gauge
12 sts and 24 rows (12 ridges) = 4 inches/10cm in garter st
To save time, take time to check gauge

Pattern Stitch
Diamond Lace
(Multiple of 18 sts + 5)
Row 1–6: Knit.
Row 7: *K2tog, yo; rep from * across, end last rep k1.
Row 8–12: Knit.
Row 13: K10, *k2tog, yo, k16; rep from * across, end last rep k11.
Row 14 and all even-numbered rows: Knit.
Row 15: K9, *k2tog, yo, k1, yo, ssk, k13; rep from * across, end last rep k9.
Row 17: K8, *k2tog, yo, k3, yo, ssk, k11; rep from * across, end last rep k8.

Row 19: K7, *k2tog, yo, k5, yo, ssk, k9; rep from * across, end last rep k7.
Row 21: K6, *k2tog, yo, k7, yo, ssk, k7; rep from * across, end last rep k6.
Row 23: K5, *k2tog, yo, k9, yo, ssk, k5; rep from * across row.
Row 25: K4, *k2tog, yo, k11, yo, ssk, k3; rep from * across, end last rep k4.
Row 27: K6, *yo, ssk, k7, k2tog, yo, k7; rep from * across, end last rep k6.
Row 29: K7, *yo, ssk, k5, k2tog, yo, k9; rep from * across, end last rep k7.
Row 31: K8, *yo, ssk, k3, k2tog, yo, k11; rep from * across, end last rep k8.
Row 33: K9, *yo, ssk, k1, k2tog, yo, k13; rep from * across, end last rep k9.
Row 35: K10, *yo, sl 1, k2tog, psso, yo, k15; rep from * across, end last rep k10.

Row 37: K11, yo, ssk, k16; rep from * across, end last rep k10.
Row 39–42: Knit.
Rep Rows 7–42 for pat.

Afghan
Cast on 149 sts.
Work even in Diamond Lace pat until afghan measures 60 inches.
Bind off loosely, do not cut yarn.

Edging
Rnd 1: With crochet hook, sc in every st along cast-on and bound-off edges and every other row on side edges. Join with sl st, do not turn.
Rnd 2: Working from left to right, work 1 sc in each sc of previous rnd. Join with sl st, fasten off. ◆

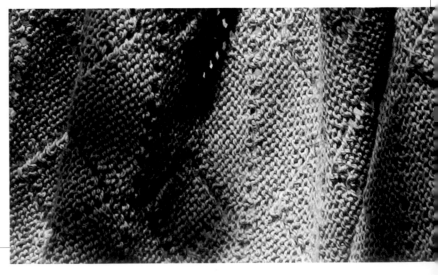

SPECIAL TECHNIQUES

Fringe

Cut a piece of cardboard half as long as specified in instructions for strands plus ½ inch for trimming. Wind yarn loosely and evenly around cardboard. When cardboard is filled, cut yarn across one end. Do this several times then begin fringing. Wind additional strands as necessary.

Single Knot Fringe

Hold specified number of strands for one knot together, fold in half. Hold project to be fringed with right side facing you. Use crochet hook to draw folded end through space or stitch indicated from right to wrong side.

Pull loose ends through folded section.

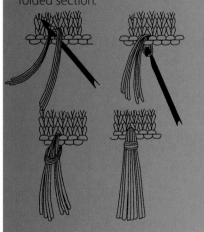

Draw knot up firmly. Space knots as indicated in pattern instructions.

Double Knot Fringe

Begin by working Single Knot Fringe completely across one end of piece. With right side facing you and working from left to right, take half the strands of one knot and half the strands of the knot next to it and knot them together.

Triple Knot Fringe

Work Double Knot Fringe across. On the right side, work from left to right tying a third row of knots.

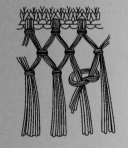

correspond most closely to knitting needle sizes.

Crochet Hook	Knitting Needle
E	4
F	5
G	6
H	8
I	9
J	10
K	10½

To work this type of cast-on, start with a crochet chain one or two stitches more than the number of stitches to be cast on for the pattern you are working. If the edge is to be decorative or removed to work in the opposite direction then the chain should be made with a contrasting color.

Once the chain is completed, with a knitting needle, pick up and knit in the back bump of each chain (Photo 1) until the required number of stitches is on the needle. Continue to work the pattern as given in the instructions.

Some instructions indicate that the provisional cast-on be removed so the piece can be worked in the opposite direction. In this case, hold the work with the cast-on edge at the top. Undo one loop of the crochet chain, inserting the knitting needle into the stitch below the chain. (This stitch is on the original first row of knitting). Continue to undo the crochet chain until all the stitches are on the needle. (Photo 2) This provides a row of stitches ready to work in the opposite direction.

Blanket Stitch

This stitch is worked along edge of piece. Bring needle up and make a counterclockwise lp. Take stitch as indicated, keeping the thread beneath the point of needle. Pull through to form stitch. Continue in same manner around outer edge.

Provisional Cast-On

The provisional cast-on has a variety of uses. It starts with a crochet chain on a crochet hook about the same size as the knitting needle. A chart is given below of crochet hooks that

Photo 1

Photo 2

Twisted Cord

Items sometimes require a cord as a drawstring closing or strap. The number of lengths and weight of yarn determine the thickness of the cord.

To form the cord hold the number of cords indicated together matching ends. Attach one end to a doorknob or hook. Twist the other end in one direction until the length is tightly twisted and begins to kink.

Sometimes the lengths are folded in half before twisting. In this case the loose ends are attached to the doorknob and a pencil is slipped into the folded loop at the other end. Turn the pencil to twist the cord.

Once the cord is tightly twisted, continue to hold the twisted end while folding the yarn in the middle. Remove the end from the knob or hook and match the two ends, then release them allowing the cord to twist on itself.

Trim the cord ends to the desired length and knot each end. If the cord is woven through eyelets, it may be necessary to tie a second knot in the end to prevent it from slipping back through the eyelet opening.

3-Needle Bind Off

Use this technique for seaming two edges together, such as when joining a shoulder seam. Hold the edge stitches on two separate needles with right sides together.

With a third needle, knit together a stitch from the front needle with one from the back.

Repeat, knitting a stitch from the front needle with one from the back needle once more.

Slip the first stitch over the second.

Repeat knitting, a front and back pair of stitches together, then bind one off.

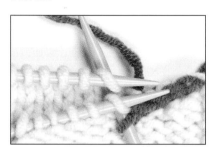

Crochet Class

For the times when you need a little crochet to trim or edge your knit project, look here.

Some knit items are finished with a crochet trim or edging. Below are some abbreviations used in crochet and a review of some basic crochet stitches.

Crochet Abbreviations

ch	chain stitch
dc	double crochet
hdc	half double crochet
lp(s)	loop(s)
sc	single crochet
sl st	slip stitch
yo	yarn over

Single Crochet (sc)

Insert the hook in the second chain through the center of the V. Bring the yarn over the hook from back to front.

Draw the yarn through the chain stitch and onto the hook.

Again bring yarn over the hook from back to front and draw it through both loops on hook.

For additional rows of single crochet, insert the hook under both loops of the previous stitch instead of through the center of the V as when working into the chain stitch.

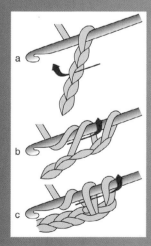

Double Crochet (dc)

Yo, insert hook in st, yo, pull through st, (yo, pull through 2 lps) 2 times.

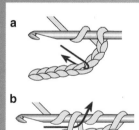

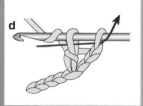

Reverse Single Crochet (reverse sc)

Working from left to right, insert hook under

both loops of the next stitch to the right.

Bring yarn over hook from back to front and draw through both loops on hook.

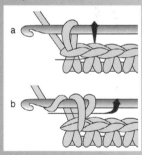

Slip Stitch (sl st)

Insert hook under both loops of the stitch, bring yarn over the hook from back to front and draw it through the stitch and the loop on the hook.

SPECIAL THANKS

Laura Andersson
Big Needle Scarf Set, 14

Svetlana Avrakh
Nifty Plaid Bag, 35

Bernat & Patons Design Studio
His Weekend Pullover, 166
Dashing Scarf, 10
Terrific Texture Scarf, 9

Uyvonne Bigham
Counterpane Yoke Sweater, 72
Rolled Brim Hat & Mitts, 24
Two-Color Scarf & Hat, 22

Dixie Butler
Five Easy Cables, 207
Gray Rose, 216

Caron International
Clever Collar Scarf, 12
Fall Comfort Coat, 179
It's All About Shine, 131
Warm-as-Toast Sweater, 122

Kathy Cheifetz
Chocolate Mousse, 204

Sue Childress
Snazzy Striped Purses & Scarves, 50

Whitney Christmas
Sassy Ruffled Skirt, 80

Anita Closic
Bold Macaw Throw, 256
Flash of Gold Shoulder Shawl, 56
Seaside Sunset Throw, 280
Retro 1930's Boudoir Throw, 260

Coats & Clark
Snazzy Stripes, 185

Ellen Drechsler
Wraparound Purse Cover, 43

Edie Eckman
Fingerpaint Fun, 278
Heathered Denim Pullover, 163
Homespun Jacket, 82
Homespun Stripes, 246
Rainbow Eyeglass Case, 28

Joyce Englund
Celtic Tradition, 199
Cross-Stitch Squares, 249

Nazanin Fard
Autumn Blaze, 208
Diamond Lace Throw, 298
Funky Foursome, 244

Bonnie Franz
Chunky Turtleneck Tunic, 119
Winter Walks, 20
My Dog & Me, 152

Julie Gaddy
Gossamer Lace, 54
Unisex Scarf, 26

Laura Gebhardt
Razzle Dazzle Sweater, 116

Fatema Habibur-Rahman
Acorn Afghan, 230

Sara Louise Harper
Feelin' Good Bolero, 138
Tangerine Smoothie, 85

Lynnette Harter
Blue Christmas Afghan, 276

Shari Haux
Climbing Roses, 268
Raspberry Afghan, 196
Wool Felted Purse, 30

Lainie Hering
Glitzy Glamour Throw, 292

Frances Hughes
Hyacinth Beauty, 214
Safari Traveler Bag, 48

Katharine Hunt
Casual Hooded Pullover, 135
Moss Stitch Diamonds, 156
Sporty Squares, 283

Kathleen Power Johnson
Baby Cable Sweater, 188
By the Sea, 232
Summer Garden Coverlet, 192
Flora Dora, 211

Melissa Leapman
Dappled Forest Glen, 113

Patsy Leatherbury
Fiesta Grande Shawl, 58
Fun & Fashionable Purse, 40

Mark Marik
All Occasion Shell, 67

Carol May
Quick Lacy Throw, 226

N.Y. Yarns
Island Sensation, 88
Multicolor Dream, 175
Stylish Tunic, 107

Carolyn Pfeifer
Fireside Warmer Afghan, 262

Laura Polley
Sand Dunes Afghan, 242
Stained Glass Squares, 288
Starflower Sweater, 125

Plymouth Yarns
Ebony Camisole, 78
Fun & Fashionable Hat, 40

Sandi Prosser
Glittering Cashmere, 285

Janet Rehfeldt
Jewel Tones, 228
Morning Sunlight, 234

Linda Roper
Luxury Lap Afghan, 252
Simple Sensation, 294

S. R. Kertzer
Enjoy the Festivities, 105
Smartly Fitted Top, 70

Kathleen Sasser
Heart of Mine, 223

Jean Schafer-Albers
Mood-Boosting Tunic, 128
Satin Tweed Fitted Blouse, 98

Pauline Schultz
Weekend in the Woods, 169

Darla Sims
Little Bows Top & Wraps, 61

E. J. Slayton
Rio Grande Stripes, 273

Colleen Smitherman
"The Bomb" in Stripes, 141

South West Trading Co.
Diva Darling, 110
Felted Rose Bags, 38
Fine Lines Pullover, 182

Scarlet Taylor
Chic Little Tote, 32
Day & Night Ensemble, 94
Flirty in Lime, 172
Relaxed V-Neck, 161

Kennita Tully
Cat's Eye Topper, 90
Complementary Geometrics, 250
Silk Cabled Shell, 64
Yukon Pullover, 101

JoAnne Turcotte
Sawtooth Stripes, 258

Barbara Venishnick
Flying Cables, 200
Jiffy Rib Afghan, 254
Lazy Man's Plaid, 270
This Way & That Way, 239
Tibetan Check Afghan, 236
Wishbone, 194

Lois Young
Dotted Stripes, 218
Fun in the Sun, 75
Garter Ridge Bag, 46
Guy's Guernsey Afghan, 202
Reversible Winter Warmers, 17
Velvet Stripes Lap Robe, 267

Diane Zangl
Confident Zip Jacket, 146
Lace Blocks, 296
Monet Miters Throw, 221
Patchwork Trio Afghan, 264
Zip Vest, 149

STANDARD ABBREVIATIONS

[ ] work instructions within brackets as many times as directed

( ) work instructions within parentheses in the place directed

** repeat instructions following the asterisks as directed

* repeat instructions following the single asterisk as directed

" inch(es)

approx approximately

beg begin/beginning

CC contrasting color

ch chain stitch

cm centimeter(s)

cn cable needle

dec decrease/decreases/decreasing

dpn(s) double-pointed needle(s)

g gram

inc increase/increases/increasing

k knit

k2tog knit 2 stitches together

LH left hand

lp(s) loop(s)

m meter(s)

M1 make one stitch

MC main color

mm millimeter(s)

oz ounce(s)

p purl

pat(s) pattern(s)

p2tog purl 2 stitches together

psso pass slipped stitch over

p2sso pass 2 slipped stitches over

rem remain/remaining

rep repeat(s)

rev St st reverse stockinette stitch

RH right hand

rnd(s) rounds

RS right side

skp slip, knit, pass stitch over—one stitch decreased

sk2p slip 1, knit 2 together, pass slip stitch over the knit 2 together; 2 stitches have been decreased

sl slip

sl 1k slip 1 knitwise

sl 1p slip 1 purlwise

sl st slip stitch(es)

ssk slip, slip, knit these 2 stitches together—a decrease

st(s) stitch(es)

St st stockinette stitch/stocking stitch

tbl through back loop(s)

tog together

WS wrong side

wyib with yarn in back

wyif with yarn in front

yd(s) yard(s)

yfwd yarn forward

yo yarn over